SECOND EDITION

STRATEGY AND THE BUSINESS LANDSCAPE

Pankaj Ghemawat

with

Bruno Cassiman
David J. Collis
Jan W. Rivkin

PEARSON

Prentice
Hall

Upper Saddle River, New Jersey 07458

A CIP catalog record for this book can be obtained from the Library of Congress.

VP/Editorial Director: Jeff Shelstad
Senior Acquisitions Editor: David Parker
Assistant Editor: Richard Gomes
Marketing Manager: Anke Braun
Marketing Assistant: Patrick Danzuso
Associate Director, Production: Judy Leale
Production Editor: Suzanne Grappi
Permissions Supervisor: Charles Morris
Manufacturing Buyer: Michelle Klein
Production Manager, Manufacturing: Arnold Vila
Cover Design Manager: Jayne Conte
Composition/Full-Service Project Management: Patty Donovan, Pine Tree
   Composition, Inc.
Printer/Binder: Bind-Rite Graphics

Pearson Prentice Hall™ is a trademark of Pearson Education, Inc.
Pearson® is a registered trademark of Pearson plc
Prentice Hall® is a registered trademark of Pearson Education, Inc.

Pearson Education LTD.
Pearson Education Singapore, Pte. Ltd
Pearson Education Canada, Ltd. Pearson
Pearson Education-Japan
Pearson Education Australia PTY, Limited
Pearson Education North Asia Ltd
Educación de Mexico, S.A. de C.V.
Pearson Education Malaysia, Pte. Ltd

10 9 8 7 6 5 4 3 2
0-13-143035-1

To my parents, Dr. Mahipal Singh Ghemawat and Mrs. Shanta Ghemawat,
for engraining in me the desire to learn and to teach

Contents

Preface

The second edition of *Strategy and the Business on Landscape* has been thoroughly updated as well as expanded to include two new chapters, competitive dynamics and corporate-level strategy, for which there seemed to be a significant demand. Like the first edition, however, it is grounded in my experience of teaching strategy to MBA students and executives at the Harvard Business School since the early 1980s. And it continues to emphasize relevance and readability as well as rigor.

In terms of rigor, *Strategy and the Business Landscape* is based on contemporary research in the field of strategy and adopts a value-focused, firm-centered perspective that is consistent with recent work on value addition and appropriation. In addition to tying together the discussions in the different chapters, this perspective promotes an analytical approach to strategy. At the same time, though, the book also begins with and maintains an explicitly historical perspective on strategy as a field. The hope is that an understanding of the history of the field may foster an ability to sort through the continual barrage of new ideas—some good and others bad—about strategy.

That last point relates as much to relevance as to rigor. *Strategy and the Business Landscape* is meant to be relevant to practitioners or practitioners-to-be, for whom it has been written as a short introduction to or refresher on strategy. That target readership has influenced decisions about how much detail to go into regarding academic research, and how much to draw on insights from business and consulting. Each of the chapters except the historical introduction concludes with a section that offers guidance for the strategy development process in terms of steps to follow or tests and principles to apply. And this conscious striving for relevance is reinforced by readability.

Readability is enhanced, most obviously, by the fact that, despite the two new chapters, this book is still much shorter than most trade books, let alone strategy textbooks. In addition, the maintenance of a unified perspective helps avoid unnecessary twists and turns. And last but not least, there are many richly detailed examples, including some featuring "inside" perspectives.

The first edition of *Strategy and the Business Landscape* included a set of Harvard Business School cases that were meant to illustrate, deepen, and extend the concepts developed in the text. Given trends in case usage, affording users flexibility in this regard seemed a superior option for the second edition. However, a suggested case map is included on the front inside cover of the text for reference.

It would have been impossible to prepare this book without aid and support from a number of different quarters. My most obvious debt is to my coauthors on the individual chapters in this book, Bruno Cassiman, David J. Collis, and Jan W. Rivkin (twice over). Each pushed the chapter(s) in which he was involved to a new level and also provided copious feedback on some of the other chapters in this book. None of the three, however, should be presumed to have signed off on the entire end-product.

I am also indebted to other current and former colleagues at Harvard Business School and at IESE Business School, Barcelona, for very helpful comments on one or more of the chapters in this book, particularly Bharat Anand, Adam Brandenburger, Estelle Cantillon, Ramon Casadesus-Masanell, Giovanni Gavetti, Tarun Khanna, Cynthia Montgomery, Felix Oberholzer-Gee, Gary Pisano, Joan Ricart i Costa, Michael Rukstad, Jordan Siegel, John Wells, Dennis Yao, and Pai-Ling Yin. And Tom King of Progressive Insurance provided a practitioner's perspective on the entire book.

In addition, I am very grateful to a number of reviewers for their guidance:

Robert Black, Houghton College

Ralph Biggadike, Columbia University

Thomas Chandy, Binghamton University

Tim Dacin, Texas A&M University

Constance Helfat, Dartmouth College

Gary Judd, Rensselaer Polytechnic Institute

Daniel E. Levinthal, University of Pennsylvania

Joseph Mahoney, University of Illinois at Urbana-Champaign

George Puia, Indiana State University

John A. Seeger, Bentley College

Mark Shanley, Northwestern University

Richard Spinello, Boston College

John Stevens, Lehigh University

Duane Windsor, Rice University

Todd Zenger, Washington University

I should also thank my high-powered research associate, Ken Mark, and my exceptionally able administrative assistant, Sharilyn Steketee, for invaluable help pushing this revised edition to completion, and David Parker and his editorial team at Prentice Hall for their patient pursuit of this project as I insisted on revising the chapters "one last time." And, as always, my wife, Anuradha Mitra Ghemawat, and my daughter, Ananya Maumita Ghemawat, provided support and animation.

Finally, a book such as this would have been infeasible without the work of all the scholars that underlies it, as well as all the students and practitioners that I have interacted with and learned from about these topics. They are owed many thanks as well.

Cambridge, MA
February 2005

About the Author

Pankaj Ghemawat is the Jaime and Josefina Chua Tiampo Professor of Business Administration at Harvard University's Graduate School of Business Administration. After receiving his A.B. in Applied Mathematics (Phi Beta Kappa) and his Ph.D. in Business Economics from Harvard University, he worked at McKinsey & Company in London in 1982—83, and has taught at the Harvard Business School since then. In 1991, Professor Ghemawat was appointed the youngest full professor in the Business School's history. There, his responsibilities have included spear heading the School's core strategy course for first-year MBAs and its strategy unit. In the past several years, he has also worked to develop a new course on international business strategy.

Professor Ghemawat's other publications include *Commitment* (1991) and *Games Businesses Play* (1997) as well as several dozen articles, book chapters and case studies. His current research focuses on competitive dynamics and on international business strategy. He serves as the department editor for *Strategy for Management Science,* as well as in a number of other editorial positions.

The Origins
of Strategy

If we wish to increase the yield of grain in a certain field and on analysis it appears that the soil lacks potash, potash may be said to be the strategic (or limiting) factor.

— *Chester I. Barnard*

The term "strategy" ... is intended to focus on the interdependence of the adversaries' decisions and on their expectations about each other's behavior.

— *Thomas C. Schelling*

Strategy can be defined as the determination of the basic long-term goals and objectives of an enterprise, and the adoption of courses of action and the allocation of resources necessary for carrying out those goals.

— *Alfred D. Chandler, Jr.*

This chapter reviews the history of strategic thinking about business through the mid-1970s. The historical perspective maintained throughout this book is attractive for at least three reasons:

➤ Despite thoughtful attempts over the decades to define **strategy** (see the quotations at the beginning of the chapter), a rash of manifestos continue to emerge that purport to redefine the term.[1] It would therefore be idiosyncratic to begin by tossing another definition onto the pile. Examining the history of strategic ideas and practice constitutes a less arbitrary approach to the study of strategy.

➤ The historical perspective organizes changing conceptions of strategy as envisioned or enacted by the participants in this field—academics, managers, and consultants—allowing us to identify patterns in what might otherwise seem to be the chaotic churn of ideas. Patterns of this sort are evident in all the chapters of this book: co-evolution with the environment, the development and diffusion of particular strategic paradigms, paradigm shifts, the recycling of earlier ideas, to name a few.

➤ Most ambitiously, the idea of path-dependence (one of the rallying cries of academic strategists since the mid-1980s) suggests that understanding of the history of ideas about strategy is essential to developing a more informed sense of where the field might go in the future.

In this chapter, we briefly discuss the origins of strategic ideas. We begin with some background, including military antecedents, and then move on to discuss the ideas about strategy, especially portfolio planning, that were developed and disseminated by academics and consultants in the 1960s and early 1970s. We conclude by reviewing the dissatisfaction with the state of the field that had developed by the second half of the 1970s. In particular, the underdevelopment of the two basic dimensions of portfolio planning grids—environmental attractiveness and competitive positioning—set the stage for much of the subsequent work on these topics that is discussed in Chapters 2 and 3, respectively, and revisited from a corporate-strategy perspective in Chapter 6. Chapters 4 and 5 address the other weakness of portfolio planning by emphasizing the dynamic dimension of strategic thinking.

BACKGROUND

"Strategy" is a term that can be traced back to the ancient Greeks, who used the word *strategos,* from which it is derived, to designate a chief magistrate or a military commander-in-chief. Over the next two millennia, refinements of the concept of strategy continued to focus on its military aspects. Carl von Clausewitz's attempted synthesis in the first half of the nineteenth century is an especially notable example: He wrote that whereas "tactics . . . [involve] the use of armed forces in the engagement, strategy [is] the use of engagements for the object of the war."[2] The adaptation of strategic terminology to a business context, however, had to await the Second Industrial Revolution, which began in the second half of the nineteenth century but really took off only in the twentieth century.[3]

The First Industrial Revolution (which spanned the mid-1700s to the mid-1800s) failed to induce much in the way of strategic thinking or behavior. This failure can be chalked up to the fact that while the period was marked by intense competition among industrial firms, virtually none of them had the power to influence market outcomes to any significant extent. Most businesses remained small and employed as little fixed capital as possible. The chaotic markets of this era led economists such as Adam Smith to describe market forces as an "invisible hand" that remained largely beyond the control of individual firms. Such firms required little or no strategy in any of the senses described in the quotations at the beginning of this chapter.

The Second Industrial Revolution, which began in the last half of the nineteenth century in the United States, saw the emergence of strategy as a way to shape market forces and affect the competitive environment. In the United States, the construction of key railroads after 1850 made it possible to build mass markets for the first time. Along with improved access to capital and credit, mass markets encouraged large-scale investment to exploit economies of scale in production and economies of scope in distribution. In some capital-intensive industries, Adam Smith's "invisible hand" came to be supplemented by what Alfred D. Chandler, Jr., a famous historian, has termed the "visible hand" of professional managers. By the late nineteenth century, a new type of firm began to emerge, first in the United States and then in Europe: the large, vertically integrated company that invested heavily in manufacturing and marketing, and in management hierarchies to coordinate those functions. Over time, the largest companies of this sort began to alter the competitive environment within their industries and even to cross industry boundaries.[4]

The need for explicitly strategic thinking was first articulated by high-level managers at these large companies. For example, Alfred Sloan, the chief executive of General Motors from 1923 to 1946, devised a successful strategy based on the perceived strengths and weaknesses of his company's critical competitor, the Ford Motor Company, and wrote it up after he retired.[5] And in the 1930s, Chester Barnard, a senior executive with New Jersey Bell, argued that managers should pay very close attention to "strategic factors," which depend on "personal or organizational action."[6]

World War II supplied a vital stimulus to strategic thinking in business as well as in the military domain, because it sharpened the problem of allocating scarce resources across the entire economy. New operations research techniques (e.g., linear programming) were devised, which paved the way for the use of quantitative analysis in formal strategic planning. In 1944, John von Neumann and Oskar Morgenstern published their classic work, *The Theory of Games and Economic Behavior,* which solved the problem of zero-sum games (many military ones, from an aggregate perspective) and framed the issues surrounding non-zero-sum games (most business situations, as discussed further in these terms in Chapter 4). The concept of the **learning curve,** first noted in the military aircraft industry in the 1920s and 1930s as manufacturers realized that direct labor costs decreased by a constant percentage as the cumulative number of aircraft produced doubled also became an important tool for production-planning efforts in wartime.

Wartime experiences encouraged not only the development of new tools and techniques, but also, in the view of some observers, the use of formal strategic thinking to guide management decisions. Peter Drucker, writing about this period, argued that "management is not just passive, adaptive behavior; it means taking action to make the desired results come to pass." He noted that economic theory had long treated markets as impersonal forces, beyond the control of individual entrepreneurs and organizations. In the age of large corporations, however, managing "implies responsibility for attempting to shape the economic environment, for planning, initiating, and carrying through changes in that economic environment, for constantly pushing back the limitations of economic circumstances on the enterprise's freedom of action."[7] This insight became the key rationale for business strategy—that is, by consciously using formal planning, a company could exert some positive control over market forces.

These insights into the nature of strategy seemed, however, to lie fallow through the 1950s. In the United States, rationing or outright bans on production during World War II combined with high levels of private savings to create excess demand for many products. The Korean War provided a further boost in demand. Europe and Japan experienced even more severe postwar dislocations, which induced greater governmental control of what Lenin had called the "commanding heights" of an economy, namely its key industries and enterprises. Similar increases in governmental control, as opposed to reliance on market forces, were observed in poorer countries, including many of the new ones that emerged as colonialism unwound itself.[8]

A more direct bridge to the development of strategic concepts for business applications was provided by interservice competition in the U.S. military after World War II. During this period, American military leaders began debating the arrangements that would best protect legitimate competition among the four military services while still maintaining the needed integration of strategic and tactical planning. Many argued that the Army, Navy, Marine Corps, and Air Force would be more efficient if they were unified into a single organization. As the debate raged, Philip Selznick, a sociologist, noted, that the Navy Department "emerged as the defender of subtle institutional values and tried many times to formulate the distinctive characteristics of the various services." In essence, "Navy spokesmen attempted to distinguish between the Army as a 'manpower' organization and the Navy as a finely adjusted system of technical, engineering skills—a 'machine-centered' organization. Faced with what it perceived as a mortal threat, the Navy became highly self-conscious about its distinctive competence."[9] The concept of **distinctive competence** would turn out to have great resonance for strategic management, as we will see.

ACADEMIC UNDERPINNINGS

Eminent economists produced some of the earliest academic writings about strategy. For example, John Commons, an institutionalist, wrote in his 1934 book about the focus of business firms on strategic or limiting factors in a way that was picked up a few years later—potash example and all—by Chester Barnard (see the first quotation at the beginning of this chapter).[10] Ronald Coase, who might be called the first organizational economist, published a provocative article in 1937 that asked why firms exist—an article that continues to be cited seventy-five years later, and that garnered its author a Nobel Prize.[11] Joseph Schumpeter, a technologist, discussed in his 1942 book the idea that business strategy encompassed much more than the price-setting contemplated in orthodox microeconomics.[12] And a book published in 1959 by Edith Penrose explicitly related the growth of business firms to the resources under their control and the administrative framework used to coordinate their use.[13] Overall, however, economists had much less direct impact on the early evolution of academic thinking about business strategy than did academics located in business schools.

The Second Industrial Revolution had witnessed the founding of many elite business schools in the United States, beginning with the Wharton School in 1881. The Harvard Business School, founded in 1908, was one of the first to promote the idea that managers should be trained to think strategically rather than just act as functional administrators, although strategy itself was not explicitly invoked until the 1960s. In 1912, Harvard introduced a required second-year course in "Business Policy" that was designed to integrate the knowledge gained in functional areas like accounting, operations, and finance. The goal was to give students a broader perspective on the strategic problems faced by corporate executives. A course description from 1917 claimed that "an analysis of any business problem shows not only its relation to other problems in the same group, but also the intimate connection of groups. Few problems in business are purely intradepartmental." Also, the policies of each department were supposed to maintain a "balance in accord with the underlying policies of the business as a whole."[14]

In the early 1950s, two professors of business policy at Harvard, George Albert Smith, Jr. and C. Roland Christensen, encouraged students to question whether a firm's strategy matched its competitive environment. In reading cases, students were taught to ask the following question: Do a company's policies "fit together into a program that effectively meets the requirements of the competitive situation?"[15] Students were told to address this problem by asking, "How is the whole industry doing? Is it growing and expanding? Is it static? Is it declining?" Then, having "sized up" the competitive environment, the student was to ask still more questions: "On what basis must any one company compete with the others in this particular industry? At what kinds of things does it have to be especially competent, in order to compete?"[16]

In the late 1950s, another Harvard business policy professor, Kenneth Andrews, expanded upon this thinking by arguing that "every business organization, every sub-unit of organization, and even every individual [ought to] have a clearly defined set of purposes or goals which keeps it moving in a *deliberately chosen direction* and prevents its drifting in undesired directions" (emphasis added). Like Alfred Sloan at General Motors, Andrews thought that "the primary function of the general manager, over time, is supervision of the continuous process of determining the nature of the enterprise and setting, revising, and attempting to achieve its goals."[17] His conclusions were motivated by an industry note and company cases that Andrews prepared on Swiss watchmakers, which uncovered significant differences in performance associated with different strategies for competing in that industry.[18] This format of combining industry notes with company cases soon became the norm in Harvard's Business Policy course.[19]

In the 1960s, classroom discussions in business schools began to focus on matching a company's "strengths" and "weaknesses"—its distinctive competence—with the "opportunities" and "threats" (or risks) that it faced in the marketplace. This framework, which came to be referred to by the acronym **SWOT,** represented a major step forward in bringing explicitly competitive thinking to bear on questions of strategy. Kenneth Andrews combined these elements in a way that emphasized that competencies or resources had to match environmental needs to have value (see Exhibit 1.1).[20]

In 1963, a business policy conference was held at Harvard that helped diffuse the SWOT concept in both academia and management practice. Attendance at the conference was heavy, but the ensuing popularity of SWOT—which is still used by many firms in the twenty-first century—did not bring closure to the problem of actually defining a firm's distinctive competence. To solve this problem, strategists had to decide which aspects of the firm were "enduring and unchanging over relatively long periods of time" and which were "necessarily more responsive to changes in the marketplace and the pressures of other environmental forces." This distinction was crucial, because "the *strategic* decision is concerned with the long-term development of the enterprise" (emphasis added).[21] When strategy choices were analyzed from a long-range perspective, the idea of "distinctive competence" took on added importance because most long-run investments involved greater risks. Thus, if the opportunities a firm was pursuing appeared "to outrun [its] present distinctive competence," then the strategist had to consider a firm's "willingness to gamble that the latter can be built up to the required level."[22]

The debate over a firm's "willingness to gamble" on its distinctive competence in its pursuit of an opportunity continued throughout the 1960s, fueled by a booming stock market and corporate strategies that were heavily geared toward growth and diversification. In a classic 1960 article that anticipated this debate, titled "Marketing Myopia," Theodore Levitt had been sharply critical of any firm that focused too narrowly on delivering a specific product, presumably exploiting its distinctive competence, rather than consciously serving the customer. Levitt argued that when companies fail, "it usually means that the product fails to adapt to the constantly changing patterns of consumer needs and tastes, to new and modified marketing institutions and practices, or to product developments in complementary industries."[23]

Another leading strategist, Igor Ansoff, disagreed with this position, arguing that Levitt asked companies to take unnecessary risks by investing in new products that might not match the firm's distinctive competence. Ansoff suggested that a company should

Exhibit 1.1 Andrew's Strategy Framework

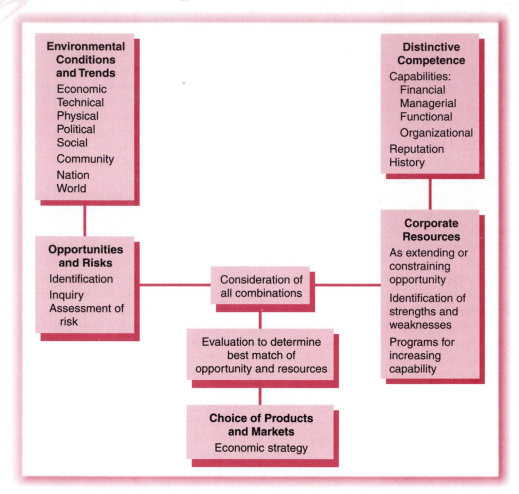

first ask whether a new product had a "common thread" with its existing products. He defined the common thread as a firm's "mission"—its commitment to exploit an existing need in the market as a whole.[24] According to Ansoff, "sometimes the customer is erroneously identified as the common thread of a firm's business. In reality a given type of customer will frequently have a range of unrelated product missions or needs."[25] To enable a firm to maintain its strategic focus, Ansoff suggested four categories for defining the common thread in its business/corporate strategy, as depicted in Exhibit 1.2.[26] Ansoff and others also worked to translate the logic built into the SWOT framework into complex flowcharts of concrete questions that needed to be answered in the development of strategies.[27]

In the 1960s, diversification and technological changes increased the complexity of the strategic situations that many companies faced, and their need for more sophisticated measures that could be used to evaluate and compare many different types of

Exhibit 1.2   Ansoff's Product/Mission Matrix

	Present Product	New Product
Present Mission	Market penetration	Product development
New Mission	Market development	Diversification

businesses. Because academics at business schools remained strongly wedded to the idea that strategies could be analyzed only on a case-by-case basis that accounted for the unique characteristics of every business, corporations turned elsewhere to satisfy their craving for standardized approaches to strategy making.[28] According to a study conducted by the Stanford Research Institute, most large U.S. companies had set up formal planning departments by 1963.[29]

General Electric (GE) served as a bellwether in developing planning techniques. It used business school faculty quite extensively in its executive education programs, but also developed an elaborate computer-based "Profitability Optimization Model" (PROM) on its own in the early 1960s that appeared to explain a significant fraction of the variation in the return on investment afforded by its various businesses.[30] Over time, GE, like many other companies, also sought the help of consulting firms. Although consultants made multifaceted contributions to business (e.g., to planning, forecasting, logistics, and long-range research and development), the next section focuses on their impact on mainstream strategic thinking.

THE RISE OF STRATEGY CONSULTANTS

The 1960s and early 1970s witnessed the rise of a number of strategy consulting practices. In particular, the Boston Consulting Group (BCG), founded in 1963, had a major impact on the field by applying quantitative research to problems of business and corporate strategy. BCG's founder, Bruce Henderson, believed that a consultant's job was to find "meaningful quantitative relationships" between a company and its chosen markets.[31] In his words, "good strategy must be based primarily on logic, not . . . on experience derived from intuition."[32] Indeed, Henderson was convinced that economic theory would eventually lead to the development of a set of universal rules for strategy. As he explained, "in most firms strategy tends to be intuitive and based upon traditional patterns of behavior which have been successful in the past." In contrast, "in growth industries or in a changing environment, this kind of strategy is rarely adequate."[33]

In order to help executives make effective strategic decisions, BCG drew on the existing knowledge base in academia: one of its first employees, Seymour Tilles, was formerly a lecturer in Harvard's Business Policy course. BCG also struck off in a new direction that Bruce Henderson described as "the business of selling powerful oversimplifications."[34] In fact, BCG came to be known as a "strategy boutique"—early in its history, its business was largely based on a single concept: the experience curve (discussed below). Using a single concept proved valuable because "in nearly all problem solving there is a universe of alternative choices, most of which must be discarded without more than cursory attention." Hence, some "frame of reference is needed to screen the . . . relevance of data, methodology, and implicit value judgments" involved in any strategy decision. Given the complexities of decision making, the most useful "frame of reference is the concept. Conceptual thinking is the skeleton or the framework on which all other choices are sorted out."[35]

BCG and the Experience Curve

BCG first developed its version of the learning curve—what it labeled the **experience curve**—in 1965–1966. According to Bruce Henderson, "it was developed to try to explain price and competitive behavior in the extremely fast growing segments" of industries for clients such as Texas Instruments and Black and Decker.[36] As BCG consultants studied these industries, they naturally asked, "[why does] one competitor [outperform] another (assuming comparable management skills and resources)? Are there basic rules for success? There, indeed, appear to be rules for success, and they relate to the impact of accumulated experience on competitors' costs, industry prices and the interrelation between the two."[37]

BCG's standard claim for the experience curve was that, for each doubling of cumulated output, *total* costs would decline roughly 20 percent because of economies of scale, organizational learning, and technological innovation. Exhibit 1.3 illustrates an 84 percent experience effect, implying a 16 percent cost reduction associated with each doubling of experience, for Ford's Model T. The strategic implications, according to BCG, were that "the producer . . . who has made the most units should have the lowest costs and the highest profits."[38] Bruce Henderson claimed that with the experience curve, "the stability of competitive relationships should be predictable, the value of market share change should be calculable, [and] the effects of growth rate should [also] be calculable."[39]

From the Experience Curve to Portfolio Planning

By the early 1970s, the experience curve had led to another "powerful oversimplification" by BCG: the so-called growth-share matrix, which represented the first use of **portfolio planning.** The relative potential of a diversified company's portfolio of business units as areas for investment was compared by plotting them on the grid shown in Exhibit 1.4.[40]

BCG's basic strategy recommendation was to maintain a balance between "cash cows" (that is, mature businesses) and "stars," while allocating some resources to fund "question marks" (that is, potential stars). "Dogs" were to be sold off. Using more sophisticated language, a BCG vice president explained that "since the producer with the

Exhibit 1.3   Experience Curve for Ford's Model T, 1910–1926

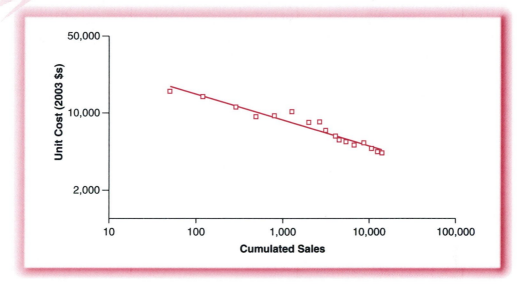

largest stable market share eventually has the lowest costs and greatest profits, it becomes vital to have a dominant market share in as many products as possible. However, market share in slowly growing products can be gained only by reducing the share of competitors who are likely to fight back." In a rapidly growing product market, in contrast, "a company can gain share by securing most of the growth. Thus, while competitors grow, the company can grow even faster and emerge with a dominant share when growth eventually slows."[41]

Exhibit 1.4   BCG's Growth-Share Matrix

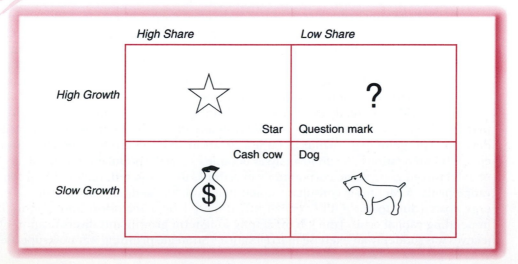

Strategic Business Units and Portfolio Planning

Numerous other consulting firms developed their own grids for portfolio planning at roughly the same time as BCG. McKinsey & Company's effort, for instance, began in 1968 when Fred Borch, the CEO of GE, asked McKinsey to examine GE's corporate structure. At the time, GE consisted of 200 profit centers and 145 departments arranged around ten groups. The boundaries for these units had been defined according to theories of financial control, which the McKinsey consultants judged to be inadequate. They argued instead that the firm should be organized on more strategic lines, with greater concern for external conditions and a more future-oriented approach than was possible using measures of past financial performance. McKinsey's study recommended a formal strategic planning system that would divide the company into "natural business units," which Borch later renamed **strategic business units (SBUs).**

After spending two years implementing this advice, GE asked McKinsey for help evaluating the strategic plans that were being devised by the company's many SBUs. GE had already considered using the BCG growth-share matrix to decide the fate of its SBUs, but its top management had then decided that they could not set priorities on the basis of just two performance measures. After studying the problem, a McKinsey team produced what came to be known as the GE/McKinsey nine-block matrix (see Exhibit 1.5).[42] The nine-block matrix used approximately one dozen measures to screen for industry attractiveness and another dozen to screen for competitive position, although the weights attached to the measures were not specified.[43]

Another, more quantitative approach to portfolio planning was developed at roughly the same time under the aegis of the "Profit Impact of Market Strategies" (PIMS) program. PIMS was the multicompany successor to the PROM program that GE had started a decade earlier. By the mid-1970s, PIMS contained data on 620 SBUs drawn from fifty seven diversified corporations.[44] These data were originally used to explore the determinants of returns on investment by regressing historical returns on several dozen variables, including market share, product quality, investment intensity, and marketing and R&D expenditures. The regressions established what were supposed to be benchmarks for the potential performance of SBUs with particular characteristics against which their actual performance might be compared.

In all these applications, segmenting diversified corporations into SBUs came to be recognized as an important precursor to analyzing economic performance.[45] This step forced "deaveraging" of cost and performance numbers that had previously been calculated at more aggregated levels. In addition, it was thought that with such approaches, "strategic thinking was appropriately pushed 'down the line' to managers closer to the particular industry and its competitive conditions."[46]

In the 1970s, virtually every major consulting firm used some sort of portfolio planning—either a variant on the two matrices already discussed or its own internally developed program (e.g., Arthur D. Little's 24-box life-cycle matrix)—to generate strategy recommendations. Portfolio analyses became especially popular after the oil crisis of 1973 forced many large corporations to rethink, if not discard, their existing long-range plans. A McKinsey consultant noted that with "the sudden quadrupling of energy costs [due to the OPEC embargo], followed by a recession and rumors of impending capital crisis, [the job of] setting long-term growth and diversification objectives was suddenly an exercise in irrelevance." Strategic planning was now supposed

Exhibit 1.5   The Industry Attractiveness-Business Strength Matrix

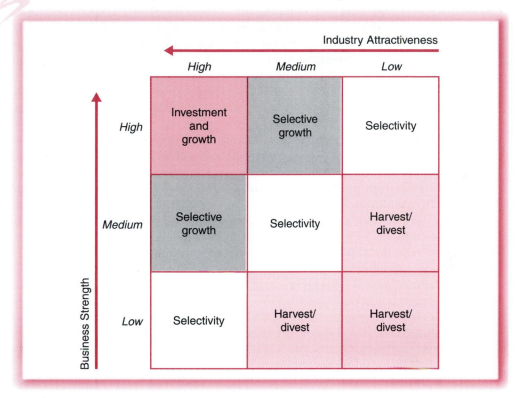

to involve "sorting out winners and losers, setting priorities, and husbanding capital." In a climate where "product and geographic markets were depressed and capital was presumed to be short,"[47] portfolio planning gave executives a ready excuse to get rid of underperforming business units while directing more funds to the "stars." By 1979, a survey of the *Fortune 500* industrial companies concluded that 45 percent of those firms had introduced portfolio planning techniques of some sort.[48]

PROBLEMS AND PROMISE

Somewhat ironically, the very macroeconomic conditions that (initially) increased the popularity of portfolio planning also inspired questions about the experience curve. The high inflation and excess capacity (due to downturns in demand) induced by the oil shocks of 1973 and 1979 disrupted historical experience curves in many industries, suggesting that Bruce Henderson had oversold the concept in a 1974 pamphlet entitled *Why Costs Go Down Forever.* Another problem with the experience curve was pinpointed by a classic 1974 article by William Abernathy and Kenneth Wayne, which argued that "the consequence of intensively pursuing a cost-minimization strategy [for example, one based on the experience curve] is a reduced ability to make innovative changes and to respond to those introduced by competitors."[49] Abernathy and Wayne pointed to Henry Ford's obsession with reducing the costs of the Model T, which left his company vulnerable to the strategy of product innovation initiated by Alfred Sloan at General Motors. The experience curve also drew criticism for treating cost reductions as automatic rather than something to be managed, for assuming that most experience could be kept proprietary, for mixing up different sources of cost reduction with very different strategic implications (e.g., learning versus scale versus vertical integration), and for leading to stalemates as multiple competitors pursued the same experience-based strategy.[50]

In the late 1970s, portfolio planning came under attack as well. One problem was that the strategic recommendations for an SBU were often inordinately sensitive to the specific portfolio planning technique employed. For instance, when an academic study applied four different portfolio techniques to a group of 15 SBUs owned by the same *Fortune 500* corporation, it found that only one out of the 15 SBUs fell in the same area of each of the four matrices and only five of the SBUs were classified similarly in three of the four matrices.[51] This level of agreement was only slightly higher than would have been expected if the 15 SBUs had been classified randomly four separate times!

Second and more seriously, even if one could figure out the "right" technique to employ, the mechanical determination of resource-allocation patterns on the basis of historical data was inherently problematic, as was the implicit assumption that financial capital was *the* scarce resource on which top management had to focus. Some consultants readily acknowledged these problems. In 1979, Fred Gluck, the head of McKinsey's strategic management practice, ventured the opinion that "the heavy dependence on 'packaged' techniques [has] frequently resulted in nothing more than a tightening up, or fine tuning, of current initiatives within the traditionally configured businesses." Even worse, technique-based strategies "rarely beat existing competition" and often leave businesses "vulnerable to unexpected thrusts from companies not previously considered competitors."[52] Gluck and his colleagues sought to loosen some of the constraints imposed by mechanistic approaches by proposing that successful companies' strategies progress through four phases (depicted in Exhibit 1.6) that involve grappling with increasing levels of dynamism, multidimensionality, and uncertainty, and therefore become less amenable to routine quantitative analysis.[53]

An even more stinging attack on the analytical techniques popularized by strategy consultants was offered by two Harvard Business School professors, Robert Hayes and William Abernathy, in 1980. They argued that "these new principles [of management], despite their sophistication and widespread usefulness, encourage a preference for (1) analytic detachment rather than the insight that comes from 'hands on experience' and (2) short-term cost reduction rather than long-term development of technological competitiveness."[54] Hayes and Abernathy particularly criticized portfolio planning as a tool that led managers to focus on minimizing financial risks rather than investing in new opportunities that required a long-term commitment of resources.[55]

These criticisms notwithstanding, portfolio planning had a lasting influence on subsequent work on business strategy because it focused attention on the need for more careful analysis of the two basic dimensions of the portfolio planning grid shown in Exhibit 1.7: industry attractiveness and competitive position. Although these two dimensions had been identified earlier—in the General Survey Outline developed by McKinsey

Exhibit 1.6   Four Phases of Strategy

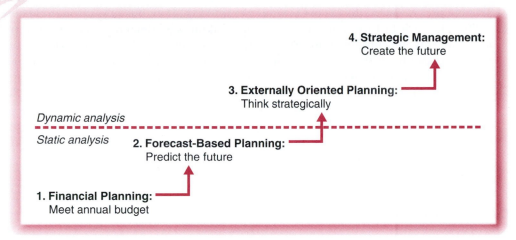

1. **Financial Planning:**
   Meet annual budget

2. **Forecast-Based Planning:**
   Predict the future

Static analysis

Dynamic analysis

3. **Externally Oriented Planning:**
   Think strategically

4. **Strategic Management:**
   Create the future

& Company for the internal use of its consultants in 1952, for example—portfolio planning underscored their usefulness in analyzing the effects of competition on business performance. Specifically, a business's performance could be thought of as the sum of the average profitability of the industry in which it operated plus its competitive advantage (or minus its competitive disadvantage) relative to the average competitor within that industry. Subsequent work aimed to dig deeper into the determinants of industry attractiveness and competitive position, as discussed in Chapters 2 and 3 respectively. But the attractions of an explicitly competitive perspective, involving direct comparisons with reference competitors, had already overcome traditional scruples based on the uniqueness of companies and their implied incommensurability.

Exhibit 1.7   Two Detriments of Profitability

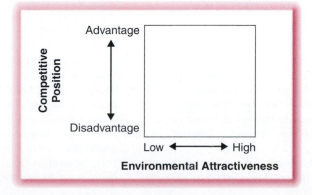

SUMMARY

This chapter reviewed the history of strategic thinking about business through the mid-1970s. The early history of business-strategic thinking was affected in many ways by military concepts and considerations. Sociology, with its construct of distinctive competence, seems to have been the academic field that wielded the most influence on the early elaborations of the concept of strategy in business, mostly by professors at business schools.[56] Consulting firms disseminated academic insights and developed sets of tools to help top managers (even of very highly diversified companies) monitor the strategies of the business units under them. Although disillusionment with specific tools was quick to set in, this line of work nevertheless framed the agenda for future research and development in the field of strategy.

GLOSSARY

- distinctive competence
- experience curve
- learning curve

- portfolio planning
- strategic business units (SBUs)

- strategy
- SWOT

NOTES

1. Consult, for instance, the two McKinsey Award winners from the 1996 volume of the *Harvard Business Review:* "Strategy as Revolution" by Gary Hamel and "What Is Strategy?" by Michael E. Porter.

2. Carl von Clausewitz, *On War,* trans. and ed. Michael Eliot Howard and Peter Paret (1976; reprint, Princeton, N.J.: Princeton University Press, 1984), p. 128.

3. For a depiction of business history in terms of these industrial revolutions and a third one, see Thomas K. McCraw, ed., *Creating Modern Capitalism: How Entrepreneurs, Companies, and Countries Triumphed in Three Industrial Revolutions* (Cambridge, Mass.: Harvard University Press, 1997). For an extended account of the evolution of business strategies through to the end of the twentieth century, see Pankaj Ghemawat, "Competition and Business Strategy in Historical Perspective," *Business History Review,* 76 (Spring 2002): 37–74.

4. Alfred Chandler, Jr., *Strategy and Structure: Chapters in the History of the Industrial Enter-* *prise* (Cambridge, Mass.: MIT Press, 1962) and *Scale and Scope: The Dynamics of Industrial Capitalism* (Cambridge, Mass.: Belknap Press of Harvard University Press, 1990).

5. See Alfred P. Sloan, *My Years with General Motors.* (New York: Doubleday, 1963).

6. Chester Barnard, *The Functions of the Executive* (1938; reprint, Cambridge, Mass.: Harvard University Press, 1968), pp. 204–205.

7. Peter Drucker, *The Practice of Management* (New York: Harper, 1954), p. 11.

8. Daniel Yergin and Joseph Stanislaw, *The Commanding Heights: The Battle between Government and the Marketplace That Is Remaking the Modern World* (New York: Simon & Schuster, 1998).

9. Philip Selznick, *Leadership in Administration: A Sociological Interpretation* (New York: Harper & Row, 1957), pp. 49–50.

10. John Rogers Commons, *Institutional Economics; Its Place in Political Economy* (New York: Macmillan Co., 1934); Barnard, *Functions of the Executive.*

11. Ronald H. Coase, "The Nature of the Firm," *Economica* 4, no. 16 (1937): 386–405. Reprinted in George Joseph Stigler and Kenneth E. Boulding, eds., *Readings in Price Theory* (Chicago: Richard D. Irwin, 1952). In addition to Coase's article, which influenced thinking about both strategy and organizations, a number of other authors made pioneering contributions to organizational theory that cannot be fully recognized here: Henri Fayol on administrative theory, Elton Mayo and Melville Dalton on human relations, and Herbert Simon and James March on information processing, to cite just a few.

12. Joseph Schumpeter, *Capitalism, Socialism, and Democracy* (New York: Harper, 1942).

13. Edith Penrose, *The Theory of the Growth of the Firm* (Oxford: Basil Blackwell, 1959).

14. Official Register of Harvard University, March 29, 1917, pp. 42–43.

15. George Smith and C. Roland Christensen, *Suggestions to Instructors on Policy Formulation* (Chicago: Richard D. Irwin, 1951), pp. 3–4.

16. George Smith, *Policy Formulation and Administration: A Casebook of Top-Management Problems in Business* (Chicago: Richard D. Irwin, 1951), p. 14.

17. Kenneth Andrews, *The Concept of Corporate Strategy* (Homewood, Ill.: Richard D. Irwin, 1971), p. 23.

18. See Edmund Learned, C. Roland Christensen, and Kenneth Richmond Andrews, *Problems of General Management; Business Policy: A Series Casebook* (Homewood, Ill.: Richard D. Irwin, 1961), pt. I.

19. Interview with Kenneth Andrews, April 2, 1997.

20. Kenneth Andrews, *The Concept of Corporate Strategy*, rev. ed. (Homewood, Ill.: Richard D. Irwin, 1980), p. 69.

21. Ibid. (1971 ed.), p. 29.

22. Ibid., p. 100.

23. Theodore Levitt, "Marketing Myopia," *Harvard Business Review* 53, no. 5 (1975): 45–56.

24. H. Igor Ansoff, *Corporate Strategy: An Analytic Approach to Business Policy for Growth and Expansion* (New York: McGraw-Hill, 1965), pp. 106–109.

25. Ibid., pp. 105–108.

26. Exhibit 1.2 is based on Henry Mintzberg's adaptation of Ansoff's matrix. Henry Mintzberg, "Generic Strategies," in *Advances in Strategic Management* (Greenwich, Conn.: JAI Press, 1988), p. 2. For the original, see Ansoff, *Corporate Strategy*, p. 128.

27. Michael E. Porter, "Industrial Organization and the Evolution of Concepts for Strategic Planning," in *Corporate Strategy: The Integration of Corporate Planning Models and Economics*, ed. Thomas H. Naylor (New York: North-Holland, 1982), p. 184.

28. Adam M. Brandenburger, Michael E. Porter, and Nicolaj Siggelkow, "Competition and Strategy: The Emergence of a Field" (paper presented at the McArthur Symposium, Harvard Business School, October 9, 1996), pp. 3–4.

29. Stanford Research Institute, *Planning in Business*, Menlo Park, Calif., 1963.

30. Sidney E. Schoeffler, Robert D. Buzzell, and Donald F. Heany, "Impact of Strategic Planning on Profit Performance," *Harvard Business Review* 52, no. 2 (1974): 137–145.

31. Interview with Seymour Tilles, October 24, 1996. Tilles credits Henderson for recognizing the competitiveness of Japanese industry at a time, in the late 1960s, when few Americans believed that Japan or any other country could compete successfully against American industry.

32. Bruce D. Henderson, *The Logic of Business Strategy* (Cambridge, Mass.: Ballinger, 1984), p. 10.

33. Bruce D. Henderson, *Henderson on Corporate Strategy* (Cambridge, Mass.: Abt Books, 1979), pp. 6–7.

34. Interview with Seymour Tilles, October 24, 1996.

35. Henderson, *Henderson on Corporate Strategy*, p. 41.

36. Bruce Henderson explained that unlike earlier versions of the learning curve, BCG's experience curve "encompasses all costs (including capital, administrative, research, and marketing) and traces them through technological displacement and product evolution. It is also

based on cash flow rates, not accounting allocation." Bruce D. Henderson, preface to Boston Consulting Group, *Perspectives on Experience* (1968; reprint, Boston: BCG, 1972).

37. Ibid., p. 7.

38. Patrick Conley, *Experience Curves as a Planning Tool,* BCG Pamphlet (1970), p. 15.

39. Henderson, preface to *Perspectives on Experience.*

40. See George Stalk and Thomas M. Hout, *Competing against Time: How Time-Based Competition Is Reshaping Global Markets* (New York: Free Press, 1990), p. 12.

41. Conley, *Experience Curves as a Planning Tool,* pp. 10–11.

42. Arnoldo C. Hax and Nicolas S. Majluf, *Strategic Management: An Integrative Perspective* (Englewood Cliffs, N.J.: Prentice Hall, 1984), p. 156.

43. Interview with Mike Allen, April 4, 1997.

44. Sidney E. Schoeffler, Robert D. Buzzell, and Donald F. Heany, "Impact of Strategic Planning on Profit Performance," *Harvard Business Review* 52, no. 2 (1974): 137–145.

45. See Walter Kiechel, "Corporate Strategies under Fire," *Fortune,* December 27, 1982.

46. Frederick W. Gluck and Stephen P. Kaufman, "Using the Strategic Planning Framework," McKinsey internal document in *Readings in Strategy* (1979), pp. 3–4.

47. J. Quincy Hunsicker, "Strategic Planning: A Chinese Dinner?" (McKinsey staff paper, December 1978), p. 3.

48. Philippe Haspeslagh, "Portfolio Planning: Uses and Limits," *Harvard Business Review* 60, no. 1 (1982): 58–73.

49. William J. Abernathy and Kenneth Wayne, "Limits of the Learning Curve," *Harvard Business Review* 52, no. 5 (1974): 109–119.

50. Pankaj Ghemawat, "Building Strategy on the Experience Curve," *Harvard Business Review* 63, no. 2 (1985): 143–149.

51. Yoram Wind, Vijay Mahajan, and Donald J. Swire, "An Empirical-Comparison of Standardized Portfolio Models," *Journal of Marketing* 47, no. 2 (1983): 89–99. The statistical analysis of Wind et al.'s results is based on an unpublished draft by Pankaj Ghemawat.

52. Gluck and Kaufman, "Using the Strategic Planning Framework," pp. 5–6.

53. Adapted from Frederick W. Gluck, Stephen P. Kaufman, and A. Steven Walleck, "The Evolution of Strategic Management," McKinsey staff paper (October 1978), p. 4. Reproduced in modified form in the same authors' "Strategic Management for Competitive Advantage," *Harvard Business Review* 58, no. 4 (1980): 154–161.

54. Robert H. Hayes and William J. Abernathy, "Managing Our Way to Economic Decline," *Harvard Business Review* 58, no. 4 (1980): 67–77.

55. Ibid., p. 71.

56. The doctrine of distinctive competence was recycled, with great success, in the 1990s. See the discussion of core competence in Chapter 6.

Mapping the Business Landscape

Pankaj Ghemawat and David Collis[1]

When an industry with a reputation for difficult economics meets a manager with a reputation for excellence, it is usually the industry that keeps its reputation intact.

—WARREN BUFFET

Warren Buffet may have overstated the case. Nevertheless, there is considerable evidence to support the idea—explicit in the techniques for portfolio analysis discussed in Chapter 1—that the industry in which a business operates has a strong influence on its economic performance. Statistical analyses show that 10–20 percent of the variation in businesses' accounting profitability reflects the industries in which they operate.[2] The key implication for managers—that the industry environment matters—is illustrated in Exhibit 2.1, which summarizes the extent to which average profitability has differed across broad industry groups over nearly two decades.[3] Note that the vertical axis subtracts out the estimated costs of (equity) capital from reported profitability (return on equity) so as to focus on economic profitability instead of accounting profitability. And the horizontal axis, which maps the size of each industry group in terms of the amount of equity capital invested in it, links measures of economic profitability to total economic value created or destroyed.

In addition, Exhibit 2.1 suggests a way of visualizing the profit potential afforded by a business environment—by mapping it into a landscape in which the vertical dimension captures the level of economic profitability (or unprofitability).[4] A two-dimensional landscape, such as the one shown in Exhibit 2.1, permits inclusion of just one dimension of choice—in this case, which industry to compete in. A three-dimensional landscape, such as the one in Exhibit 2.2, allows for two dimensions of choice—for example, where to compete along one dimension and how to compete along the other.

17

Exhibit 2.1   Average Economic Profits of U.S. Industry Groups (1984–2002)

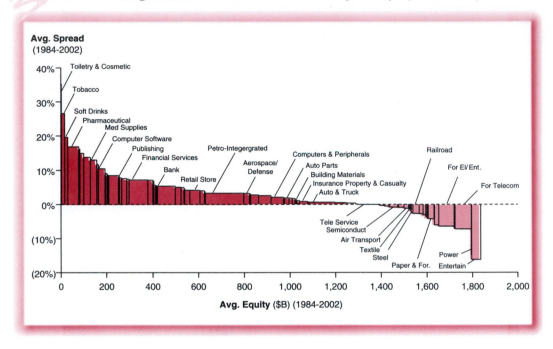

Exhibit 2.2   A Three-Dimensional Business Landscape

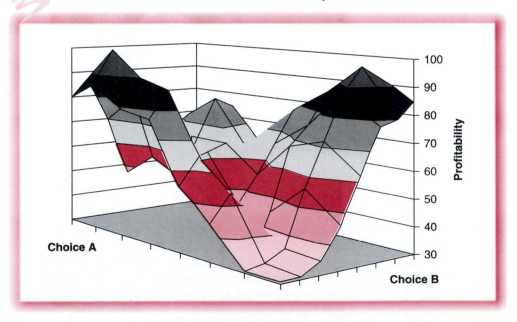

Most businesses are best envisioned as operating in a high-dimension space of choices, with each location in this space representing a different business strategy—that is, a different set of choices about what to do and how to do it. A **business landscape** maps each business strategy's elevation according to its economic profitability. The central challenge of strategy is to guide a business to a relatively high point on this landscape.

The chapters that follow will elaborate further on the landscape metaphor. In the context of this chapter, it can be used to highlight the fact that the profitability of direct competitors tends to have a common industry-specific component. Because of this industry-specific component, the average height above (or below) the zero-margin line—the average economic margin—will vary systematically across different industries. Recast in these terms, Exhibit 2.1 suggests that in the last twenty years or so, more than half of all the equity capital employed in U.S. industry has been invested in industry groups with average returns on equity and costs of equity capital that fell within four percentage points of one another. It is also clear, however, that businesses in some industry groups (e.g., pharmaceuticals) have generally operated on profit plateaus, whereas businesses in others (e.g., steel) have mostly remained stuck in deep troughs.

Managers' first-hand experience of such differences in average profitability across industries largely explains why many tend to take Warren Buffet seriously, despite his somewhat constraining view of what they can achieve. But managers need to do more than recognize how profitable particular industry arenas have proved in the past. They also need to understand the reasons behind such effects in order to decide where and how their firms will compete, to assess the implications of major changes in the relevant parts of the business landscape, and to adapt to or, better yet, shape the business landscape.

Such ambitions combine with the complexities of the real world to place a sizable premium on finding simple, yet structured ways of thinking about business landscapes. This chapter begins by describing three successively more general structures that have been proposed as solutions to this problem: the **supply-demand analysis** of individual markets, the **"five forces" framework** for industry analysis developed by Michael Porter, and the **value net** devised by Adam Brandenburger and Barry Nalebuff.[5] We then examine the actual process of mapping a business landscape in more detail.

The concept of the business landscape is deliberately meant to be broader than the usual conception of an "industry." Although this chapter focuses on so called industry-level (or population-level) effects on performance, we want to explore such effects within a broader set of relationships than the ones that have come to be associated with traditional industry analysis.

SUPPLY-DEMAND ANALYSIS

Supply and demand are the grandparents of all attempts at landscape analysis. The idea that the interplay of supply and demand determines a natural price goes back—at least in Western culture—to the scholastic professors (mostly clerics) of the Middle Ages.[6] Although many of the elements of supply-demand analysis were formalized by the scholastics and their successors, Alfred Marshall (in the late nineteenth century) was the first to combine them into the conventional supply-demand diagram depicted in Exhibit 2.3.

Exhibit 2.3   Supply-Demand Analysis

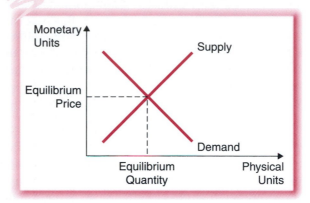

The development of the "Marshallian scissors" was motivated by the continuing debate about whether "value" was governed by supply-side costs or demand-side willingness to pay. This debate seemed no more reasonable to Marshall than disputes about whether the lower (or the upper) blade of a pair of scissors is the one that actually cuts paper. He suggested that price would instead be determined by the "equilibrium" point at which the **demand curve** for a particular product, summed across its buyers in decreasing order of their willingness to pay, intersected with its **supply curve,** summed across its suppliers in increasing order of their costs of production.[7]

The downward-sloping demand curve that underpins this line of analysis was treated as self-evident by Marshall, who also introduced the notion of the **price-elasticity of demand.** Demand is said to be relatively price-elastic if changes in price induce relatively large changes in the aggregate quantity demand (i.e., if the demand curve is close to horizontal); it is deemed relatively price-inelastic if the reverse is true (i.e., if the demand curve is close to vertical). On the supply side, Marshall argued that upward-sloping supply curves tend to become flatter—or even become horizontal—as the period lengthens. He had trouble, however, with his attempts to analyze supply curves that slope downward rather than upward (i.e., display increasing returns to scale). Additionally, his analysis assumed that individual buyers and sellers would be small in relation to the size of the overall market and homogenous in the sense that a given buyer would have the same willingness to pay for the product of each supplier, and a given supplier would face the same costs in supplying its product to each buyer.

Supply-demand analysis was incorporated relatively quickly into economics and marketing courses at business schools. It seems to have had less impact on the teaching and practice of business strategy until the recessions of the 1970s and early 1980s, when downward shifts in demand curves reinforced the importance of developing a more thorough understanding of supply curves or, more precisely, cost curves that could help determine where prices would settle down.

For an example of this sort of analysis, consider Exhibit 2.4, which traces the cost curve for hospitals in the Greater Boston area in 1991, as developed by Bain and Company, a consulting firm. This simple piece of analysis helped sensitize the high-cost Harvard Medical Center (HMC) teaching hospitals to the dire implications of the expected

Exhibit 2.4   Supply Curve for Boston Hospitals

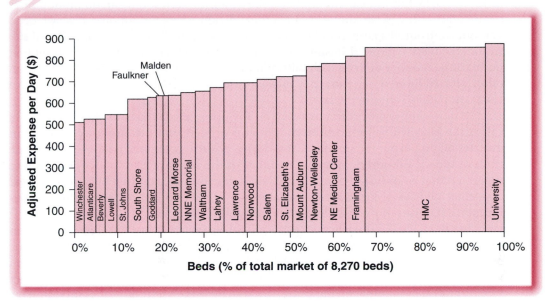

decrease in hospital utilization rates in Massachusetts from 80 percent in 1991 to 40–60 percent by 1999, as "hospital bed days" per person declined from 1.2 per year toward the national average of 0.6 per year.[8] Note that with 40–60 percent utilization, the HMC hospitals were all stuck farther out on the cost curve than its point of intersection with demand.

This example also illustrates the limitations of Marshallian supply-demand analysis. First, it is unrealistic to treat the hospitals in the local market as individually small and lacking market power. In fact, the two largest teaching hospitals affiliated with the HMC, Massachusetts General Hospital and Brigham and Women's Hospital, decided to join forces in the aftermath of Bain's study to attain a combined market share of 21 percent and improve their "clout." Second, the example also violates the assumption of homogeneity. Patients' needs differ, as do hospitals' relative effectiveness in fulfilling those needs, to an extent that can only partially be controlled for by adjusting hospitals' costs on the basis of their case mix. It would therefore be useful to generalize the specializing assumptions associated with supply-demand analysis in this case and many others. The attempt to do so that has met with the greatest success in the business community is considered next, in its own historical context.

THE "FIVE FORCES" FRAMEWORK

The large-numbers assumption built into conventional supply-demand analysis had already been relaxed more than half a century before Marshall offered his synthesis. In 1838, Antoine Cournot provided the first analytical characterizations of equilibrium prices under monopoly and with duopolists (two sellers) independently deciding how much to produce.[9] The homogeneity assumption was relaxed in two books published in 1933, one by Edward Chamberlin and the other by Joan Robinson, on monopolistic competition—that is, situations in which the individual firm monopolized its own products but confronted a large number of competitors, similarly situated, that offered substitute products.[10] From a business-strategic perspective, however, these attempts to posit a large number of firms with different products that otherwise resembled one another offered limited benefits: they missed the subtleties of **oligopolistic competition** (i.e., competition among the few).

A more important role was reserved for other economists in what came to be called the Harvard School, whose proponents argued that the structure of some industries might permit incumbent firms to earn positive economic profits over long periods of time.[11] Edward S. Mason, a member of the Harvard Economics Department, suggested that an industry's structure would determine the conduct of buyers and sellers—their choices of key decision variables—and, by implication, the industry's performance in terms of profitability, efficiency, and innovation.[12]

Joe Bain, also of the Harvard Economics Department (but unrelated to the consulting firm of the same name), sought to uncover relationships between industry structure and performance through empirical work focused on a limited number of structural variables. Two studies he published in the 1950s were particularly notable. The first study found that manufacturing industries in which the eight largest competitors accounted for more than 70 percent of sales were nearly twice as profitable as industries with eight-firm concentration ratios less than 70 percent.[13] The second study explained how, in certain industries, "established sellers can persistently raise their prices above a competitive level without attracting new firms to enter the industry."[14] Bain identified three basic types of **entry barriers:** (1) an absolute cost advantage for an established firm (an enforceable process patent, for instance); (2) a significant degree of product differentiation; and (3) economies of scale.

Bain's insights enabled the rapid growth of a new subfield of economics, known as **industrial organization (IO),** that explored the structural reasons why some industries were more profitable than others. By the mid-1970s, IO economists had carried out several hundred inter-industry empirical studies. Although the relationships between structural variables and performance proved more complicated than earlier work had suggested,[15] these studies confirmed that some industries have inherently higher long-run profitability, or "attractiveness," than others.

IO's immediate impact on business strategy was limited by the focus of Bain and his successors on public, rather than private, policy and by their emphasis on using a short list of structural variables to explain industry profitability in a way that slighted business strategy. Both problems were addressed by Michael Porter, who had worked with another IO economist at Harvard, Richard Caves, to study industry structure and business strategy. In 1974, Porter prepared a "Note on the Structural Analysis of Industries" that represented his first attempt to turn IO on its head by focusing on the business policy objective of profit maximization, rather than the public policy objective of minimizing "excess" profits.[16] In 1980, he published *Competitive Strategy,* a book that owed much of its success to his "five forces" framework. This framework, which is reproduced in Exhibit 2.5, sought to relate the average profitability of the participants in an industry to five competitive forces.

Exhibit 2.5   The "Five Forces" Framework for Industry Analysis

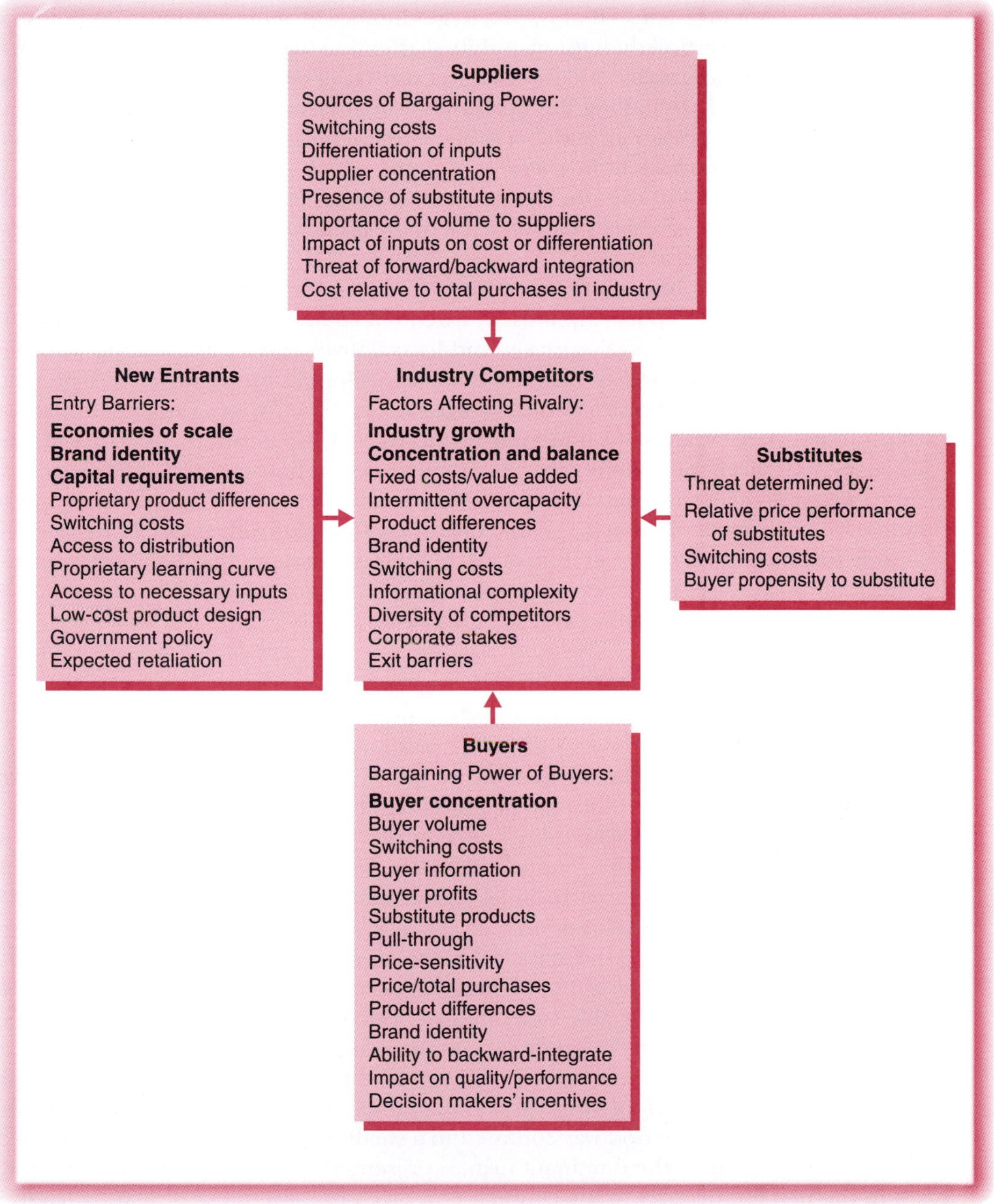

Suppliers

Sources of Bargaining Power:

Switching costs
Differentiation of inputs
Supplier concentration
Presence of substitute inputs
Importance of volume to suppliers
Impact of inputs on cost or differentiation
Threat of forward/backward integration
Cost relative to total purchases in industry

New Entrants

Entry Barriers:

Economies of scale
Brand identity
Capital requirements
Proprietary product differences
Switching costs
Access to distribution
Proprietary learning curve
Access to necessary inputs
Low-cost product design
Government policy
Expected retaliation

Industry Competitors

Factors Affecting Rivalry:

Industry growth
Concentration and balance
Fixed costs/value added
Intermittent overcapacity
Product differences
Brand identity
Switching costs
Informational complexity
Diversity of competitors
Corporate stakes
Exit barriers

Substitutes

Threat determined by:

Relative price performance
   of substitutes
Switching costs
Buyer propensity to substitute

Buyers

Bargaining Power of Buyers:

Buyer concentration
Buyer volume
Switching costs
Buyer information
Buyer profits
Substitute products
Pull-through
Price-sensitivity
Price/total purchases
Product differences
Brand identity
Ability to backward-integrate
Impact on quality/performance
Decision makers' incentives

Porter's framework for industry analysis generalized the supply-demand analysis of individual markets in several respects. First, it relaxed the assumptions of both large numbers and homogeneity—that is, of a large number of representative competitors. Second, along the vertical dimension, it shifted attention from two-stage vertical chains, each consisting of a supplier and a buyer, to three-stage chains made up of suppliers, rivals, and buyers. Third, along the horizontal dimension, it accounted for potential entrants and substitutes as well as direct rivals. These generalizations did, however, force Porter to reach beyond scientific evidence into the realm of common sense. Indeed, a survey of empirical IO in the late 1980s—more than a decade after Porter first developed his framework—revealed that only a few of the influences that Porter flagged commanded strong empirical support.[17]

Despite such problems, the "five forces" framework's focus on business concerns rather than public policy, its emphasis on **extended competition** for value rather than just competition among existing rivals, and its (relative) ease of application inspired numerous companies as well as business schools to adopt its use. A survey by Bain (the consulting firm) suggested a 25 percent usage rate in 1993.[18] Given the clear impact of this framework, we will discuss it in some detail. We will also illustrate the structural influences on industry profitability that the framework emphasizes by comparing two industry groups—steel and pharmaceuticals—located at the opposite ends of the business landscape depicted in Exhibit 2.1. While the discussion starts with the degree of **rivalry** among direct competitors in an industry, keep in mind that perhaps the most valuable contribution of Porter's "five forces" framework is its suggestion that rivalry is only one of several forces that determine industry attractiveness.

Force 1: The Degree of Rivalry

The degree of rivalry is the most obvious of the five forces in an industry—and the one on which strategists have focused historically. It influences the extent to which the value created by an industry will be dissipated through direct competition. Several types of structural determinants of rivalry can be identified. One set concerns the number and relative size of competitors. The more concentrated the industry, the more likely that competitors will recognize their mutual interdependence and so will restrain their rivalry. If, in contrast, the industry includes many small players, each will be apt to think that its effect on others will go unnoticed and so may be tempted to grab additional market share, thereby disrupting the market. For similar reasons, the presence of one dominant competitor rather than a set of equally balanced competitors may lessen rivalry: the dominant player may be able to set industry prices and discipline defectors, while equally sized players may try to outdo one another to gain an advantage.

A good example of these influences is seen in the U.S. steel industry, which was much more profitable before World War II than it has been in the postwar years. Competition in the prewar period was confined to a small number of domestic players led by U.S. Steel, which, as the dominant firm, represented an important source of stability. In the first few decades of the century, U.S. Steel, like a number of market leaders in other U.S. industries, helped prop up prices despite the erosion of its own market share over time.[19]

A second set of structural attributes that influence rivalry is more closely related to the industry's basic conditions. In capital-intensive industries, for example, the level of capacity utilization directly influences firms' incentive to engage in price competition to fill their plants. More generally, high fixed costs, excess capacity, slow growth, and lack of product differentiation all increase the degree of rivalry. In recent years, all of these attributes have been implicated as factors in the low profitability of the U.S. steel industry. In this industry, the ratio of fixed capital costs to value added is one of the highest in the U.S. economy, labor is largely a fixed cost, demand has been flat, and product differentiation is relatively limited, so that excess capacity has proved chronic and catastrophic in its effects.

The pharmaceutical industry presents a very different sort of picture. Fixed manufacturing costs are limited as a percentage of sales or value added. In fact, gross margins range above 90 percent for some blockbuster drugs. Demand has grown at double-digit rates, and differences among products, brand identity, and switching costs—discussed at greater length in the section "Force 4: Buyer Power"—have created insulation among competitors that is reinforced by patent protection.

Finally, the degree of rivalry also has behavioral determinants. If competitors are diverse, attach high strategic value to their positions in an industry, or face high exit barriers, they are more likely to compete aggressively. In steel, for instance, foreign competitors have, by adding diversity, helped shatter the domestic oligopolistic consensus. Strategic stakes have been high, because each domestic integrated steel maker has historically focused on steel as its core business. In addition, exit barriers have been compounded by the costs of cleaning up decommissioned sites. In pharmaceuticals, in contrast, both U.S. and non-U.S. firms have been able to effectively coordinate lobbying and other market-enhancement activities in the lucrative U.S. market under the auspices of the Pharmaceutical Research and Manufacturers of America association.

Force 2: The Threat of Entry

Average industry profitability is influenced by both potential and existing competitors. The key concept in analyzing the threat of entry is entry barriers, which prevent an influx of firms into an industry whenever profits, adjusted for the cost of capital, rise above zero. Entry barriers exist whenever it is difficult or not economically feasible for an outsider to replicate the incumbents' positions. Entry barriers usually rest on irreversible resource commitments, as discussed below and elaborated in Chapter 5.

Exhibit 2.5 illustrates the diverse forms that entry barriers can take. Some barriers reflect intrinsic physical or legal obstacles to entry. The most common forms of entry barriers, however, are usually the scale and the investment required to enter an industry as an efficient competitor. For example, when incumbent firms have well-established brand names and clearly differentiated products, a potential entrant may find it uneconomical to undertake the marketing campaign necessary to introduce its own products effectively. The magnitude of the required expenditures may be only part of the entrant's problem in such a situation: it may take years for the firm to build a reputation for product quality, no matter how large its initial advertising campaign. Also, entry barriers are not given exogenously: they can be contrived along these dimensions and many others. Credible threats of retaliation by incumbents represent perhaps the clearest example.

To illustrate the difference that entry barriers can make, consider two very different **strategic groups**—as in firms following two very different business strategies—within the pharmaceutical industry: research-based pharmaceutical companies versus manufacturers of generic pharmaceuticals. Research-based companies have been far more profitable on average, largely because they are protected by higher entry barriers. These barriers, some of which are discussed in more detail in Chapter 5, include patent protection, a new-drug development process that costs hundreds of millions of dollars and stretches over more than a decade, carefully cultivated brand identities backed, in some cases, by substantial advertising campaigns, and large sales forces that call on individual doctors. In contrast, the generic drug segment of the industry is characterized by a lack of product patents, much smaller requirements of capital and time for product development, weak to nonexistent brand identities, and distribution efforts that focus on serving large accounts that purchase in bulk at low prices.

The steel industry suggests that barriers to entry, like other elements of industry structure, can change over time. Integrated U.S. steel makers that manufactured steel from iron ore were long protected from competition by domestic entrants by the billion-plus dollars of capital required to build an efficiently scaled integrated steel mill. Since the 1960s, however, integrated steel makers have come under intense pressure from minimills, which make steel from scrap rather than from iron ore. Minimill technology has essentially reduced the scale required for efficient operation by a factor of 10 (or more) and the investment required per ton of capacity by another factor of 10—leading, in some sense, to barriers to entry one-hundredth as high as before. As a result, profitability has collapsed in the segments of the steel industry that minimills have been able to penetrate.

Force 3: The Threat of Substitutes

The threat that **substitutes** pose to an industry's profitability depends on the relative price-to-performance ratios of the different types of products or services to which customers can turn to satisfy the same basic need. The threat of substitution is also affected by switching costs—that is, the costs in areas such as retraining, retooling, or redesign that are incurred when a customer switches to a different type of product or service. In many cases, the substitution process follows an S-shaped curve. It starts slowly as a few trendsetters risk experimenting with the substitute, picks up steam if other customers follow suit, and finally levels off when nearly all of the cost-effective substitution possibilities have been exhausted.

Substitute materials that are putting pressure on the steel industry include aluminum, plastics and ceramics. Consider, for example, the substitution of aluminum for steel in the metal can industry. Aluminum's lighter weight and superior lithographic characteristics enable it to take volume away from steel despite higher prices. The costs to can makers of switching from steel to aluminum did slow down substitution initially. Since the 1980s, however, substitution sped up so that steel currently holds only a small share of the market, in niches such as food cans.

It is worth emphasizing that any analysis of the threat of (demand-side) substitution must look broadly at all the different ways of performing similar functions for customers, not just at physically similar products. Thus, the steel industry also must reckon with the substitution threat associated with less-intensive use of steel in smaller, lighter cars. And substitutes for pharmaceuticals, broadly construed, might include preventive medical care and hospitalization. Indeed, there may be some truth to the pharmaceutical industry's assertions that one reason for its profitability and growth is the fact that pharmaceuticals represent a more cost-effective form of health care, in many cases, than hospitalization.

Conceptually, analysis of the substitution possibilities open to buyers should be supplemented by considering the possibilities available to suppliers.[20] Supply-side substitutability influences suppliers' willingness to provide required inputs, just as demand-side substitutability influences buyers' willingness to pay for products. Thus, while minimills historically did relatively well in the U.S. market, the spike demand for scrap as well as steel in China has, by providing scrap suppliers with substitute outlets, significantly impaired minimill performance—to such an extent that in early 2004, the United States imposed export controls on steel scrap!

Force 4: Buyer Power

Buyer power is one of the two vertical forces that influence the appropriation of the value created by an industry. It allows customers to squeeze industry margins by compelling competitors to either reduce prices or raise the level of service offered without recompense.

Probably the most important determinants of buyer power are the size and the concentration of customers. Such considerations help explain why auto makers, in particular, have historically enjoyed considerable leverage in dealing with steel makers. Other reasons include the extent to which they were well informed about steel makers' costs and the credibility of their threats to integrate backward into steel making (a strategy once adopted by Ford). In contrast, none of these sources of buyer power—concentration, good information, or the ability to backward-integrate—were evident, historically, in the pharmaceutical industry.

Buyer bargaining power can obviously be offset in situations in which competitors are themselves concentrated or differentiated. Both conditions have helped manufacturers of stainless and other specialty steels achieve higher rates of profitability than large, integrated steel makers. In the pharmaceutical industry, no substitutes are available for many (recently) patented drugs: they must be purchased from a single manufacturer.

It is also often useful to distinguish potential buyer power from the buyer's willingness or incentive to use that power. For example, the U.S. government is potentially a very powerful purchaser of pharmaceuticals through its Medicaid and Medicare programs. Historically, however, it has refrained from exercising its potential power—a fortunate state of affairs for the pharmaceutical industry but an unfortunate one for taxpayers. In fact, the prescription drug benefit added to Medicare in late 2003 is seen as a windfall for the pharmaceutical firms because it explicitly prohibits Medicare from using its purchasing power to bargain for lower prices!

To explain why buyers do or do not have the incentive to use their inherent power, we must look at other, more behavioral conditions. One of the most important factors in this regard in a market context is the share of the purchasing industry's cost accounted for by the products in question. Purchasing decisions naturally focus on larger-cost items first. This fact of life has been a curse for the steel industry: steel represents a major slice of the costs of many of the end-products in which it is used, from cans to cars.

Another important factor is the perceived risk of failure associated with a product's use. In pharmaceuticals, patients often lack enough information to evaluate competing drugs and must take into account the high personal cost of any substitute's failure. This high personal cost of failure is also a consideration for doctors who prescribe drugs: the medical profession is quite concerned about malpractice suits. Generics tend to be seen as particularly risky, a perception that has not been alleviated by scandals involving some firms' substandard manufacturing practices. As a result, high-priced brands have been able to retain significant shares in many product categories even after satisfactory generic substitutes have reached the market.

The pharmaceutical industry example also highlights the importance of studying the decision-making process when analyzing buyer power. The interests and incentives of all the players involved in the purchase decision must be understood if we are to predict the price-sensitivity of that decision. Many doctors and patients have traditionally lacked incentives to hold down the prices paid for drugs because a third party—an insurance company—actually footed the bill. These incentives are changing, however, as the spread of managed care increases price-sensitivity.

Force 5: Supplier Power

Supplier power is the mirror image of buyer power. As a result, the analysis of supplier power typically focuses first on the relative size and concentration of suppliers relative to competitors and second on the degree of differentiation in the inputs supplied. The ability to charge competitors—suppliers' buyers—different prices in line with the differences in the value created for each of them usually indicates that the market is characterized by high supplier power.

None of these considerations was much of a problem for the pharmaceutical industry in the past. For conventional drugs (as opposed to biotechnological products), inputs are usually available from several commodity chemical companies. The U.S. integrated steel industry, in contrast, has been ravaged by the way in which supplier power, particularly the power of workers unionized by the United Steel Workers, has been wielded. Through collective action, these employees have historically been able to bargain their wages to levels well in excess of other manufacturing industries while protecting jobs. Toward the beginning of the period considered in Exhibit 2.1, excess compensation and employment swallowed up as much as one-fourth of steel makers' total revenues!

We conclude this section by noting that relationships with buyers and suppliers have important cooperative as well as competitive elements. To foreshadow an example that will be looked at in more detail in the discussion of holdup in Chapter 5, General Motors and other U.S. automobile companies lost sight of this fact when they pushed their parts suppliers to the wall by playing them against one another. Japanese car manufacturers, in contrast, committed themselves to long-run supplier relationships that paid off in terms of higher quality and faster new product development. The importance of both **cooperation** and competition is further highlighted by the template for landscape analysis, the value net, that is discussed in the next section.

THE VALUE NET AND OTHER GENERALIZATIONS

The years since Porter first developed his "five forces" framework have seen the rearrangement and incorporation of additional variables (e.g., import competition, multimarket contact, and collaborative institutions such as trade associations) into the determinants of the intensity of each of the five competitive forces (rivalry, in the case of these examples). Even more important, the framework itself can be generalized as necessary by bringing new types of players into the analysis. The most successful attempt to do so involves the value net framework devised by Adam Brandenburger and Barry Nalebuff (see Exhibit 2.6).[21]

The value net highlights the critical role that **complementors**—participants from which customers buy complementary products or services, or to which suppliers sell complementary resources—can play in influencing business success or failure. Complementors are defined as being the mirror image of competitors (including new entrants and substitutes as well as existing rivals). On the demand side, they increase buyers' willingness to pay for products; on the supply side, they decrease the price that suppliers require for their inputs.

To see why it is important to include complementors in the picture, reconsider the pharmaceutical industry example. Doctors greatly influence the success of pharmaceutical manufacturers through their prescribing of drugs, but they cannot, in most cases, be considered buyers: gifts aside, money typically does not flow directly from them to the pharmaceutical manufacturers. Thus they are more naturally thought of as complementors who increase buyers' willingness to pay for particular products.

An even more powerful example is provided by the personal computer landscape, to which we will keep returning for examples in this section. Note that Microsoft's Windows XP operating system is more valuable on a laptop computer equipped with an Intel Centrino microprocessor than one containing another chip, and vice versa. Yet Microsoft and Intel wouldn't show up on one another's "five forces" screens! Common sense nevertheless suggests that Intel should regard Microsoft as an important player in the business landscape on which it operates, and vice versa. The importance of this insight is reinforced by recent reports of wobbles in the "Wintel" axis as the interests of these two players have diverged. Intel, at least, has incorporated complementors into its analyses of its business landscape.[22]

The next chapter will characterize more precisely the value that cooperation with complementors and other types of players can add. Here we will simply emphasize that

Exhibit 2.6   The Value Net

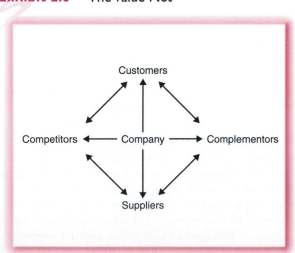

cooperating with complementors to expand the size of the pie should be combined with some consideration of competing with them to claim slices of that pie. Common sense suggests a number of rules of thumb for assessing the relative bargaining power of complementors. Several are based on considerations of relative competitive intensity: on how much competition there is among complementors, versus among rivals:

➤ *Relative concentration.* Complementors are more likely to have the power to pursue their own agenda when they are concentrated relative to competitors and are less likely to be able to do so when they are relatively fragmented. Examples include Microsoft's and Intel's sway over the much more fragmented manufacturers of personal computers. Or for that matter, their attempts to support AMD and Linux respectively, to weaken the other's hold on the industry.

➤ *Relative buyer/supplier switching costs.* When the costs to buyers or suppliers of switching across complementors are greater than their costs of switching across competitors, that increases complementors' ability to pursue their own goals. For instance, the cost of switching software on your personal computer is likely to be significantly higher than the cost of switching your Internet service provider, with clear implications for how much of the economic pie these two classes of players can hope to capture. And within software, switching costs tend to be significantly higher for operating systems than for most types of application programs, which is why many of the latter can be (and are) purchased independently.

➤ *Relative complementor/competitor switching costs.* Also related to the differentiation of complementors' versus competitors' product are differences in the ease with which complementors themselves can switch to working with different competitors versus the ease with which competitors can switch to working with different complementors. In particular, if complementors play a significant role in pulling through demand (e.g., through differentiation) or supply (e.g., through volumes commanded), their power is likely to expand. Intel's "Intel Inside" campaign is an example of an attempt by a complementor to build up independent pull-through on the demand side.

➤ *Asymmetric integration threats.* Complementors are likely to have more power when they can threaten to invade competitors' turf more credibly than competitors can threaten to invade complementors' turf. Thus Intel's forward integration into chipsets and even motherboards brings it into more direct competition with personal computer manufacturers, who do not seem to have any offsetting backward integration options.

➤ *Rate of growth of the pie.* From a behavioral perspective, competition with complementors to claim value is likely to be less intense when the size of the pie available to be divided among competitors and complementors is growing rapidly. Thus, it is hard not to see some of the recent tensions between Microsoft and Intel as related to the maturing of demand for high-end personal computers.

Having identified some commonsensical determinants of the relative bargaining power of complementors, it is worth remembering that the point is not to minimize complementors' bargaining power per se, by, for instance, setting up a fragmented, undifferentiated complementor network. That would be as bad as U.S. automakers' historical "divide and conquer" strategy toward their suppliers, described at the end of the preceding section, and for the same broad reason: the relationship with complementors has important cooperative as well as competitive elements. Having independent, differentiated complementors that are motivated to make investments in and support a particular platform has, in fact, proved critical in the personal computer landscape: Microsoft was able to beat Apple with operating systems not normally considered superior partly because, unlike Apple, it encouraged independent software vendors to write applications software to run on its platform.

More broadly, a review of the templates for landscape analysis discussed so far in this chapter—supply-demand analysis, the "five forces" framework, and the value nets—suggests that one way in which each generalizes its predecessor(s) is by bringing new types of players into the analysis. The next question is obvious: can additional improvements in our ability to understand the business landscape be achieved by further broadening the types of players considered?

The answer to this question depends on the case being considered but is sometimes clearly affirmative. For example, it is often important to account for **nonmarket relationships**—such as interactions with the government, the media, activist/interest groups, and the public—that, in addition to involving not-for-profit players, may be distinguished from market relationships by such characteristics as strong norms of fairness, broad enfranchisement, and majority rule.[23] Consider the case of the pharmaceutical industry. It depends on the government as a major buyer, regulator, sponsor of basic research, and upholder of patent laws, and has increasingly had to worry about the threat to its legitimacy posed by various social as well as political movements, particularly agitation against high pharmaceutical prices and profit margins. As a result, pharmaceutical companies should—and do—pay explicit attention to nonmarket relationships with governments and with nongovernmental organizations instead of looking at them solely in terms of their implications for relationships among groups of market (or for-profit) players. Folding them into the five or six forces will not help them develop integrated strategies that explicitly address both market and nonmarket relationships.[24]

A simple theme should stand out from this discussion: it is impossible to prespecify a single, all-purpose framework or template for analyzing the business landscape. Instead, the framework must be fitted to the landscape—and the decision issue—being analyzed. The successively more general frameworks discussed so far in this chapter remind us that we must think broadly about the other players involved and suggest a process for doing so. The rest of this chapter focuses on that topic.

THE PROCESS OF MAPPING BUSINESS LANDSCAPES

Having reviewed the historical development of different approaches to the business landscape, it is time to discuss how managers can link such thinking to strategic planning and action. The purpose of mapping the business landscape is not (as is often misunderstood) to identify whether one operates on a part of it that is high above or well below economic sea level (in the terms we used in discussing Exhibit 2.1): most managers know whether they are gasping for economic breath or not. Instead, the principal purpose is to understand the reasons for such variations and to incorporate them into strategic action. We lay out a six-step process to make this happen. Although it may be necessary to cycle through these steps more than once, they are most simply considered in turn.

Step 1: Gathering Information

Mapping the business landscape in the kind of detail described above requires a great deal of information. There is, as a result, a premium on thinking broadly about souces of information. Exhibit 2.7 lists some public sources of information for industry (and competitive) analysis. Several broader points should be made about the list.

➤ The amount of publicly available information in many situations is staggering. As a result, information overload seems at least as significant a problem as information unavailability. And there is often no alternative to information filtering.

➤ The selection and prioritization of sources of public information must account for variations in their content, quality, and accessibility. For example, while the Internet has clearly transformed information gathering, indiscriminate searches on industry names will likely yield too many hits of too low a quality while missing out on deeper points.

➤ The need to supplement public information with external private information (from buyers or suppliers, consultants, or even direct or indirect contact with competitors) varies. Generally speaking, however, it is possible to map a business landscape fairly well without depending on costly or hard-to-access external private information of the sort that is more often required for competitive analysis.

➤ Given the fixed costs of undertaking such analyses from scratch, much emphasis has been placed on systems for scanning the external environment on an ongoing basis. While systems of this sort are costly, their costs can be spread across the types of analysis discussed in Chapters 3–5 as well as in this one.

➤ The process of mapping the business landscape should leverage, instead of ignoring, the extensive amounts of information about the external environment generated internally by employees accomplishing their day-to-day activities. It is important

Exhibit 2.7   Public Sources of Information for Industry (and Competitive) Analysis

- Industry studies
  - Books
  - Stock analysts' reports
  - Market research reports
  - Business school case studies
  - Trade associations
  - Special interest groups
- Company Sources
  - Annual reports
  - SEC filings
  - Websites
  - Press releases
  - White papers
- Government Sources
  - Census, legal, or tax documents
  - Antitrust/regulatory documents
- Business Press
  - General publications
  - Specialized industry trade journals
  - Local newspapers
  - Online databases (e.g. Bloomberg, OneSource, Compustat)
- Other Worldwide Web
  - Stock discussion boards
  - Blogs
  - Unarchived stories
- Directories
  - Thomas' Register
  - Dun & Bradstreet
- Miscellaneous
  - Conferences, proceedings (e.g. keynote speeches and Q&A sessions)
  - Trade shows

to have processes for capturing such information and organizational reinforcement to actually do so.

➤ The information assembled must be analyzed and have the potential to influence action to be of any use. The content of what is involved in mapping business landscapes is reviewed in the analytical steps that follow, and the content of competitive analysis (which feeds off the same broad information base, albeit with more of an emphasis on company-level as opposed to group-level analysis) in the chapters that follow.

Step 2: Drawing the Boundaries

Another precursor to the actual analysis is to decide which part of the business landscape to focus on—also known as the problem of industry definition. Operationally, the challenge for the strategist is to decide how broadly (or narrowly) to draw the boundaries.

General-purpose industry classification schemes are of some help in this regard but often have to be redrawn to be really useful. For example, one would probably want to split the "auto and truck" group in the Value Line classification system on which Exhibit 2.1 is based into "autos" and "trucks" at least, because buyers, competitors, and even suppliers differ across those two segments. Official statistical definitions such as the North American Industrial Classification System (NAICS) are better in some respects, but not by much. For example, at the five-digit level, the NAICS does distinguish between automobiles and heavy duty trucks. On the other hand, it lumps light trucks together with sports utility vehicles (SUVs) when, for at least some purposes, one would want to separate them.

A different way of drawing boundaries is to take an inside-out approach, starting with a business's served market. Usually, the boundaries of the landscape should be drawn a bit more broadly to include not only the segments that the business serves but also unserved segments with which it shares customers or technologies (or competitors). To make the same point in a different way, substitutability helps determine whether lines of business should be looked at together or separately. Thus whether to analyze cars and SUVs together depends on both demand-side substitutability and the extent to which know-how and equipment can be cross-utilized (supply-side substitutability)—and, perhaps, on the extent to which the same competitors are present in both markets. By symmetry, important complements should also be included among the markets covered.

These issues all focus attention on the choice of **horizontal scope** across product markets or segments. This choice is discussed further, in the context of corporate strategy, in Chapter 6. **Vertical scope** and **geographic scope** raise somewhat different analytical issues. As far as vertical scope is concerned, the key issue is how many vertically linked stages of the supplier→buyer chain to consider. For example, can one analyze the mining of bauxite ore, its refining into alumina, the smelting of alumina into aluminum metal, and the fabrication of aluminum products from that metal independently of one another? In general, if a competitive market for third-party sales exists between vertical stages or could be created, the stages should be analyzed separately; if not, they should be analyzed together. In this sense, the tightest coupling in the vertical aluminum chain occurs between bauxite mining and alumina refining, because most refineries can employ only one source of bauxite (as a result of which, most firms participate in both stages or in neither). The loosest coupling arises between aluminum smelting and fabrication, because fabricators can buy aluminum ingot from the London Metal Exchange as well as from different smelters. Issues related to vertical scope are discussed further in the section on holdup in Chapter 5 of this book.

In regard to geographic scope, the key issue is how broadly to define the business landscape in terms of physical locations covered. For example, is it better to look at pharmaceutical manufacturers just in the United States or at the pharmaceutical industry worldwide? Such issues arise around local and regional boundaries in addition to national ones. As before, the degree of market integration—in this case, across geographic boundaries—is key to determining whether geographies should be looked at together or separately. Of course, much also depends on the specific decision at stake: local considerations dominate certain kinds of decisions (e.g., salesforce organization in pharmaceuticals) even in industries that are, by most criteria, quite globally integrated. Still, systematic application of the market integration test does suggest, because of increasing cross-border integration, that the complexities of competing across multiple locations affect an ever broader range of decisions. Take the case of prices, which were traditionally set locally in both pharmaceuticals and steel. In pharmaceuticals, particularly in the lucrative U.S. market, pricing is much more constrained than before by the threat of imports. And in steel, the correlation between U.S. and European steel prices for a key product increased from 37 percent between 1994 and 1998 to 74 percent between 1998 and 2002. Ghemawat elaborates on how increasing, but incomplete international integration can complicate single-geography strategy.[25]

A final remark: given all the scope complexities discussed above, there often isn't any perfect way of drawing the boundaries of the business landscape. For that reason, it is more useful to focus on ensuring that the boundaries are drawn clearly and that there is consistency in the treatment of what is in versus out instead of looking for *the* right way of drawing boundaries. And sometimes, both narrow and broad-scope analysis may be necessary, with narrowness focusing attention and breadth guarding against being blindsided.

Step 3: Identifying Groups of Players

The principal groups of players that must usually be considered—direct competitors, potential entrants, substitutes, complements, buyers, and suppliers—and the importance of adding to those groups as necessary were discussed in the preceding section. There are, however, some additional procedural guidelines that are worth mentioning here.

➤ Groups of players need to be clearly and consistently labeled from the perspective of the business for which the analysis is being undertaken. It is not unknown, for instance, for case discussions to confuse rivals with suppliers on the grounds that rivals are suppliers for their own buyers!

➤ It is often useful to distinguish *within* the groups of players listed above: to explicitly separate out and consider different types of suppliers, different strategic groups within the set of direct competitors, different buyer segments, and so on. The objective is to pick up variations in bargaining power (the subject of step 4) that more aggregated perspectives might obscure. Thus, in steel, it is useful to distinguish explicitly between labor, with substantial if declining bargaining power, and other input suppliers with, typically, much less leverage over steelmakers. Similarly, the bargaining power of different types of buyers of pharmaceuticals varies greatly.

➤ Finally, there is often a tendency, in mapping business landscapes, to focus on existing players. Deliberate attempts to counteract such biases by explicitly directing attention toward new or potential players may be necessary. Note that this ties in with the theme of thinking dynamically, which is the subject of step 5.

Step 4: Understanding Group-Level Bargaining Power

Building on the preceding steps, we can now discuss the core objective of attempts to map the business landscape: understanding group-level bargaining power. It is useful to concentrate on groups or subgroups of players with particular potential to influence a business's payoffs, e.g., suppliers that account for a large percentage of the cost structure, buyers that represent a substantial share of the market, or groups that are outliers on important structural dimensions, such as degree of market concentration. Not insisting on looking at all groups in equal depth helps keep the amount of analysis manageable. And it is also important to remember that the group-level analysis described in this chapter focuses on "macro" regularities and rules of thumb. Chapters 3 through 5, in contrast, can be seen as going "micro" by burrowing beneath the group level to look at individual businesses in comparison or interaction with each other.

Group-level analysis of the sort discussed in this chapter is driven by the idea that structural analysis can help identify which groups of players will, on average, get how much of the economic pie. The "five forces" framework provides a very helpful checklist in this regard, although it often makes sense to work through the long list rather quickly to focus in on a short list of structural factors to be explored further. The version of the value net developed in the preceding section suggests that similar analytical techniques can also be applied to complementors as a group of players.

Extension of the analysis to at least certain other groups of players (e.g., governments or nonprofits) requires some modifications to the basic approach outlined above, since such players should not, even to a first approximation, be thought of as value-maximizers. It is still possible, however, to think through their interests and the amount of influence that they are likely to bring to bear in pursuing them. And thus their impact on the average profitability of direct competitors in an industry can be identified even though it may not make sense to speak of their own average profitability.

A final point about this step: this is also the juncture at which it is perhaps most useful to test the emerging understanding of the structural determinants of profitability against data about the average profitability of different groups of players or patterns in the decisions that they make. Given the constraints on the information available and the reliance on rules of thumb, there is always judgment involved in assessing group-level bargaining power and, by implication, a need for cross-checking.

Step 5: Thinking Dynamically

The point of the analysis is usually to understand the business landscape *as it will be* rather than as it is or was. Dynamic thinking about how the business landscape will change can prove extremely valuable, just as a failure to anticipate changes can be disastrous. For a very dramatic example, consider IBM's entry into the personal computer business in 1980. In an apparent rush to get in, it turned to Microsoft for the operating system (as well as to Intel for the microprocessor). Microsoft did not actually have an operating system, but bought one called QDOS (Quick and Dirty Operating System), for $50,000, renamed it MS-DOS, and supplied it to IBM. Fatefully, it also secured IBM's permission to sell it to other computer manufacturers.[26] This paved the way for the emergence of a one supplier–many competitors structure dominated by Microsoft's MS-DOS and its successor, Windows, since users preferred to standardize their operating systems. IBM, in contrast, lost market share and, eventually, market leadership in an industry that has experienced sustained overall pressure on average profitability—in large part because of Microsoft and Intel.

In thinking dynamically about the business landscape, it is useful to distinguish between the short run and the long run. Although short-run dynamics reflect transient effects, they also pick up on phenomena such as economy-wide business cycles and industry cycles that can prove very important, particularly in asset-intensive industries. In the U.S. steel industry, for example, integrated steel makers' attempts to modernize were regularly and debilitatingly interrupted by cyclical downturns. More recently, a surge in Chinese demand has driven up the price of key product grades and inputs by more than 100 percent. Amidst the general profit-taking, however, thoughtful steel companies are already beginning to think through their strategies for the hard landing that may follow this short-run spike.

In the longer run, attention needs to be paid to such dynamics as market growth, the evolution of buyer needs, the rate of product and process innovation, changes in the scale required to compete, changes in input costs, and changes in exchange rates. Many other types of long-run dynamics might be cited: Exhibit 2.8 supplies a longer list, organized in terms of the "six forces," although it must be noted that the effects of such dynamics often affect more than one force. Another way of distinguishing among long-run changes is in terms of trends, cycles, and shocks. The notion of trends is obvious. The longer-run cycle that has attracted the most attention is the product/industry life cycle, which hinges on the idea that opportunities for innovation, particularly product innovation, are likely to be depleted as an industry matures. Some researchers have argued that there is actually a typical pattern of structural changes as an industry progresses through its life cycle (see Exhibit 2.9). And shocks of various sorts can emanate from sources as diverse as technology, regulation, and adjacent industries.

To illustrate the potential usefulness of long-run analysis of this sort, think of a pharmaceutical company trying to set a strategic agenda for itself. Long-run trends that it might want to consider include:

➤ The increased viability of biotechnology and other unconventional drug-discovery methods and increased outsourcing of drug discovery to them by the major pharmaceutical companies

➤ The increased dependence of branded pharmaceutical companies on a limited number of blockbusters for profitability and mergers among them as ways of boosting product pipelines and (perhaps) achieving scale economies

➤ The heightened threat from generic manufacturers and, more generally, imitative, or "me-too," competition

➤ On the consumer side, pressure from managed care and from import threats (e.g., into the United States from cheaper sources in Canada), counterbalanced by posi-

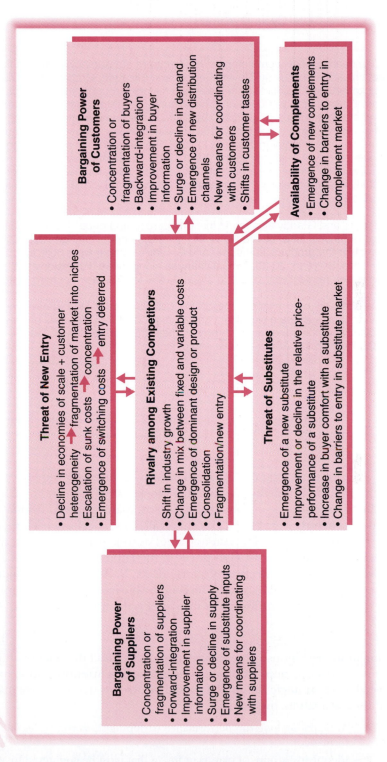

Exhibit 2.8 Common Long-Run Dynamics

Bargaining Power of Customers
- Concentration or fragmentation of buyers
- Backward-integration
- Improvement in buyer information
- Surge or decline in demand
- Emergence of new distribution channels
- New means for coordinating with customers
- Shifts in customer tastes

Availability of Complements
- Emergence of new complements
- Change in barriers to entry in complement market

Threat of New Entry
- Decline in economies of scale + customer heterogeneity → fragmentation of market into niches
- Escalation of sunk costs → concentration
- Emergence of switching costs → entry deterred

Rivalry among Existing Competitors
- Shift in industry growth
- Change in mix between fixed and variable costs
- Emergence of dominant design or product
- Consolidation
- Fragmentation/new entry

Threat of Substitutes
- Emergence of a new substitute
- Improvement or decline in the relative price-performance of a substitute
- Increase in buyer comfort with a substitute
- Change in barriers to entry in substitute market

Bargaining Power of Suppliers
- Concentration or fragmentation of suppliers
- Forward-integration
- Improvement in supplier information
- Surge or decline in supply
- Emergence of substitute inputs
- New means for coordinating with suppliers

Exhibit 2.9   Life-Cycle Dynamics

To understand how common product life-cycles are and how dramatic their effects can be, consider findings by Steven Klepper and Elizabeth Graddy. These researchers tracked 46 new products from their early history through 1981—periods covering, in some cases, nearly 100 years.[27] They found that 38 products had experienced some kind of shakeout (i.e., significant reduction in the number of producers), after periods of growth which averaged 29 years, but varied widely. Klepper and Graddy pointed out that the eight remaining products in their sample might still be expected to contract since they were relatively young (as of 1981). Even more striking, the number of producers declined by an average of 52% from the peak for the 22 products that had achieved stability along this dimension (within 11 years of the onset of the shakeout period)!

Klepper and Graddy also found that output rose and prices fell at decreasing percentage rates over time, before stabilizing. Average annual changes in the first five-year interval for the products in Klepper and Graddy's sample were 50% for output and −13% for price. By years 20-30, annual changes along these dimensions had stabilized to averages, respectively, of 2% to 3% and −2% to −3%: a very sharp contrast.

The similarity across landscapes of this constellation of life-cycle related changes—and others, such as a significant shift from product R&D towards process R&D[28]—is indicative of the importance of reviving the early work on life-cycles put forth by the consulting firm of Arthur D. Little and others.

tive changes such as the rapid growth of categories like the "life-style" or behavioral drug segment and, in the United States, relaxation of the rules on direct-to-consumer advertisting

The principal long-run cycle of concern, in line with the life-cycle hypothesis, is that the industry's pipeline of potential blockbusters appears to be emptier than before. In terms of shocks, the pharmaceutical companies have individual—often product-specific—concerns (e.g., Merck's recent recall of its blockbuster, Vioxx, which wiped out more than one-quarter of its market value) as well as broader ones, most notably, the threat of a backlash against high prices in the United States despite the industry's expensive and generally effective lobbying efforts. Note, once again, that this chapter has focused on "macro" analysis at the level of the business landscape; more "micro" analysis of dynamics at the individual or firm level is the topic of Chapters 4 and 5.

Step 6: Adapting to/Shaping the Business Landscape

Having drawn the industry boundaries and understood the relationships—current and future—between groups of players, the manager's attention must turn to using this knowledge for strategic action.[29] It should be obvious that there are many possible uses of landscape analysis, including:

➤ Anticipating long-run performance (stripping short-run cycles out of current performance)

➤ Identifying groups of players or forces that must be countered to achieve good performance

> ➤ Testing decisions to enter, invest in, or exit from an industry
> ➤ Assessing the effects of a major change in the business landscape so as to be able to adapt to it
> ➤ Identifying ways to shape the business landscape

Some of these uses are obvious or have already been discussed at some length. But the notions of adaptation and shaping shaping strategies should be elaborated further.

For an example of **adaptation,** consider the recent changes at the major accounting firms.[30] The profitability of their audit business, in particular, had been eroded over time by the rivalry between what were originally the Big Eight firms, which resembled each other in terms of size and the intent of becoming market leader, and by price pressure from the typical purchaser, a company CFO, for whom the audit fee typically represented the single largest item on the budget. Mergers since the mid-1980s that consolidated the Big Eight into the Big Five helped mitigate some of this pressure. The big payoff, however, came after the collapse of Arthur Andersen, one of what was by then the Big Five, in the wake of the Enron scandal in 2001. After this shock, the remaining Big Four were able to divide Andersen's clients in such a way as to increase their concentrations in many industry sectors and geographies well above the levels that would normally be permitted by the U.S. Department of Justice on antitrust grounds. In addition, they appear to have had some success in shifting the purchase of audit services away from CFOs and toward clients' CEOs and audit committees, which are substantially less price-sensitive given their newfound liability, under the Sarbanes-Oxley Act, for accounting inaccuracies. As a result, the average audit fee increased from 9 basis points in 2000 to 16 basis points in 2002, the year the Sarbanes-Oxley Act was passed. And increases in concentration by industry sector explain about half the observed increases in fees, suggesting that the increases in fees reflect more than just the increased cost of audits. As a partner at one of the Big Four put it, "We regained pricing power after . . . the U.S. government just about blew up a fifth of the industry."

Adaptation of this sort, while important, is not the only strategic posture that might be adopted in dealing with the business landscape. A business might, instead, strive more actively to shape its environment. Such shaping is most obvious in fluid environments that are still taking form (e.g., multimedia), but is also evident in older, apparently more mature contexts. Consider De Beers's dominance of the diamond industry.[31]

De Beers grew out of Cecil Rhodes's takeover, in 1888, of South African mines that produced 95 percent of the world's diamonds. Over the course of the next 100 years, South Africa's production share dropped below 15 percent. De Beers nevertheless continued to regulate the flow of new diamonds to the market—and to dominate and shape it—by using its Central Selling Organization (CSO) to buy and, if necessary, stockpile other suppliers' rough diamonds. The CSO cleared markets by deciding who would get which stones; stabilized prices to prevent boom-and-bust cycles from wrecking its suppliers' (or the trade's) finances or customer confidence; sorted diamonds into standard grades; arranged financing, security, and transportation; and built demand by advertising the category and developing new markets (Japan was the most recent major example) and new products (e.g., tennis bracelets). All these functions expanded the total size of the pie available to the industry. In addition, it provided incentives for others to play along: the diamond trade was highly lucrative for the major supplier countries and, at the individual level, for the CSO's several hundred dealers. But suppliers and dealers had to agree to restrictive contracts and intensive monitoring. And there was a note of menace to the scene as well: De Beers had a well-developed reputation for ruthlessness in punishing transgressors, that is, in bringing sticks as well as carrots to bear. We think that explicit consideration of the relevant groups of players and how the relationships among them might evolve is more helpful in identifying such strategies for shaping the business landscape of this sort than simple exhortations to be insightful.

By way of update, however, it is worth noting the problems that developed relatively recently with De Beers's strategy, and the changes that have been made to it since the late 1990s. Starting in the early 1980s, rough diamond supply exploded as additional (primarily non-De Beers) mines came on line, and created chronically large inventories for the CSO. In response, De Beers has finally stopped supporting the industry by paying for and stockpiling everyone's diamonds and has focused instead, on pursuing a strategy of becoming "the supplier of choice" by pumping up advertising and focusing it on its own brand, further tightening controls on the trade, integrating forward into jewelry retailing in a joint venture with Louis Vuitton, capitalizing on its superior infrastructure and information to address social concerns about "conflict diamonds" that fuel civil wars in Africa, and trying to clean up its image with the public and with governments. In other words, De Beers has embarked on a strategy of reshaping the diamond business.

These recent changes at De Beers suggest, more generally, a need to move beyond looking at environmental attractiveness—the first of the two determinants of profitability in the profitability grid in Exhibit 1.7—to considering competitive positioning, the second of the two determinants. This move requires a shift from industry-level analysis to firm-level analysis. We can visualize this shift in landscape terms. Instead of looking at the landscape from a high altitude, where only the principal features of its various parts, such as the average height above (or below) sea level, stand out, we will zoom in for a much closer look. Our scrutiny will reveal that the landscape often looks very rugged with a higher degree of resolution as well: variations in the profitability of direct competitors tend to be even larger than the common components of their profitability examined in this chapter. Understanding such differences in competitive positioning and figuring out how to create competitive advantage are the principal topics of the next chapter.

SUMMARY

Landscape analysis helps make part of the older SWOT (strengths-weaknesses-opportunities-threats) paradigm a more systematic process for strategic planning by elucidating the opportunities and threats confronting individual businesses, some of which they share with their direct competitors.

Landscape analysis is not, however, confined to direct competitors: it usually involves looking beyond them. Supply-demand analysis focuses attention on product markets—that is, on exchange relationships between suppliers and buyers. The "five forces" framework extends the analysis to three-stage (supplier → competitor → buyer) vertical chains and to explicit consideration of substitution possibilities. The value net draws complementors into the picture. Even more groups of players may need to be added, depending on the context. The broader point is that it is important to fit the framework used to the situation being studied, rather than the other way around.

Identification of the relevant groups of players paves the way for actually understanding their relative bargaining power and, at a deeper level, the relationships among them. Both the cooperative and the competitive components of such relationships must be taken into account—otherwise, this task would be a lot simpler. The "five forces" framework offers a number of helpful heuristics with its structural determinants of industry attractiveness. So does the value net, as developed in this chapter. It is also worth emphasizing that any such understanding of group-level profitability must be dynamic, because relationships between groups of players can and do change over time, as a result of cycles, trends, shocks, and other factors.

The ultimate object of such exercises is to affect the actions that businesses take. The analytical frameworks and steps discussed in this chapter are helpful in this regard, but not, by themselves, complete. As the SWOT framework reminds us, perceptions of common opportunities and threats must be integrated with consideration of the strengths and weaknesses of individual players. The next chapter expands on this insight.

GLOSSARY

- adaptation
- business landscape
- buyer power
- complementors
- cooperation
- demand curve
- dynamic thinking
- endogenous sunk costs
- entry barriers
- exogenous sunk costs
- extended competition
- external fit
- "five forces" framework
- geographic scope
- horizontal scope
- industrial organization or IO
- industry definition
- nonmarket relationships
- oligopolistic competition
- price-elasticity of demand
- rivalry
- "shaping" strategies
- strategic groups
- substitutes
- supplier power
- supply curve
- supply-demand analysis
- value net
- vertical scope

NOTES

1. This chapter has benefited enormously from the help of Adam Brandenburger and Jan Rivkin, who developed many of the ideas that it covers, allowed us to draw on their unpublished materials, and offered comments on earlier drafts.

2. See, for example, Richard Schmalensee, "Do Markets Differ Much?" *American Economic Review* 75, no. 3 (June 1985): 341–351; Richard P. Rumelt, "How Much Does Industry Matter?" *Strategic Management Journal* 12, no. 3 (Mar. 1991): 167–185; A. M. McGahan and M. E. Porter, "What Do We Know About Variance in Accounting Profitability?"

Management Science 48, no. 7 (Jul 2002): 834–851.

3. Uta Werner of Marakon Associates deserves our thanks for helping make these data available.

4. The landscape metaphor originated in biology more than fifty years ago. See Stuart A. Kauffman, *At Home in the Universe: The Search for Laws of Self-Organization and Complexity* (New York: Oxford University Press, 1995) for a discussion in that context. The last four chapters of his book also discuss applications to issues concerning human organizations. For other applications of landscape-based models to strategy, see

Daniel A. Levinthal, "Adaptation on Rugged Landscapes," *Management Science* 43, no. 7 (July 1997): 934–950; Jan W. Rivkin, "Imitation of Complex Strategies," *Management Science* 46, no. 6 (June2000): 824–844; and Pankaj Ghemawat and Daniel Levinthal, "Choice Structures, Business Strategy and Performance: A Generalized Nk-Simulation Approach" (Harvard Business School Working Paper no. 01-012, 2000).

5. This discussion builds on Adam Brandenburger's unpublished note, "Models of Markets" (Harvard Business School, January 1998).

6. Jurg Niehans, *A History of Economic Theory: Classic Contributions, 1720–1980* (Baltimore: Johns Hopkins University Press, 1990).

7. Alfred Marshall, *Principles of Economics,* bk. 5 (London New York: Macmillan, 1890).

8. For additional details, see Gary P. Pisano and Maryam Golnaraghi, "Partners Healthcare System, Inc. (A)" (Harvard Business School Case no. 696–062, Boston, 1996). Also note that the implications of a decline in capacity utilization would be even more severe than implied by this cost curve because it includes fixed as well as variable costs in its cost base.

9. Antoine A. Cournot, *Recherches sur les principes mathématiques de la tThéorie des richesses* (Paris: Hachette, 1838). The rather different characterization of outcomes when duopolists set prices rather than quantities was provided by another French savant, Jean Bertrand, in his review of Cournot's book in the *Journal des Savants* 67 (1883): 499–508.

10. See Edward Chamberlin, *The Theory of Monopolistic Competition,* Harvard Economic Studies, vol. 38. (Cambridge, Mass.: Harvard University Press, 1933), and Joan Robinson, *The Economics of Imperfect Competition* (London: Macmillan, 1933).

11. Economists associated with the University of Chicago generally doubted the empirical importance of this possibility—except as an artifact of regulatory distortions.

12. Mason's seminal work was Edward S. Mason, "Price and Production Policies of Large-Scale Enterprise," *American Economic Review* 29, no. 1 (March 1939): 61–74.

13. Joe S. Bain, "Relation of Profit Rate to Industry Concentration: American Manufacturing, 1936–1940," *Quarterly Journal of Economics* 65, no. 3 (August 1951): 293–324.

14. Joe S. Bain, *Barriers to New Competition* (Cambridge, Mass.: Harvard University Press, 1956), 3.

15. See, for instance, Harvey J. Goldschmid, H. Michael Mann, and J. Frederick Weston, *Industrial Concentration: The New Learning* (Boston: Little, Brown, 1974).

16. Michael E. Porter, "Note on the Structural Analysis of Industries" (Harvard Business School Case no. 376–054, Boston, 1975).

17. Richard Schmalensee, "Inter-Industry Studies of Structure and Performance," in *Handbook of Industrial Organization,* ed. Richard Schmalensee and Robert D. Willig (Amsterdam: North-Holland, 1989), chap. 16, pp. 951–1009. The elements in Porter's framework that are supported by Schmalensee's review of the evidence appear in bold print in Exhibit 2.5.

18. Darrell K. Rigby, "Managing the Management Tools," *Planning Review,* September-October 1994.

19. Richard E. Caves, Michael Fortunato, and Pankaj Ghemawat, "The Decline of Dominant Firms, 1905–1929," *Quarterly Journal of Economics* 99, no. 3 (August 1984): 523–546.

20. Adam M. Brandenburger and Harborne W. Stuart, Jr., "Value-Based Business Strategy," *Journal of Economics & Management Strategy* 5, no. 1 (1996): 5–24.

21. Even Porter is reported to have modified his "five forces" framework in ways suggested by the value net.

22. Andrew S. Grove, *Only the Paranoid Survive: How to Exploit the Crisis Points That Challenge Every Company and Career* (New York: Currency Doubleday, 1996), 27–29.

23. David P. Baron, "Integrated Strategy: Market and Nonmarket Components," *California Management Review* 37, no. 2 (Winter 1995 1995): 47–65, esp. p. 47. See David P. Baron, *Business and Its Environment,* 2nd ed. (Upper Saddle River, N.J.:

Prentice Hall, 1996) for an extended treatment of nonmarket strategies.

24. Ibid.

25. Pankaj Ghemawat, "Semiglobalization and International Business Strategy," *Journal of International Business Studies* 34, no. 2 (March 2003): 138–152.

26. Adam Horowitz and the editors of Business 2.0, *The Dumbest Moments in Business History: Useless Products, Ruinous Deals, Clueless Bosses and Other Signs of Unintelligent Life in the Workplace,* compiled by Mark Athitakis and Mark Lasswell (New York: Portfolio, 2004).

27. Steven Klepper and Elizabeth Graddy, "The Evolution of New Industries and the Determinants of Market Structure," *Rand Journal of Economics* 21, no. 1 (1990): 27–44.

28. James M. Utterback and William J. Abernathy, "Patterns of Industrial Innovation," *Technology Review* 80 (1978): 2–9.

29. While the basic ideas on which this subsection draws are well established, the adapter/shaper dichotomy used here and elsewhere in this book is based on recent work by the consulting firm of McKinsey & Company, as discussed at the McKinsey Strategy Forum.

30. This description of the accounting industry is based on Emilie R. Feldman, "Arthur Andersen: A Lesson in How Not to Punish an Oligopolistic Competitor" (Harvard College Senior Honors Thesis, 2004); Sharad Asthana, Steven Balsam, and Sung-soo Kim, "The Effect of Enron, Andersen, and Sarbanes-Oxley on the Market for Audit Services" (unpublished working paper, June 2004); and interviews with industry participants.

31. This description of De Beers is based on Pankaj Ghemawat and Toby Lenk, "De Beers Consolidated Mines Ltd. (A)" (Harvard Business School Case no. 391-076, 1990) and Pankaj Ghemawat, "De Beers Consolidated Mines Ltd. (B)" (Harvard Business School Case no. 702-434, 2001).

Chapter 3

Creating Competitive Advantage

Pankaj Ghemawat and Jan Rivkin

If a man ... make a better mousetrap than his neighbor, tho' he build his
house in the woods, the world will make a path to his door.
—RALPH WALDO EMERSON (ATTRIBUTED)

L
ecturing in the nineteenth century, Emerson anticipated one of the key pieces of
advice that strategists still stress at the beginning of the twenty-first: Strive for an
edge over the competition! Since Emerson's time, strategists have explored, in effect,
what makes one mousetrap better than others from the point of view of profitability. "Better" involves not just buyers' **willingness to pay** for a firm's mousetrap or the costs incurred to provide the trap, but the difference between the two. In other words, an
appreciation of the importance of a competitive edge has been elaborated into an understanding of the economics of what might be called the competitive wedge. A firm is
said to have created a **competitive advantage** over its rivals if it has driven a wider wedge
between willingness to pay and costs than its competitors have achieved.[1]

The long-standing interest in competitive advantage and its inclusion as the second
dimension of the profitability grid in Exhibit 1.7 reflect the sense that while industry- or
population-level effects have a large impact on business performance, large differences
in performance also appear *within* industries. Consider, for example, the two industries
identified as outliers in terms of performance and analyzed in Chapter 2—pharmaceuticals and steel. Exhibit 3.1 unbundles the spreads between returns on equity and
the costs of equity capital in these two industries, competitor by competitor.[2] Some
companies have historically earned less than their costs of capital even in the pharmaceutical industry, and others have historically created value even in the steel industry.

Exhibit 3.1   Average Economic Profits in the Steel Industry, 1984–2002
(*Source:* Compustat, Value Line, Marakon Associates Analysis.)

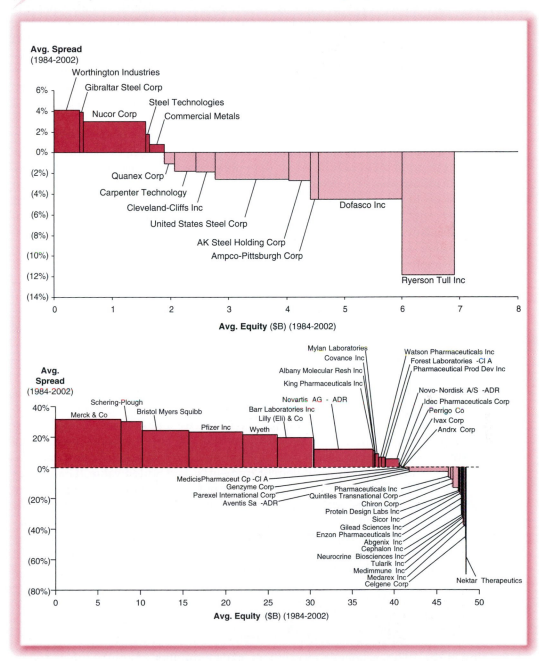

The structure within industries, often described in terms of "strategic groups," helps explain part of these differences in performance. In the pharmaceutical industry, biotechnology firms as a group have underperformed conventional pharmaceutical firms for decades. In the steel industry, minimills that make steel from scrap have outperformed conventional integrated steel makers. But there is more to the story than just group-level differences. Within the group of biotech companies, Amgen has historically outperformed its peers, and among minimills, Nucor has been a stand-out performer (although both Amgen and Nucor have come under pressure recently, foreshadowing the discussions of the dynamics of competitive advantage in Chapters 4 and 5).

More systematic research confirms that such within-industry performance differences are widespread and substantial. The research suggests, in fact, that within-industry differences in profitability may be larger than differences in the averages across industries. While industry-level effects appear to account for 10 to 20 percent of the variation in business profitability in the United States, stable within-industry effects account for 30 to 45 percent.[3] (Most of the remainder can be assigned to effects that fluctuate from year to year.) Note, however, that this is *not* an argument for ignoring industry-level effects, the other dimension of the profitability grid introduced in Exhibit 1.7 and discussed in Chapter 2. First, industry-level effects *do* account for a significant fraction of the variation in performance observed on average. Second, industry-level effects may have a more persistent influence on business-level profitability than within-industry differences.[4] Third, it may even be the case that industry characteristics play a larger role than their average contribution might suggest in determining the room for positive departures from average profitability.[5] Finally, market leaders, in particular, often confront important tensions between managing industry structure and improving their own **competitive position** within that structure.

In order to understand within-industry differences, we must zoom in from the industry level to look at the landscapes within industries. Examining intra-industry landscapes, which also turn out to be very rugged, is the focus of this chapter. The first part of the chapter reviews the historical development of the core concepts in analyzing competitive position (either advantaged or disadvantaged): competitive **cost analysis,** the analysis of **differentiation,** cost-benefit **trade-offs,** and **added value.** The second part of the chapter draws on these concepts to lay out a process for analyzing competitive positioning, illustrated with an extended example. This tack, which is primarily analytical, is not intended to deny the importance of creativity and insight in the creation of competitive advantage. Rather, it can be read as an attempt to guide entrepreneurial energies by setting up a battery of tests for new business ideas. The topic of creativity is taken up again in the next chapter.

THE DEVELOPMENT OF CONCEPTS FOR COMPETITIVE POSITIONING

Starting in the 1970s, academic researchers made a number of contributions to our understanding of positioning within industries. The IO-based approach to strategic groups, initiated at the Harvard Business School by Michael Hunt's work on broadline versus narrowline strategies in the major home appliance industry, suggested that competitors within particular industries could be grouped in terms of their competitive strategies in ways that helped explain their interactions and relative profitability.[6] And a stream of work at Purdue University by Dan Schendel and his collaborators explored the heterogeneity of competitive positions, strategies, and performance in brewing and other industries with a combination of statistical analysis and qualitative case studies.[7] The work that seems to have had the most impact on business-strategic thinking about competitive positions in the late 1970s and the 1980s, however, was more pragmatic than academic in its orientation, with consultants once again playing a leading role (particularly in the development of techniques for competitive cost analysis).

Cost Analysis

With the growing acceptance of the experience curve in the 1960s, most strategists turned to some type of cost analysis as the basis for assessing competitive positions. The interest in competitive cost analysis survived the declining popularity of the experience curve in the 1970s but was reshaped by it in two important ways. First, greater attention was paid to disaggregating businesses into their components as well as to assessing how costs in a particular activity might be shared across businesses. Second, strategists greatly enriched their menu of **cost drivers,** expanding it beyond just experience.

The disaggregation of businesses into components was motivated, in part, by early attempts to "fix" the experience curve so as to deal with the rising real prices of many raw materials in the 1970s.[8] The proposed fix involved splitting costs into the costs of purchased materials and "cost added" (value added minus profit margins) and then redefining the experience curve as applying only to the latter category. The natural next step was to disaggregate a business's entire cost structure into parts—functions, processes, or activities—whose costs might be expected to behave in interestingly different ways. (To be consistent with later sections of the chapter, we will refer to the parts as "activities.")[9] As in the case of portfolio analysis, the idea of splitting businesses into component activities diffused quickly among consultants and their clients in the 1970s. A template for activity analysis that became especially prominent is reproduced in Exhibit 3.2.

Exhibit 3.2   McKinsey's Business System[10] (*Source:* Bales et al., 1980.)

Technology	Manufacturing	Distribution	Marketing	Service
Design	Procurement	Transport	Retailing	Parts
Development	Assembly	Inventory	Advertising	Labor

Activity-based analysis also suggested a way of circumventing the "free-standing" conception of individual businesses built into the concept of strategic business units (SBUs).[11] One persistent problem in splitting diversified corporations into SBUs was that, with the exception of pure conglomerates, SBUs often shared elements of their cost structure with one another. Consulting firms—particularly Bain & Company and Strategic Planning Associates—began to emphasize the development of field maps or matrices that identified shared costs at the level of individual activities that were linked across businesses.[12]

In another important development in competitive cost analysis during the late 1970s and early 1980s, strategists began to consider a richer menu of cost drivers. Scale effects, although officially lumped into the experience curve, had long been studied independently in individual cases. Even more specific treatment of the effects of scale was now forced by activity analysis that might indicate, for example, that advertising costs were driven by national scale, whereas distribution costs were driven by local or regional scale. Field maps underscored the potential importance of economies (or diseconomies) of scope across businesses rather than scale within a given business. The effects of capacity utilization on costs were dramatized by macroeconomic downturns in the wake of the two oil shocks. The globalization of competition in many industries highlighted the location of activities as a key driver of competitors' cost positions, and so on. Cost drivers are discussed more comprehensively in the second section of this chapter.

Differentiation Analysis

Increasingly sophisticated cost analysis was followed, after a significant lag, by greater attention to customers in the process of analyzing competitive position. Of course, customers had never been entirely invisible. Even in the heyday of experience curve analysis, **market segmentation** had been an essential strategic tool—but it was often used to gerrymander markets to "demonstrate" a positive link between share and cost advantage rather than for truly analytical purposes. By one insider's recollection (that of Walker Lewis, the founder of Strategic Planning Associates), "To those who defended the classic experience-curve strategy, about 80 percent of the businesses in the world were commodities."[13] In the 1970s, this view began to change.

As strategists paid more attention to customer analysis, they began to reconsider the idea that attaining low costs and offering customers low prices was always the best way to compete. Instead, they focused more closely on *differentiated* ways of competing that might let a business command a price premium by improving customers' performance or reducing their (other) costs.[14] Although (product) differentiation had always occupied center stage in marketing, the idea of considering it in a cross-functional, competitive context that also accounted for cost levels apparently began to emerge in business strategy in the 1970s. Thus one member of Harvard's Business Policy group assigned Joe Bain's writings on entry barriers (see Chapter 2) to students in the 1970s and recalls using the concepts of cost and differentiation—implicit in two of Bain's three sources of entry barriers—to organize classroom discussions.[15] McKinsey began to apply the distinction between cost and value in its consulting activities later in the same decade.[16] The first extensive treatments of cost and differentiation, in Michael Porter's *Competitive Strategy* and in a *Harvard Business Review* article by William Hall, appeared in 1980.[17]

Porter's 1985 book, *Competitive Advantage,* suggested analyzing cost and differentiation via the **value chain,** a template that is reproduced in Exhibit 3.3. Although Porter's value chain bore some resemblance to McKinsey's business system, his discussion of this construct emphasized the importance of regrouping functions into the activities actually performed to produce, market, deliver, and support products, thinking about linkages among activities, and connecting the value chain to the determinants of competitive position in a specific way:

> Competitive advantage cannot be understood by looking at a firm as a whole. It stems from the many discrete activities a firm performs in designing, producing, marketing, delivering, and supporting its product. Each of these activities can contribute to a firm's relative cost position and create a basis for differentiation. The value chain disaggregates a firm into its strategically relevant activities in order to understand the behavior of costs and the existing and potential sources of differentiation.[18]

Exhibit 3.3 illustrates the value chain for an Internet start-up that sells and physically distributes music.

Exhibit 3.3   Value Chain for an Internet Start-Up

Firm infrastructure	Financing, legal support, accounting				Support activities
Human Resources	Recruiting, training, incentive system, employee feedback				
Technology Development	Inventory system	Site software	Pick and pack procedures	Site look and feel Customer research	Return procedures
Procurement	CDs Shipping	Computers Telecom lines	Shipping services	Media	
	Inbound shipment of top titles Warehousing	Server operations Billing Collections	Picking and shipment of top titles from warehouse Shipment of other titles from third-party distributors	Pricing Promotions Advertising Product information and reviews Affiliations with other Web sites	Returned items Customer feedback	Primary activities
	Inbound Logistics	Operations	Outbound Logistics	Marketing and Sales	Service	

Subsequent advances in the integration of cost analysis and differentiation analysis not only disaggregated businesses into activities (or processes), but also split customers into segments based on cost-to-serve as well as customer needs. Such deaveraging of customers was often said to expose situations in which 20 percent of a business's customers accounted for more than 80 percent (or even 100 percent) of its profits.[19] It also suggested new customer segmentation criteria. Thus, starting in the late 1980s, Bain & Company built a thriving "customer retention" practice based on the notion that it generally cost more to capture new customers than to retain existing ones.

Costs versus Differentiation

Porter and Hall, the first two strategists to write about both cost and differentiation, argued that successful companies usually had to choose to compete *either* on the basis of low costs *or* by differentiating products through quality and performance characteristics. Porter popularized this idea in terms of the **generic strategies** of low cost and differentiation. He also identified a **focus strategy** that cut across the two basic generic strategies (see Exhibit 3.4), and linked these strategy options to his work on industry analysis:

> In some industries, there are no opportunities for focus or differentiation—it's solely a cost game—and this is true in a number of bulk commodities. In other industries, cost is relatively unimportant because of buyer and product characteristics.[20]

The generic strategies appealed to strategists for at least two reasons. First, they captured a common tension between cost and differentiation. A firm must often incur higher costs to deliver a product or service for which customers are willing to pay more. Most customers are willing to pay more for a Toyota automobile than for a Hyundai, for

Exhibit 3.4 Porter's Generic Strategies (*Source:* Michael E. Porter, *Competitive Strategy: Techniques for Analyzing Industries and Competitors,* New York: Free Press, 1980.)

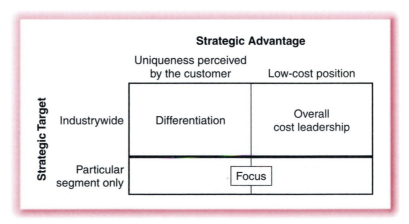

example, but the costs of manufacturing a Toyota are significantly higher than the costs of making a Hyundai. Toyota's higher profit margins derive from the fact that the price premium Toyota can command is greater than the incremental costs associated with its product.

Second, the generic strategies were also appealing because the capabilities, organizational structure, reward system, corporate culture, and leadership style needed to make a low-cost strategy succeed are, at first blush, contrary to those required for differentiation. For the sake of **internal consistency** and to ensure that it maintains a single-minded purpose, a firm might have to choose to compete either one way or the other.

Despite their appeal, the generic strategies provoked a vigorous debate among strategists, for both empirical and logical reasons. Empirically, the tension between cost and differentiation does not appear to be absolute. In the 1970s and 1980s, for instance, Japanese manufacturers in a number of industries found that, by reducing defect rates, they could make higher-quality products at lower cost. And Dell's build-to-order model for personal computers reduces the costs of components, inventories, and obsolescence, while sustaining prices as high as or even higher than rivals and building market share—indicators of superior willingness to pay. Exhibit 3.5 traces the interplay between cost and differentiation in an expanded treatment of competitive advantage that recognizes the possibility of **dual competitive advantages.**

How common are companies with dual competitive advantages? Porter argues that dual advantages are rare, typically being based on operational differences across firms that are easily copied.[21] Others contend that rejecting the trade-offs between cost and differentiation—replacing trade-offs with "trade-ons"—represents a fundamental way to transform competition in an industry.[22] The debate continues today.

Exhibit 3.5   Interplay between Cost and Differentiation

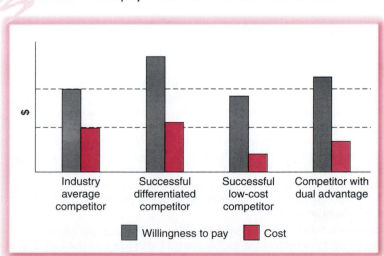

A second challenge to the notion of generic strategies is logical in nature. Although a desire for internal consistency may drive companies to the extremes of low cost and high differentiation, external considerations may pull firms back toward the center. If most customers want neither the simplest nor the most elaborate product, for instance, the most profitable strategy may be to offer a product of intermediate quality and intermediate costs. Consider Zara, the Spanish fashion retailer. Its offerings aren't nearly as upmarket as Gucci's or Armani's, although they sometimes share the same look. But Zara *is* a rung above other mass-market fashion retailers: its emphasis on within-season production and trendiness boosts willingness to pay—and production costs as well. Fortunately for Zara, the incremental willingness to pay appears to exceed the incremental costs, making its intermediate position viable.

Strategists have generally ceased to be dogmatic about generic strategies of any particular stripe. Instead, they embrace the idea that any analysis of competitive position must consider both relative cost and differentiation and recognize the tension between the two. Positioning, in this view, is or should be about driving the largest possible wedge between cost and differentiation. As differentiation rises, so, too, does cost in most instances. However, the largest gap between the two need not occur at the extremes of low costs or high price premia. The optimal position, from this perspective, represents a **choice** from a spectrum of trade-offs between cost and differentiation rather than a choice between mutually exclusive generic strategies.[23]

A few examples will help illustrate the richness of positioning possibilities.

➤ Accenture is regarded as the leader in IT consulting because of its deep experience, reinforced by its research and development, its Knowledge Xchange portal, its stringent hiring and training practices, its close relationships with the CEOs as well as the CIOs of global corporations, and its successful attempts to build its brand. Some of the activities that Accenture undertakes to differentiate itself are clearly costly: R&D and training, for instance, swallow up 5 percent of revenues, even though they have been scaled back in recent years. On the other hand, Accenture often faces no competing bids when it pitches consulting work and is able to keep its revenues per consultant high, especially by maintaining a high utilization rate (reportedly 78 percent in 2003, versus roughly 65 percent for the industry as a whole).[24] This more than compensates for the extra costs it incurs: Accenture has historically earned returns significantly higher than most other large IT services companies.

➤ Southwest Airlines has configured itself to focus on budget customers. It has standardized its fleet around fuel-efficient Boeing 737s, concentrates on short-haul point-to-point routes between midsize cities and secondary airports, offers very low ticket prices and no-frills service (no assigned seats, food service, baggage transfer, or connections with other airlines), emphasizes quick turnaround times, and manages to keep its planes in the air one-third longer each day than the average airline. Its stripped-down offering may generate slightly less willingness to pay than the offering of a full-service airline, but it incurs far lower costs than a full-service rival. As a result, Southwest is the only U.S. airline to have been consistently profitable during the last thirty years, has grown at an annual rate of 20–30 percent over the last five years, and maintains the youngest fleet and the lowest debt levels among the major carriers.

➤ Cirque du Soleil is an innovative firm that combines elements of circus and theater. In designing its performances, Cirque excluded many of the high-cost components of the traditional circus—animals, star performers, and three-ring shows—and focused on what it considered to be the three elements responsible for the lasting allure of the circus: the clowns, the tent, and the acrobatic acts. By refining the clowns' acts, glamorizing the tent, and incorporating elements from the world of theater—themes and storylines, for example—Cirque de Soleil created a new category of entertainment with which it is synonymous.[25] In 2003, more than 7 million people paid a total of $650 million to see its live performances, and the value of this privately held firm was estimated at $1.2 billion.[26]

Added Value

In the mid-1990s, Adam Brandenburger and Harborne Stuart added rigor to the idea of driving the largest-possible wedge between costs and differentiation through their characterization of added value.[27] Brandenburger and Stuart considered three-stage vertical chains (suppliers → competitors → buyers) and were precise about the monetary quantities of interest. On the demand side, they mapped differentiation into buyer willingness to pay for products or services; on the supply side, they used the exactly symmetric notion of supplier **opportunity costs** (the smallest amounts that suppliers would accept for the services and **resources** required to produce specific inputs). Given these definitions, the total **value** created by a transaction is the difference between the customer's willingness to pay and the supplier's opportunity cost. The division of this value among the three levels of the vertical chain is, in general, indeterminate. Nevertheless, an upper bound on the value captured by any player is provided by its added value—the maximum value that can be created by all the participants in the vertical chain minus the maximum value that would be created without that particular player.

More precisely, the amount of value that a firm can claim cannot exceed its added value under **unrestricted bargaining**. To see why this constraint applies, assume for a moment that a lucky firm *does* strike a deal that allows it to capture more than its added value. The value left over for the remaining participants is then less than the value that they could generate by arranging a deal among themselves. The remaining participants could, after all, break off and form a separate pact that improves their collective lot. Any deal that grants a firm more than its added value is vulnerable to such breakaway possibilities.

For an illustration of the usefulness of this style of analysis, consider the ill-starred decision in 1986 by the Holland Sweetener Company (HSC) to enter the aspartame industry, then monopolized by NutraSweet.[28] HSC's costs were probably higher, even after its initial capital investment was sunk, than those of NutraSweet because of limited scale and learning. In addition, customers' willingness to pay for HSC's aspartame was probably lower because of NutraSweet's heavy investments in building up its brand identity. HSC decided to enter the market anyway, presumably because the prices that Coca-Cola and Pepsi-Cola were paying NutraSweet were approximately three times as high as HSC's prospective costs.

As things turned out, the big winners from HSC's entry were Coke and Pepsi, which were able to extract much lower prices from NutraSweet. An explanation is suggested in Exhibit 3.6, which graphs in stylized terms the willingness to pay and the relevant post-entry costs. Evidently, HSC's entry depressed NutraSweet's added value (hence the lower prices). HSC, however, could not expect to have added value post-entry (given unrestricted bargaining) because total value created would not be reduced if the firm

Exhibit 3.6   Costs and Willingness to Pay
for Aspartame

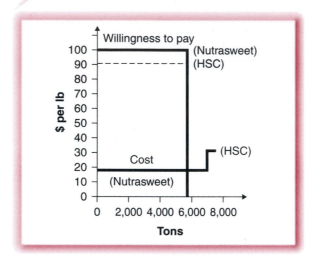

were to disappear.[29] So HSC would have had to do something more than just jump into this business if it wanted to earn profits from it. One possibility would have been to convince Coke and Pepsi to pay it to play up front, instead of relying on their "goodwill" after its entry to amortize its fixed costs.[30] Another approach would have been to communicate that HSC's market-share goals were sufficiently modest that it made no sense for NutraSweet to lower its prices across the board.[31]

Added value is sometimes quantifiable, as was approximately the case in the context of aspartame. Even when it isn't, however, it provides a useful test for judging a firm's strategy: If a firm were to disappear, would someone in its network of suppliers, customers, and complementors miss it? This question is harder-edged than older tests in the same vein—come up with a better product (à la Emerson), manage for uniqueness, focus on your distinctive competence, and so on—because it is based on an explicit model of interactions among buyers, suppliers, competitors, and complementors.

The concept of added value also helps tie together intra-industry analysis of competitive advantage and industry-level analysis of average profitability. In an industry with an "unattractive" structure, competitors' added values tend to be low, with exceptions arising only in the case of firms that have managed to create competitive advantages for themselves—that is, driven bigger wedges than most of their competitors between buyers' willingness to pay and costs. In more "attractive" industries, a firm may expect to do better than its competitive advantage alone would guarantee, through two mechanisms. First, the added values of individual competitors tend to be larger than their competitive advantages in such industry environments. Second, some industries seem to make it feasible for competitors to engage in what is politely termed "recognition of mutual dependence" and is less politely described as "tacit collusion" (an important determinant of the degree of rivalry and an important departure from the assumption of unrestricted bargaining).

A PROCESS FOR ANALYSIS

Having reviewed the development of concepts for competitive positioning, we now discuss a process for linking such concepts to strategic planning and action.[32] How can managers identify opportunities to raise willingness to pay by more than costs or to drive down costs without sacrificing too much willingness to pay? Sheer entrepreneurial insight certainly plays a large role in spotting such arbitrage opportunities. Michael Dell, for example, might see that customers are becoming comfortable with computer technology, realize that retail sales channels add more costs than benefits for many customers, and act on his insight to start a direct-to-the-customer computer business.[33] Likewise, a company such as Liz Claiborne might perceive a huge pent-up demand for a collection of medium to high-end work clothes for female professionals.[34] Dumb luck also plays a role. Engineers searching for a coating material for missiles in the 1950s discovered the lubricant WD-40, whose sales continued to generate a return on equity between 40 and 50 percent four decades later.

Most strategists believe, however, that smart luck beats dumb luck and that analysis can hone insight. To analyze competitive advantage, they typically break a firm down into discrete activities or processes and then examine how each contributes to the firm's relative cost position or comparative willingness to pay.[35] The activities undertaken to design, produce, sell, deliver, and service goods are what ultimately incur costs and generate buyer willingness to pay. Differences across firms in activities—differences in what firms actually do on a day-to-day basis—produce disparities in cost and willingness to pay and hence dictate added value. By analyzing a firm activity by activity, managers can (1) understand why the firm does or does not have added value, (2) spot opportunities to improve its added value, and (3) foresee likely shifts in its added value.

The starting point of positioning analysis is usually to catalog a business's activities. We can often facilitate the task of grouping the myriad activities that a business performs into a limited number of economically meaningful categories by referring to generic templates for activity analysis, such as the ones reproduced in Exhibits 3.2 and 3.3. Porter's value chain, which distinguishes between primary activities that directly generate a product or service and support activities that make the primary activities possible, is particularly helpful in ensuring that one considers a comprehensive array of activities. Generic templates cannot, however, be used blindly, for two reasons. First, not all of the activities they identify will be relevant in any given situation. Second, data often come prepackaged so as to favor a particular way of cataloging activities—unless a major effort to "clean up" such data is deemed necessary.

The rest of the analysis usually proceeds in three steps. First, managers examine the costs associated with each activity, using differences in activities to understand how and why their costs differ from those of competitors. Second, they analyze how each activity generates customer willingness to pay, studying differences in activities to see how and why customers are willing to pay more or less for the goods or services of rivals. Finally, managers consider changes in the firm's activities, with the objective of identifying changes that will widen the wedge between costs and willingness to pay.

The following subsections discuss these steps in this order, although it is often necessary to iterate back and forth among them in practice. To illustrate their application, we focus on a simple example: the snack cake market in the western part of Canada.[36] Between 1990 and 1995, Little Debbie grew its share of this market from

1 percent to nearly 20 percent. At the same time, Hostess, the maker of such long-time favorites as Twinkies and Devil Dogs, saw its dominant 45 percent share dwindle to 25 percent. An analysis of competitive positioning shows why Little Debbie and Hostess fared so differently and helps suggest a strategy for the latter.

Step 1: Using Activities to Analyze Relative Costs

Typically, competitive cost analysis is the starting point for the strategic analysis of competitive advantage. In pure commodity businesses, such as wheat farming, customers refuse to pay a premium for any company's product. In this type of setting, a low-cost position is the key to added value and competitive advantage. Even in industries that are not pure commodities, however, differences in cost often exert a large influence on differences in profitability.

To begin with our example, in the early 1990s, Hostess's managers struggled to understand why their financial performance was poor and their market share was plummeting. They cataloged the major elements of their value chain and calculated the costs associated with each class of activities. As Exhibit 3.7 shows, although Hostess sold the typical package of snack cakes to retailers for 72¢, raw materials (ingredients and packaging material) accounted for only 18¢ per unit. Operation of automated baking, filling, and packaging production lines (largely depreciation, maintenance, and labor costs) amounted to 15¢. Outbound logistics—delivery of fresh goods directly to convenience stores and supermarkets, and maintenance of shelf space—constituted the largest portion of costs, 26¢. Marketing expenditures on advertising and promotions added another 12¢. Thus a mere penny remained as profits for Hostess.

After calculating the costs associated with each activity, the managers determined the set of cost drivers associated with each activity, i.e., the factors that increase or decrease the cost of an activity. For instance, the Hostess managers realized that the cost of outbound logistics per snack cake fell rapidly as a firm increased its local market share,

Exhibit 3.7   Hostess's Cost Components

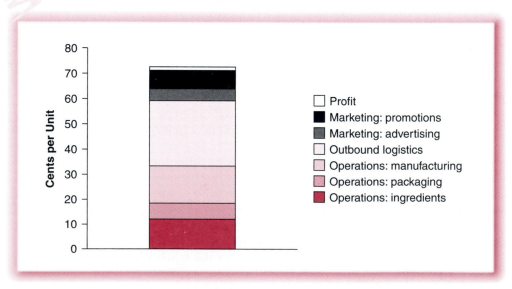

because delivery costs depended largely on the number of stops that a truck driver had to make. Thus, the larger a firm's market share, the greater the number of snack cakes a driver could deliver per stop. Urban deliveries tended to be more expensive than suburban ones, because city traffic slowed the drivers down. Outbound logistics costs also rose with product variety: the firm's broad product line made it difficult for drivers to restock shelves and remove out-of-date merchandise. Finally, the nature of the product itself affected logistics costs. For instance, snack cakes with more preservatives could be delivered less frequently. Using this information, the managers developed numerical relationships between activity costs and drivers for outbound logistics activities and for the other activities depicted in Exhibit 3.7.

Cost drivers are critical because they allow managers to estimate *competitors'* cost positions. Although one usually cannot observe a competitor's costs directly, it is often possible to study their drivers. Thus, Hostess could observe Little Debbie's market share, the portion of its sales in urban areas, the breadth of its product line, and the ingredients in its products. Using its own costs and the numerical relationships to cost drivers, this permitted estimation of the competitor's cost position.

The results of the cost analysis were sobering to Hostess's managers. Because Little Debbie used inexpensive raw materials, purchased in bulk, and tapped national-scale economies, its operations costs totaled 21¢, compared with 33¢ for Hostess. Little Debbie packed its product with preservatives so that deliveries could be made less frequently, kept its product line very simple, and benefited from growing market share. Consequently, its logistics costs per unit were less than half those of Hostess. Also, Little Debbie did not run promotions. Altogether, the managers estimated, a package of Little Debbie snack cakes cost only 34¢ to produce, deliver, and market. Exhibit 3.8 illustrates the results of the cost analysis of Hostess and its major competitors. (The comparison with the two other major competitors, Ontario Baking and Savory Pastries, was not so discouraging. Indeed, Hostess had a small cost advantage over each.)

This specific example illustrates a number of general points about relative cost analysis:[37]

➤ Managers often examine *actual* costs—rather than opportunity costs—because data on actual costs are concrete and available. Although the symmetric treatment of suppliers and buyers in the formalization of added value is useful—reminding us that competitive advantage can come from better management of supplier relations, rather than solely from a focus on downstream customers—supplier opportunity costs and actual costs are usually assumed to track one another closely. Obviously, this assumption should be relaxed when it does not make sense.

➤ When reviewing a relative cost analysis, it is important to focus on differences in individual activities, not just differences in total cost. Ontario Baking and Savory Pastries, for instance, had similar total costs per unit. The two firms had different cost structures, however, and, as we will discuss later, these differences reflected distinct competitive positions.

➤ Good cost analyses typically focus on a subset of a firm's activities. The cost analysis in Exhibit 3.8, for example, does not cover all the activities in the snack cake value chain. Effective cost analyses usually break out in greatest detail and pay the most attention to cost categories that (1) pick up on significant differences across competitors or strategic options, (2) correspond to technically separable activities, or (3) are large enough to influence the overall cost position to a significant extent.

Exhibit 3.8   Relative Cost Analysis

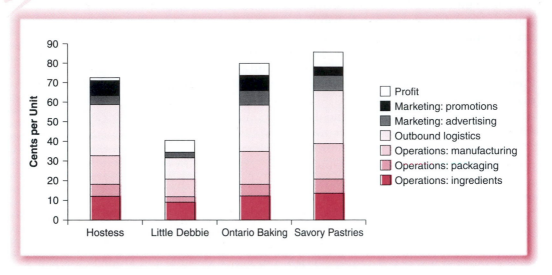

> ➤ Activities that account for a larger proportion of costs deserve more in-depth treatment in terms of cost drivers. For instance, the snack cake managers assigned several cost drivers to outbound logistics and explored them in depth. They gave less attention to the drivers of advertising costs. The analysis of any cost category should focus on the drivers that have a major impact on it.

> ➤ A cost driver should be modeled only if it is likely to vary across the competitors or in terms of the strategic options that will be considered. In the snack cake example, manufacturing location influenced wages, rates, and, therefore, operational costs. All of the rivals had plants in western Canada, however, and manufacturing elsewhere was not an option because shipping was costly and goods had to be delivered quickly. Consequently, manufacturing location was not considered as a cost driver.

> ➤ Finally, because the analysis of relative costs inevitably involves a large number of assumptions, **sensitivity analysis** is crucial. Sensitivity analysis identifies which assumptions really matter and therefore need to be honed. It also tells the analyst how much confidence to have in the results. Under any reasonable variation of the assumptions, Little Debbie had a substantial cost advantage over Hostess.

A number of references discuss cost drivers in greater detail and suggest specific ways to model them numerically.[38] The catalog of potential drivers is long. Many relate to the size of the firm—for example, economies of scale, economies of experience, economies of scope, and capacity utilization. Others relate to differences in firm location, functional policies, timing (e.g., first-mover advantages), institutional factors such as unionization, and government regulations such as tariffs. Differences in the *resources* possessed by a firm may also drive differences in activity costs. A farm with more productive soil, for instance, will incur lower fertilization costs.

A number of pitfalls commonly snare newcomers to cost analysis. Many companies—especially those that produce large quantities of distinct products in a single facility—have grossly inadequate costing systems that must be cleaned up before they can be used as reference points for estimating competitors' costs. As pointed out in courses on management accounting, conventional accounting systems often overemphasize manufacturing costs and allocate overhead and other indirect costs very poorly. As firms move toward selling services and transacting on the basis of knowledge, these outdated systems will make it increasingly more difficult to analyze costs intelligently. Also problematic is a tendency to compare costs as a percentage of sales rather than in absolute dollar terms, which mixes up cost and price differences. Another common but dangerous practice is the mixing together of recurring costs and one-time investments. Analysts sometimes also confuse differences in firms' costs with differences in their product mixes, but one can avoid this problem by comparing the cost positions of comparable products; for example, one should compare Ford's four-cylinder, mid-sized family sedan to Toyota's four-cylinder, mid-sized family sedan, rather than some imaginary "average" Ford to an "average" Toyota. Finally, a focus on costs should not crowd out consideration of customer willingness to pay—the topic of the next section.

Step 2: Using Activities to Analyze Relative Willingness to Pay

The activities of a firm do not just generate costs. They also (one hopes) make customers willing to pay for the firm's product or service. Differences in activities account for differences in willingness to pay and subsequently for differences in added value and profitability. In fact, differences in willingness to pay apparently account for more of the variation in profitability observed among competitors than do disparities in cost levels.[39]

Virtually any activity in the value chain can affect customers' willingness to pay for a product.[40] The most obvious effects are those of product design and the manufacturing activities that influence product characteristics—quality, performance, features, aesthetics. For example, consumers pay a premium for New Balance athletic shoes in part because the firm offers durable shoes in hard-to-find sizes. More subtly, a firm can boost willingness to pay through activities associated with sales or delivery—that is, via the ease of purchase, speed of delivery, availability and terms of credit, convenience of the seller, quality of presale advice, and so on. The catalog florist Calyx and Corolla, for instance, can command a premium because it delivers flowers faster and fresher than most of its competitors do.[41] Activities associated with post-sale service or complementary goods—customer training, consulting services, spare parts, product warranties, repair service, compatible products—may also matter. For example, U.S. consumers may hesitate to buy a Fiat automobile because they fear that spare parts and service will be difficult to obtain. Signals conveyed through advertising, packaging, and branding efforts can play a role in determining willingness to pay as well. Nike's advertising and endorsement activities, for instance, affect the premium it commands. Finally, support activities can have a surprisingly large, if indirect, impact on willingness to pay. Thus, the hiring, training, and compensation practices of Nordstrom create a helpful, outgoing sales staff that permits the department store to charge a premium for its clothes.

Ideally, a company would like to have a "willingness-to-pay calculator"—something that indicates how much customers would pay for any combination of activities. For a host of reasons, however, such a calculator usually remains beyond a firm's grasp. In many cases, willingness to pay depends heavily on intangible factors and perceptions that are hard to measure. Moreover, activities can affect willingness to pay in complicated (i.e., nonlinear and nonadditive) ways. And when a business sells to end-users through intermediaries rather than directly, willingness to pay depends on multiple parties.

Lacking a truly accurate calculator, most managers use simplified methods to analyze relative willingness to pay. A typical procedure is as follows. First, managers think carefully about who the *real* buyer is. This determination can be tricky. In the market for snack cakes, for instance, the immediate purchaser is a supermarket or convenience store executive. The ultimate consumer is typically a hungry school-age child. The pivotal decision-maker, however, is probably the parent who chooses among the brands.

Second, managers work to understand what the buyer or buyers want. The snack-cake-buying parent, for example, makes a purchase based on price, brand image, freshness, product variety, and the number of servings per box.[42] The supermarket or convenience store executive selects a snack cake on the basis of trade margins, turnover, reliability of delivery, consumer recognition, merchandising support, and so forth. Marketing courses discuss ways to flush out such customer needs and desires through formal or informal market research.[43] It is important for such research to identify not only what customers *want*, but also what they *are willing to pay for*. Moreover, it should reveal the needs that are most important to consumers and determine how they trade them off.

Third, managers assess how successful the firm and its competitors are at fulfilling customer needs. Exhibit 3.9 shows such an analysis for the snack cake market that helps us understand both the statics and the dynamics of the marketplace. Little Debbie stands out on an attribute that customers value highly (low price), while Hostess is not superior on any of the customer needs. This sort of analysis helps explain the large shifts in share observed in the market. Ontario Baking enjoys the best brand image—a position for which it has paid via relatively heavy advertising and promotion. Savory Pastries delivers the freshest product, as reflected in its high manufacturing and raw materials cost. Further analysis (not carried out in the snack cake example) can actu-

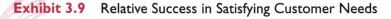

Exhibit 3.9   Relative Success in Satisfying Customer Needs

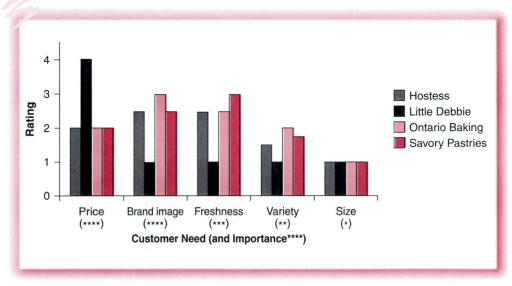

ally assign dollar values to the various customer needs. For example, it can estimate how much a customer will pay for a product that is one day fresher.

Fourth, managers relate differences in success in meeting customer needs back to company activities. Savory Pastries' high score on the freshness need, for instance, can be tied directly to specific activities regarding procurement and selection of ingredients, manufacturing, and delivery.

At this point, managers should have a refined idea of how activities translate, through customer needs, into willingness to pay. They should also understand how activities alter costs. Now they are prepared to take the final step—the analysis of different strategic options. Before moving on to that step, however, we should highlight some guidelines concerning the analysis of willingness to pay.

A major challenge in analyzing willingness to pay is narrowing the long list of customer needs down to a manageable roster. In general, we can ignore needs that have little bearing on customer choice. Likewise, needs that are equally well satisfied by all current and contemplated products can usually be neglected. If the group of competing products plays a small role in satisfying a need relative to other products outside the group, the need can often be removed from the list as well.

So far, we have treated all customers as identical. In reality, of course, buyers differ in what they want and how badly then want it. Some customers in a bookstore want novels, while others look for business books. (This type of disparity, in which different customers rank products differently, is known as **horizontal differentiation.**) Among those customers who want J. K. Rowling's new *Harry Potter* novel, some will pay for the more expensive hardback edition, while others are content to wait for the less expensive soft-cover version. (**Vertical differentiation** arises when customers agree on which product is better—the hardback edition, in this example—but differ in how much they will pay for the better product.)

The analysis of willingness to pay becomes trickier, but more interesting, when customers are either horizontally or vertically differentiated. The usual response is **segmentation:** one first finds clumps of customers who share preferences and then analyzes willingness to pay on a segment-by-segment basis. In our experience, firms that identify segments tend to pinpoint between two and twelve clusters of customers. Diversity in customer needs and ease in customizing the firm's product or service typically increase with the number of segments that the analysis considers. Some observers have even argued that companies should move beyond segmentation to embrace **mass customization.**[44] In this approach, enabled by information and production technologies, companies begin to tailor their products to individual customers. Thus, Blinds to Go receives up to 20,000 custom orders for window blinds and shades per day that it promises to process within forty-eight hours. New approaches to customization have enabled it build up a business with more than $100 million in revenues and 20 percent net margins.[45]

Finally, we want to emphasize the limits to analyzing willingness to pay. In some settings, it is possible to quantify willingness to pay quite precisely. For example, when a firm provides an industrial good that saves its customers a well-understood amount of money, it is relatively easy to calculate this amount. Calculations become much more difficult, however, when buyer choice includes a large subjective component, when customer tastes are evolving rapidly, and when the benefits that the customer derives from the product are hard to quantify. A wide range of market research techniques—such as surveys, hedonic pricing, attribute ratings, and conjoint analysis—have been designed to overcome such problems. Nevertheless, we remain wary, especially when market research asks people to assess their willingness to pay for new products that they have never seen or for the satisfaction of needs that they themselves may not recognize. Fine market research "proved" that telephone answering machines would sell poorly, for instance.[46] In some settings, creative insight may have to replace analysis. In all settings, analysis should serve to hone insight, and not to displace it.

Step 3: Exploring Different Strategic Options and Making Choices

The final step in the analysis of cost and willingness to pay involves the search for ways to widen the wedge between the two. To this point, the management team has researched how changes in activities will affect added value. The goal now is to find favorable options. Because the generation of options is ultimately a creative act, it is difficult to lay down many guidelines for it. We can, however, suggest a few patterns from past experience:

1. It is often helpful to distill the essence of what drives each competitor. Little Debbie, for instance, saw that preservatives could substitute for fast delivery. By adding preservatives to its physical product, the company was able to reduce its delivery costs substantially. This approach also reduced customers' willingness to pay, but the reduction was smaller than the corresponding cost savings. Such distillation often suggests new ways to drive wedges between costs and willingness to pay. Savory Pastries, for instance, was tapping a willingness to pay for freshness. The Hostess managers, however, felt that Savory was not exploiting this customer need fully; a product even fresher than what was available from Savory might command a large premium that might serve as the basis for substantial added value.

2. When considering changes in activities, it is crucial to consider competitor reactions. In the snack cake example, Hostess's managers felt that Little Debbie would readily launch a price war against any competitor that tried to match its low-cost, low-price position. They were less concerned about an aggressive response from Savory Pastries, whose managers were distracted by an expansion into a different business. Such reactions and, more generally, competitive dynamics are the topic of the next chapter.

3. Managers often tend to fixate on a few product characteristics and think too narrowly about benefits to buyers. They rarely consider the full range of ways in which all of their activities can create added value. One way to avoid a narrow focus is to draw out not only one's own value chain, but also the value chains of one's customers and suppliers and the linkages between the chains.[47] Such an exercise can highlight ways to reduce buyers' costs, improve buyers' performance, reduce suppliers' costs, or improve suppliers' performance. Some apparel manufacturers, for instance, have found new ways to satisfy department store buyers that have nothing to do with the physical character of the clothes. By shipping clothes on the proper hangers and in certain containers, for example, these manufacturers can greatly reduce the labor and time required to transfer clothes from the department store's loading dock to the sales floor.

4. In rapidly changing markets, it is often valuable to pay special attention to leading-edge customers *if* their demands presage the needs of the larger marketplace. Yahoo!, the Internet search engine firm, releases test versions of new services to sophisticated users to shake down software and sense the future needs of the wider market.[48] Similarly, under-

served customer segments often represent a significant opportunity. And the Southwest example reminds us that overserved customers can offer an opportunity as well.

5. More generally, one of the most potent ways that a firm alters its added value is by adjusting the *scope* of its operations—that is, changing the range of customers it serves or products it offers within an industry.[49] Broad scope in an industry tends to be advantageous when there are significant economies of scale, scope, and learning (including vertical bargaining power based on size), when customers' needs are relatively uniform across market segments, and when it is possible to charge different prices in different segments. Of course, broader is not always better: there may be diseconomies rather than economies of size, and attempts to serve heterogeneous customers may introduce compromises into a firm's value chain or blur its external or internal message by creating cognitive conflicts in the minds of customers or employees.[50] And even when broader *is* better, there tend to be a variety of ways in which a firm can expand its reach, some of which (such as licensing, franchises, or strategic alliances) fall short of an outright expansion of scope. Chapter 6 discusses related issues in depth, but in the context of corporate strategy (in what range of industries should a diversified corporation participate?) rather than business-unit strategy (within an industry, what range of customers should a firm serve and what range of products should it offer?).

6. We have laid out a process in which a management team develops a comprehensive grasp of how its activities affect costs and willingness to pay, and *then* considers options to widen the wedge between the two. In practice, it is often efficient and effective to reverse this process: to start with a set of options, articulate what each option implies for activities, then analyze the impact of each alternative configuration of activities on the wedge between costs and willingness to pay. By reverse-engineering the analyses they do from the options they face, managers can focus on the analyses that truly matter. Of course, this alternative process works best when managers start with a good grasp of the options available to them.

In general, a firm should scour its business system for, and eliminate, activities that generate costs without creating commensurate willingness to pay. It should also search for inexpensive ways to generate additional willingness to pay, at least among a segment of customers.

THE WHOLE VERSUS THE PARTS

The analysis described in the preceding section focuses on decomposing the firm into parts—that is, discrete activities. In the final step of exploring options, however, the management team must work vigilantly to build a vision of the whole. After all, competitive advantage comes from an *integrated set* of choices about activities. A firm whose choices do not fit together well is unlikely to succeed.

The importance of internal consistency can be visualized, once again, in terms of our metaphor of the business landscape. What particularly complicate the search for high ground—or added value—on this landscape are the interactions among choices: production decisions affect marketing choices, distribution choices need to fit with operations decisions, compensation choices influence a whole range of activities, and so forth. Graphically, the interactions make for a **rugged landscape** characterized by lots of local peaks, each of which depicts a coherent bundle of mutually reinforcing choices.[51]

The ruggedness of the business landscape has several vital implications. First, it suggests that incremental analysis and incremental change may not lead a firm to a new, fundamentally higher position. Rather, a firm may have to consider changing many of its activities in unison to attain a higher peak. To improve its long-run prospects, it may even have to step down and tread through a valley. (Consider the wrenching and far-reaching changes required to turn around IBM, for instance.)

Second, ruggedness implies that more than one internally consistent way to do business often exists within the same industry. Although only a limited number of viable positions are available, more than one high peak usually appears when the interactions among choices are rich. In the retail brokerage business, for instance, both Merrill Lynch and Edward Jones have succeeded historically, but they have done so in very different ways. Merrill Lynch operates large offices in major cities, provides access to a full range of securities, advertises nationally, offers in-house investment vehicles, and serves corporate clients. Edward Jones operates thousands of one-broker offices in rural and suburban areas, handles only conservative securities, markets its services through door-to-door sales calls, produces none of its own investment vehicles, and focuses almost exclusively on individual investors.[52]

Third, the landscape metaphor reminds us that the creation of competitive advantage involves *choice*. In occupying one peak, a firm forgoes an alternative position. Relatedly it can be used to visualize the role of competition. There is often more added value to occupying one's own separate peak than from piling on to a heavily populated summit. And finally, it provides additional perspective on the techniques for industry analyses that were discussed in Chapter 2. It suggests, at least to us, additional emphasis on deaveraging: somewhat less emphasis on analyzing average industry attractiveness—which might be envisioned as the average height of the landscape above sea level—and more emphasis on understanding the industry features that influence the locations of peaks and troughs and their evolution over time.

SUMMARY

The analysis in this chapter helps systematize part of the older SWOT (strengths-weaknesses-opportunities-threats) paradigm for strategic planning because strengths and weaknesses often vary substantially, even among direct competitors. As a result, within-industry differences in performance tend to be significant, and businesses that aim to be very successful must typically position themselves to create competitive advantages within their industries.

Competitive advantage depends on driving a wider wedge between buyers' willingness to pay and costs than one's competitors can. The concept of added value helps integrate considerations of competitive advantage/disadvantage and industry-level conditions into assessments of the likely profitability of individual businesses. A business has added value when the network of customers, suppliers, and complementors in which it operates is better off with it than without it—that is, when the firm offers something unique and valuable in the marketplace.

To achieve a competitive advantage or a higher added value than its rivals, a business must do things differently from them on a day-to-day basis. These differences in activities, and their effects on relative cost position and relative willingness to pay, can be analyzed in detail and used to generate and assess options for creating competitive advantage.

In addition to decomposing the business into activities, however, its managers must also craft a vision of an integrated whole. Much power can be derived, in particular, from positive, mutually reinforcing linkages among activities that make the whole more than the sum of its parts.

Finally, we must emphasize that discussions of positioning risk being static instead of dynamic. Some of this risk flows from the terminology itself. It would probably be better to talk about targeting a path for continuous improvement than to discuss settling into a position for all time. Additionally, positioning has a connotation of choosing from a preset, well-specified set of possibilities, whereas coming up with new positions—fundamentally new ways of competing—can have very high payoffs and therefore demands strategic attention. And perhaps most important, while achieving lower costs or delivering greater benefits than competitors can lead to competitive advantage, how is a competitive advantage—or disadvantage—likely to evolve over time? This question is the focus of the next two chapters of the book, on dynamics.

GLOSSARY

- added value
- competitive advantage
- competitive position
- cost analysis
- cost drivers
- differentiation
- dual competitive advantage
- focus strategy
- generic strategies
- horizontal differentiation
- internal consistency
- market segmentation
- mass customization
- opportunity costs
- resources
- rugged landscape
- segmentation
- sensitivity analysis
- strategic options
- trade-offs
- unrestricted bargaining
- value
- value chain
- vertical differentiation
- willingness to pay

NOTES

1. For further discussion of the definition of competitive advantage, see Steven Postrel, "Competitive Advantage: A Synthesis" (paper presented at the Atlanta Competitive Advantage Conference, Atlanta, June 17, 2004).

2. Uta Werner of Marakon Associates deserves our thanks for helping make these data available.

3. Richard P. Rumelt, "How Much Does Industry Matter?" *Strategic Management Journal* 12, no. 3 (March 1991): 167–185 and Anita M. McGahan and Michael E. Porter, "How Much Does Industry Matter, Really?" *Strategic Management Journal* 18 (July 1997): 15–30.

4. Anita M McGahan and Michael E Porter, "The Persistence of Shocks to Profitability: Comparing the Market-Structure and Chicago Views," *Review of Economics and Statistics* 81 (1999): 43–53.

5. Richard Caves and Pankaj Ghemawat, "Identifying Mobility Barriers," *Strategic Management Journal* 13 (1992): 1–12; Jan W. Rivkin, "Reconcilable Differences: The Relationship Between Industry Conditions and Firm Effects," manuscript, Harvard Business School (1997).

6. See Michael S. Hunt, "Competition in the Major Home Appliance Industry" (D.B.A. thesis, Harvard University, 1972). Two other dissertations at Harvard—Howard

H. Newman, "Strategic Groups and the Structure-Performance Relationship: A Study with Respect to the Chemical Process Industries," and Michael E. Porter, "Retailer Power, Manufacturer Strategy and Performance in Consumer Good Industries"—elaborated and tested the notion of strategic groups. A theoretical foundation for strategic groups was provided by R. E. Caves and M. E. Porter, "From Entry Barriers to Mobility Barriers: Conjectural Decisions and Contrived Deterrence to New Competition," *Quarterly Journal of Economics* 91, no. 2 (May 1977): 241–262.

7. See, for instance, Kenneth J. Hatten and Dan E. Schendel, "Heterogeneity within an Industry: Firm Conduct in the U.S. Brewing Industry, 1952–71," *Journal of Industrial Economics* 26, no. 2 (1977): 97–113.

8. This conclusion is based on Pankaj Ghemawat's experience working at BCG at the beginning of the 1980s.

9. Michael E. Porter, *Competitive Advantage: Creating and Sustaining Superior Performance* (New York: Free Press, 1985), chap. 2.

10. Adapted from Carter F. Bales, P. C. Chatterjee, Donald J. Gogel and Anupam P. Puri, "Competitive Cost Analysis," McKinsey Staff Paper (January 1980), p. 6.

11. For a review of activity-based analysis from the perspective of cost accounting, see Robin Cooper and Robert S. Kaplan, "Profit Priorities from Activity-Based Costing," *Harvard Business Review* 69, no. 5 (May–June 1991): 130–135.

12. Interestingly, the founders of both Bain and SPA had worked on a BCG study of Texas Instruments that was supposed to have highlighted the problem of shared costs. See Walter Kiechel III, "The Decline of the Experience Curve," *Fortune,* October 5, 1981, p. 139.

13. Quoted in ibid.

14. The term "differentiated" is often misused. When we say that a firm has differentiated itself, we mean that it has boosted the willingness of customers to pay for its output and can command a price premium. We do not mean simply that the company is different from its competitors.

Similarly, it is a common error to say that a company has differentiated itself by charging a lower price than its rivals. A firm's choice of price does not affect how much customers are intrinsically willing to pay for a good—except when price conveys information about product quality.

15. Interview with Joseph Bower, April 25, 1997.

16. Interview with Fred Gluck, February 18, 1997.

17. Michael E. Porter, *Competitive Strategy: Techniques for Analyzing Industries and Competitors* (New York: Free Press, 1980), chap. 2; William K. Hall, "Survival Strategies in a Hostile Environment," *Harvard Business Review* 58, no. 5 (September–October 1980): 75.

18. Porter, *Competitive Advantage*, p. 33.

19. Talk by Arnoldo Hax at Massachusetts Institute of Technology, April 29, 1997.

20. Porter, *Competitive Strategy,* pp. 41–44.

21. Ibid., chap. 2. Michael E. Porter, "What Is Strategy?" *Harvard Business Review* 74, no. 6 (November–December 1996): 61–78.

22. Adam Brandenburger and Barry Nalebuff, *Co-Opetition* (New York: Doubleday, 1996), pp. 127–130.

23. See, for instance, Pankaj Ghemawat, *Commitment: The Dynamic of Strategy* (New York: Free Press, 1991), chap. 4. For some empirical studies that seem to support this conclusion, see Lynn W. Phillips, Dae R. Chang, and Robert D. Buzzell, "Product Quality, Cost Position and Business Performance: A Test of Some Key Hypotheses," *Journal of Marketing* 47, no. 2 (Spring 1983): 26–43; Danny Miller and Peter H. Friesen, "Porter's (1980) Generic Strategies and Performance: An Empirical Examination with American Data. Part I: Testing Porter," *Organization Studies* 7, no. 1 (1986): 37–55.

24. Accenture Q4 2003 conference call.

25. W. Chan Kim and Renée Mauborgne, "Blue Ocean Strategy," *Harvard Business Review* 82, no. 10 (October 2004): 76.

26. Matthew Miller, "The Acrobat," *Forbes,* March 15, 2004, p. 100.

27. Adam M. Brandenburger and Harborne W. Stuart, Jr., "Value-Based Business Strat-

egy," *Journal of Economics & Management Strategy* 5, no. 1 (1996): 5–24.

28. Adam M. Brandenburger, Maryellen Costello, and Julia Kou, "Bitter Competition: The Holland Sweetener Co. Vs. Nutrasweet (A)" (Harvard Business School Case no. 794-079, Boston, 1993).

29. This conclusion assumes, of course, that NutraSweet would continue to expand its capacity in line with rapidly growing demand—something that might have appeared quite uncertain to HSC. One limiting feature of added value analysis in its current form is that it doesn't allow for informational complexities of this sort, although it may turn out to be generalizable.

30. In the event, HSC was able, later on, to get paid to stay.

31. Such expedients have variously been referred to as "judo economics" and the "puppy-dog ploy." See Judith R. Gelman and Steven C. Salop, "Judo Economics: Capacity Limitation and Coupon Competition," *Bell Journal of Economics* 14, no. 2 (Autumn 1983): 315–325; Drew Fudenberg and Jean Tirole, "The Fat-Cat Effect, the Puppy-Dog Ploy, and the Lean and Hungry Look," *American Economic Review* 74, no. 2 (May 1984): 361–366.

32. This section draws heavily on ideas first developed in Porter, *Competitive Advantage,* especially chaps. 2–4. Also see Ghemawat, *Commitment,* chap. 4.

33. Das Narayandas and V. Kasturi Rangan, "Dell Computer Corp." (Harvard Business School Case no. 596-058, Boston, 1995).

34. Nicolaj Siggelkow, "Change in the Presence of Fit: The Rise, the Fall, and the Renaissance of Liz Claiborne," *Academy of Management Journal* 44, no. 4 (August 2001): 838–857.

35. Porter, *Competitive Advantage,* chaps. 2–4; Porter, "What Is Strategy?"

36. The authors thank Roger Martin, formerly of Monitor Company, for this example. Details about the companies and other items have been altered substantially to protect proprietary information.

37. See Ghemawat, *Commitment,* chap, 4, for a more extensive list of general guidelines.

38. See Porter, *Competitive Advantage,* chap. 3; David Besanko, David Dranove, and Mark Shanley, *The Economics of Strategy* (New York: John Wiley, 1996), chap. 13.

39. Richard E. Caves and Pankaj Ghemawat, "Identifying Mobility Barriers," *Strategic Management Journal* 13, no. 1 (January 1992): 1–12. Of course, this general pattern may not hold up in a particular setting.

40. See Porter, *Competitive Advantage,* chap. 4; Besanko, Dranove, and Shanley, *Economics of Strategy,* chap. 13.

41. Walter J. Salmon and David Wylie, "Calyx & Corolla" (Harvard Business School Case no. 592-035, Boston, 1991).

42. We present "low price" as an attribute that buyers seek. This statement should not be misunderstood as meaning that price determines willingness to pay. Rather, price is included as an attribute in surveys of customer needs so that one can calibrate the willingness of customers to pay a price premium for the other attributes in the survey (such as freshness).

43. See, for instance, Philip Kotler, *Marketing Management: Analysis, Planning, Implementation, and Control,* 8th ed. (Englewood Cliffs, N.J.: Prentice-Hall, 1994).

44. B. Joseph Pine II, *Mass Customization: The New Frontier in Business Competition* (Boston: Harvard Business School Press, 1992).

45. Larry Menor and Ken Mark, "Blinds to Go: Invading the Sunshine State" (Richard Ivey School of Business Case no. 901D04, 2001).

46. Oren Harari, "The Myths of Market Research," *Small Business Reports* 19, no. 7 (July 1994): 48–52.

47. Porter, *Competitive Advantage.*

48. Marco Iansiti and Alan MacCormack, "Developing Products on Internet Time," *Harvard Business Review* 75, no. 5 (September–October 1997): 108–117.

49. Scope has a number of dimensions—horizontal, vertical, and geographic—that were discussed in Chapter 2. The discussion here focuses on horizontal and geographic scope. Vertical scope, which raises a different set of issues, is discussed at

greater length in Chapter 5, in the context of hold up.

50. Porter, "What Is Strategy?"

51. Daniel A. Levinthal, "Adaptation on Rugged Landscapes," *Management Science* 43, no. 7 (July 1997): 934–950; Jan W. Rivkin, "Imitation of Complex Strategies," *Management Science* 46, no. 6 (June 2000): 824–844. The landscape metaphor is de-rived from evolutionary biology, especially Stuart A. Kauffman, *The Origins of Order: Self-Organization and Selection in Evolution* (New York: Oxford University Press, 1993).

52. Richard Teitelbaum, "The Wal-Mart of Wall Street," *Fortune,* October 13, 1997, pp. 128–130.

Anticipating Competitive Dynamics

Bruno Cassiman and Pankaj Ghemawat

Know your enemy, know yourself, and you can fight a hundred battles with no danger of defeat. When you are ignorant of the enemy but know yourself, your chances of winning and losing are equal. If you don't know your enemy or yourself, you are bound to perish in all battles.
                                        —SUN TZU, *THE ART OF WAR*

Mapping the business landscape and pursuing a peak or advantaged position on it are necessary but not sufficient for business success over time. Unless a business can count on all its competitors being inept or inert, it needs to recognize that even as it tries to maximize its own payoffs, competitors may be similarly engaged, with significant implications for what it ought to do. Interactions with buyers, suppliers, and other players striving to improve their own positions can have similar implications. Strategists are confronted, therefore, with the challenge of anticipating important interactions with all these types of players. That said, most of the discussion in this chapter will focus on anticipating interactions with direct competitors, although many of the same principles apply to dynamics involving other types of players. The chapter is intended to provide a better answer to the broad question: "What moves or strategy shifts are identifiable competitors—or significant others—likely to make?"

While the conceptual importance of such dynamic thinking is clear, managers still do not seem to engage in much of it. According to one survey, for example, while 70–75 percent say they consider competitors in making product and pricing decisions, only 8 percent report thinking through *future* competitive behavior in the context of product introductions, and 15 percent in the context of price changes.[1] The most commonly cited reason is that the real world is far too uncertain for such anticipations to be folded into action. But even if this were correct—and there is no evidence that it is—competitors do not stand still, which suggests that ignoring their moves is *not* the answer. It seems better to make use of the available techniques for anticipating competitive dynamics, even though they are partial, on the grounds that in the land of the blind, the one-eyed can be king. And if competitors also display strategic foresight, myopia on one's own part is even more likely to be problematic. Put differently, the advantages of anticipating competitive dynamics do *not* depend on those advantages being widely overlooked—a theme that we return to toward the end of this chapter.

The obvious way to analyze competitive dynamics among a few players is to use detailed information about them to forecast what they will do, with a view to preventing moves that harm one's interests while promoting those that help. This requires managers to put themselves in the shoes of other players instead of viewing competitive situations solely from the egocentric perspectives of their own businesses. This chapter focuses on two broad approaches have been proposed for this purpose: **game theory** and **competitor profiling.** Game theory takes an economic perspective by focusing on incentives under conditions of competition, whereas competitor profiling takes more of a behavioral perspective by trying to identify competitors' predispositions. Put differently, game theory tries to answer this question by focusing on what competitors *should* do under some (reasonable) baseline assumptions, while competitor profiling brings in considerations related to what competitors really want, what they might—given their beliefs—see themselves doing to accomplish their goals, and what they have tended to do historically in similar situations.

While they obviously involve very different kinds of analysis, the two approaches are generally complementary: game theory is worth considering unless you expect your competitors to succumb their predispositions with probability one, and competitor profiling unless you expect them to be entirely economically rational.

The chapter begins by using detailed examples to illustrate how to apply game theory to the challenge of forecasting what competitors will do, and how to fold the insights afforded into one's own choice of strategy. It then discusses competitor profiling and ways of melding it with game-theoretic analysis, so as to increase predictive power by reducing the uncertainty surrounding competitive dynamics. The chapter concludes by proposing some ways of opening up the process of analyzing competitive dynamics in order to enhance its applicability to real-world situations involving a small number of identifiable players. Situations in which players are numerous or faceless are addressed in the next chapter.

SIMPLE GAMES

Game theory is the study of interactions among players whose **payoffs** depend on one another's choices and who recognize the interdependence in trying to maximize their respective payoffs. The historical development of game theory is outlined in Exhibit 4.1. In this chapter we focus on *non-cooperative* game theory.[2] A real-world application, to a pricing study for a major pharmaceutical company, will illustrate the building blocks of the theory, its perspective on interactions, and guidelines for applying it.

Consider, therefore, the pharmaceutical case study. One of the most profitable products sold by the incumbent (hereinafter, *I*) dominated its category but faced the introduction of a substitute product by a major competitor. As the late-mover, the en-

Exhibit 4.1   The Historical Development of Game Theory

The Jewish Talmud supplies what is apparently the first application of game theory when it discusses the death of a man whose estate is too small to cover the (different) payments specified in separate marriage contracts with his three wives. The Talmud recommends apparently different ways of dividing the estate—depending on the size of the shortfall—that have perplexed scholars for the better part of two millennia. Two decades ago, game-theorists realized that the Talmudic solutions correspond to a particular solution concept from **coalitional** (or what is sometimes known as **cooperative) game theory.**[3]

The notion of coalitional games was formalized in 1944 in the celebrated book *The Theory of Games and Economic Behavior* by John von Neumann, a mathematician also regarded as the father of modern computing, and Oskar Morgenstern, an economist.[4] Von Neumann and Morgenstern also advanced the analysis of **strategic** or **non-cooperative game theory**—the theory of moves (as opposed to combinations) that has attracted more attention in the formal development of game theory. Specifically, they supplied a general theory of the purely adversarial case of two-person **zero-sum games,** in which one player's gain is exactly equal to the other player's loss (e.g., chess).

Very few games in business—or elsewhere—seem to be strictly zero-sum, however, so modern game theory has come to focus on nonzero-sum or, more accurately, **nonconstant-sum games** that afford opportunities for cooperation as well as competition. While we still lack a general theory of such games, a broad organizing principle is provided by the work of mathematician John Nash, who won the Nobel Prize in economics in 1994 and whose life was exposed to a broader audience in the book/movie "A Beautiful Mind." In two papers published in 1950 and 1951, Nash proved the existence of a strategic equilibrium for non-cooperative games—the **Nash equilibrium**—and proposed that cooperative games be studied by reducing them to non-cooperative form.[5]

Subsequent theorizing has focused mainly on refinements and extensions of the Nash equilibrium. Thus, Nash's co-winners of the Nobel Prize, for work done in the 1960s, were Reinhard Selten, who suggested using the refinement of subgame perfection (backward induction or looking ahead and reasoning back) to select from the frequently large number of Nash equilibria in dynamic games, and John Harsanyi, who developed the concept of a Bayesian Nash Equilibrium for games with incomplete information, thereby laying the foundations for a vast literature on signaling and, more broadly, information economics.[6]

Harsanyi and Selten also collaborated in the 1980s to develop a general theory of equilibrium selection in non-cooperative games.[7] Work on this broad topic continues. In addition, recent years have seen an interest in learning, evolutionary processes, and the incorporation of behavioral and experimental insights into game theory, as discussed in the latter sections of this chapter.

trant (hereinafter, E) was expected to launch its own product at a very large discount. It was uncertain exactly how low E's launch price would be, and whether I should reduce its own prices in anticipation or reaction. The cash flows involved were large enough, however, to compel careful analysis of I's options.

The analysis began with the specification of the **players** in the game: I and E. In fact, there were a total of five players, including E, in the product category. However, two players were excluded from the analysis on the grounds that they were marginal players without a discernible impact on market outcomes, and a third, because unique product characteristics insulated it from interactions between I and E. The number of players can sometimes also be reduced—and game-theoretic analysis greatly simplified—by aggregating players with similar economics and objectives.

The second step in applying game theory to this problem involved specifying the possible actions of both players: their **strategies.**[8] The final analysis focused on four strategies involving different levels of discounting for *E*'s launch price and four strategies for *I*'s own (relative) price.[9] The latter were bounded by the alternatives of holding *I*'s price level constant (which would entail a very large price advantage for *E*) and of neutralizing *E*'s price advantage. Thinking broadly about possible options and outcomes is very important and is discussed further in the last section of this chapter.

As a third step, payoffs were assigned to the different combinations of strategies for *I* and *E*. This involved, first of all, assessing the two players' objectives: was *E* likely to maximize profits, or would it emphasize growth and gaining share? Based on considerations discussed below in the section on competitor profiling, *E* was deemed to be a profit-maximizer, like *I*. Next, players' objectives were mapped into numerical payoffs associated with each outcome from each player's perspective. Experts gauged the market shares implied by each pair of prices and combined them with knowledge of *I*'s costs and estimates of *E*'s to calculate the net present values (NPVs) of the two products for the two players. Note that if *E* had been deemed to be a sales-maximizer, further analysis might have been couched in terms of NPVs for *I* and some measure based on sales revenue for *E*.

Because there were only two players, the information on their strategies and payoffs could conveniently be captured in a **payoff matrix,** as depicted in Exhibit 4.2, with the rows representing *I*'s strategic options, and the columns *E*'s. The first entry in each cell corresponds to the estimated NPV, in millions of dollars, for *I*, and the second entry to the estimated NPV for *E;* the three shaded cells were judged to be arithmetically infeasible.[10] Within this set-up, firms select strategies—rows or columns—and not individual outcomes, as in particular cells. It is in this sense that payoff matrixes capture the dependence of each firm's payoff on its rival's strategy as well as its own.

Use of the payoff matrix to derive strategic recommendations required additional specification of the **rules** of the game. In this game, as in many others, the timing of moves was critical: were the players making **simultaneous moves,** or was there more of a dynamic structure to their interactions? As a first cut, it was assumed that *I* and *E* would simultaneously and independently choose their pricing strategies—although the assumption of simultaneity as opposed to sequentiality was revisited later in the analytical process, as described below.

This structure provided the basis for *I* to think through its interactions with *E* *before E* entered the market. In particular, the payoff matrix raised questions about the business plan that firm *I* had in place, which assumed that *E* would launch with a high price and that *I* would not change its price at all. The matrix suggested that this "base case" was unlikely to materialize. Specifically, if *E* launched with a high price, leaving its price unchanged was *not* a **best response** for *I*. Instead, *I* could, by neutralizing *E*'s price advantage, achieve an expected NPV of $669 million versus $624 million in the base case. Similarly, the base case also failed to coincide with a best response for *E*. With no price change anticipated on the part of *I*, *E* had a large incentive to charge a very low price instead and achieve an estimated NPV of $190 million versus $116 million in the base case. So, in the supposed base case, neither firm would actually be using its best response to the other, making it a highly implausible outcome.

The game-theoretic idea of the elimination of **dominated strategies,** strategies that do not maximize payoffs for one player no matter what the other player does, was

Exhibit 4.2   The Pharmaceutical Payoff Matrix (millions of dollars for *I, E*)

Incumbent (*I*'s) Price	Entrant's (*E*'s) Price			
	Very Low	Low	Moderate	High
No price change	358,190	507,168	585,129	624,116
Large Price Advantage for *E*	418,163	507,168		
Small Price Advantage for *E*	454,155	511,138	636,126	
Neutralization of *E*'s Price Advantage	428,50	504,124	585,129	669,128

used to further narrow the possible outcomes. In the payoff matrix in Exhibit 4.2, charging a high price was a dominated strategy for *E* because, irrespective of *I*'s choice among the rows, *E* would do better, in terms of its choice among the columns, by setting a moderate price instead of a high price. The implication is that *I* should not expect *E* to set a high price—in other words, that it should eliminate the outcomes in the last column of the payoff matrix from the space of possibilities. Also discernible is the idea of **iterated elimination** of dominated strategies: once the high launch-price strategy was ruled out for *E*, *I*'s dominant strategy, the strategy that maximized I's payoffs no matter what E did, became leaving *E* a small price advantage, in the sense of affording it higher expected NPVs than each of the three other rows (now dominated strategies), regardless of *E*'s choice among the three remaining columns. Note the effect that this has of narrowing the space of possible outcomes to the first three cells in the third row, in which *I* concedes *E* a small price advantage.

Pressing forward, another round of iterated elimination of dominated strategies, this time from *E*'s perspective, pinned down—in this case, but not necessarily in general—a unique **Nash equilibrium:** a strategy pair, one for each player, from which neither player had an incentive to deviate unilaterally. Note that if *E* launched with a very low price, and *I* conceded *E* a small price advantage, each player would be playing its best response to the other's strategy: given *E*'s strategy, *I* would have no incentive to change its own strategy, and vice versa. As a result, unilateral deviations from this strategy pair would be costly—imposing a penalty of at least $17 million in NPV terms on each player (= $155 million - $138 million for *E*), up to nearly $100 million on *I* ($454 million – $358 million for *I*), depending on the precise deviation.

But while this was the only Nash equilibrium that did not make it very enticing from the perspective of *I*'s managers, some of whom were more inclined to see it as threatening to their careers. After all, compared to the (admittedly unrealistic) business plan, it implied a shortfall of $166 million, or 27 percent of "base case" NPV of $624 million. In response, *I*'s managers began to explore whether they could make a **credible**

precommitment to a (relative) pricing strategy for their product before *E* committed to a particular launch price. If feasible, this would effectively change the rules of the game from simultaneous moves to sequential moves, with *I* becoming the **first mover.** In particular, a credible precommitment to ceding a large price advantage to *E* might, given the payoff matrix, persuade *E* to launch with a low price rather than a very low price (*E* stood to make 3 percent more, or $168 million instead of $163 million by doing so) and increase *I*'s payoffs from 73 percent of base case payoffs to 81 percent (i.e., to $507 million). And a credible precommitment to neutralizing *E*'s price advantage was even more likely to persuade *E* not to launch with a very low price: it stood to make an extra $73–79 million, more than doubling its NPV, by entering with a low-to-moderate price instead. In particular, if *I* committed to neutralize and *E* entered with a low price, *I*'s payoffs would approximate 81 percent of the base case; if *E* entered with a moderate price instead, *I*'s payoffs would increase by another $80 million, to 94 percent of base case payoffs. Subsequent work centered on the legal and practical feasibility of credibly communicating the "neutralization strategy" to *E*.

In addition to illustrating the payoffs from modeling business situations as simple, quantifiable games, the pharmaceutical example highlights the broader contribution that game theory can make to business strategy: game theory forced *I*'s managers to think about the launch price that would maximize *E*'s profits—*E*'s best response—instead of fixating on the high launch price that they would have *liked* to see *E* set. And *E*, too, stood to gain from thinking through *I*'s best response—that is, recognizing that *I* might react to *E*'s entry instead of leaving its price unchanged. In effect, each firm had to derive a **reaction function** identifying its rival's best responses to different pricing choices that it might make. Such reaction functions, by themselves, offer useful insights into competitors' incentives. For example, if one player is able to move first, as *I* aspired to do by the end of the study, it can try to maximize its payoffs by selecting the point that it prefers off its rival's reaction function instead of waiting for things to settle down at an intersection of the reaction functions of *I* and *E* respectively—the predicted outcome of a simultaneous move game. The next section uses another detailed example to advance the analysis of such explicitly **dynamic games**.

DYNAMIC GAMES

To state the obvious, strategic decision-making happens over time and not all at once. Game theory also lets us structure and study strategic interactions over time, as dynamic games in which moves are sequential and uncertainty about competitor behavior or other elements of the environment unfolds as time passes, allowing firms to adjust their decisions along the way. Note that this dynamic extension is essential to studying such issues as timing advantages, credible threats and promises, and the implications of commitment or irreversibility for strategy. Our next example illustrates the usefulness of game theory in a dynamic context.

The example concerns the interactions between Boeing (*B*) and Airbus (*A*) around the superjumbo (SJ), a multibillion-dollar commitment that required careful strategic analysis and took the better part of a decade to unfold—a complex example that, even better, yields some counterintuitive implications when viewed game-theoretically. The discussion is based on a teaching case prepared by Benjamin Esty that was analyzed by Esty and Ghemawat.[11]

In December 2000, Airbus entered the new millennium by formally committing to spending $11.9 billion to develop a 555-seat superjumbo, the A380. The company had about fifty firm orders and options on another forty-two units. This move threatened the lucrative monopoly that Boeing held, with the Boeing 747 or jumbo, in very large aircraft (VLA) capable of accommodating more than 400 passengers. Should Boeing have been the competitor to build the superjumbo? And even if it couldn't have changed the outcome of the game at this level, what did it do or what could it have done to mitigate the impact of Airbus's entry into the VLA market? Game theory provides powerful insights into these and other difficult questions.

Following the analysis in the preceding section, we represent the interaction between Boeing and Airbus around the introduction of the superjumbo as a two-player game. However, given the dynamic nature of the game, each player's choice set is more complex than a "simple" decision to develop or not develop the superjumbo. We start the game before either player has committed to the decision to develop the superjumbo and depict its unfolding in terms of the **game tree** in Exhibit 4.3. (This, like the matrix representation in the preceding section, is simply a visual aid to better understand the structure of the game and play it more effectively.)[12] The order of decisions is as follows. First B decides whether or not to make a credible and visible commitment to the development of the superjumbo (Node I).[13] This decision results in two possible **subgames.** At node II.1, A decides whether or not to commit to its own superjumbo development project, knowing that B is not developing a superjumbo, while at node II.2, A faces a similar decision, but against the backdrop of B's having decided to commit to

Exhibit 4.3 The Superjumbo Development Game: Present Values of Expected Operating Profits ($ millions)*

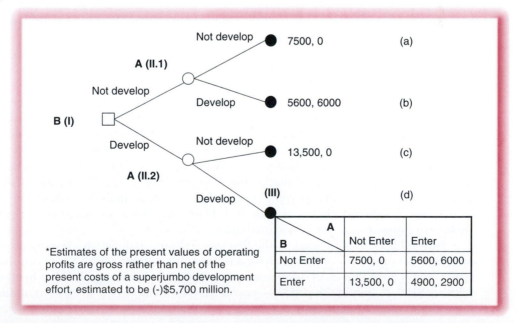

B \ A	Not Enter	Enter
Not Enter	7500, 0	5600, 6000
Enter	13,500, 0	4900, 2900

*Estimates of the present values of operating profits are gross rather than net of the present costs of a superjumbo development effort, estimated to be (-)$5,700 million.

the superjumbo. Finally, at node III, both *A* and *B* have completed any development efforts that they started and, conditional on completion, have to decide whether to compete in the VLA market by selling superjumbos.

Given the cardinal principle of dynamic game theory, **look ahead and reason back,** it is useful to begin by pinning down the payoffs at the tips of the game tree. The numbers reported in Exhibit 4.3 are estimates of the present values of the operating profits contingent on each of the four possible development paths, based on assumptions and calculations summarized in Exhibit 4.4, with the first entry representing the payoff for *B* (including the profits from the sales of 747 jumbos as well as superjumbos, potentially), and the second the payoff for *A*.[14] It is important to remember that these operating payoff estimates do *not* account for the net present value of the costs to develop a superjumbo, estimated to be −$5,700 million. Development costs will be netted in as we reason back to decision-making about development efforts.

Along three of the four possible development paths (cases a–c), the outcomes to the last stage of decision-making, as in who will compete in which product market, are obvious. Case (d), in contrast, involves multiple possible outcomes. Game-theoretic reasoning along the same lines as in the pharmaceutical example, to which the matrix in Exhibit 4.3 bears a structural resemblance, helps sort through the possibilities. Note that *A* has a dominant strategy: it always enters the superjumbo market if it gets to this point in the game tree. The situation for *B* is quite different: given that entry is a dominant strategy for *A,* entry by *B* as well into superjumbos not only creates tough competition there, but also hurts *B*'s sales of jumbos. The best outcome for *B* would be to monopolize both the jumbo and superjumbo categories, but this outcome seems very unlikely. Under the assumption that *A* will enter the superjumbo market, *B* should not enter, even though the superjumbo prototype is assumed to be paid for and ready by this stage: the drop in operating profits on jumbos is not offset by the profits generated by competing to sell superjumbos. Therefore, if we reach this stage of the game, we expect *B* not to enter the superjumbo market, and to earn $5,600 million from its jumbos, while *A* does enter and earns an estimated $6,000 million in operating profits in present-value terms from superjumbos.

Having determined that the top right-hand cell in the payoff matrix (*A* enters, *B* does not) is the outcome in case (d), we can now fold back the last stage of decisions in the game tree in Exhibit 4.3 to look at earlier-stage decisions about whether or not to develop the superjumbo. The game tree that follows in Exhibit 4.5 nets out the costs of development—$5.7 billion in present-value terms—as appropriate from the operating profits associated with the ends of the previous game tree. Once again, *A* has a dominant strategy—in this case, to embark on development. To see this, note that even if *B* does decide to develop a superjumbo (node II.1), *A* can develop its own version and expect to capture the superjumbo market for a net payoff of $300 million (since *B* would not wish to participate in a superjumbo duopoly). The same analysis applies to the subgame where *B* stays out, that is, at node II.2. Therefore, *A* has an incentive to develop the superjumbo irrespective of what *B* does.

Now fold the analysis back to the first stage: should *B* decide to develop a superjumbo? Based on the preceding analysis, *A* will develop and introduce a superjumbo no matter what (since that is *A*'s dominant strategy), so *B* can either go head-to-head with *A*, losing $100 million in the process—payoff (d)—or it can decide to stay out of the superjumbo market and generate operating profits of $5.6 billion from jumbos—payoff

Exhibit 4.4   Boeing versus Airbus in Superjumbos: Possible Product Market Payoffs

The outcomes in Exhibit 4.3 are most simply described in increasing order of complexity, from top to bottom. The numbers reported, in particular, are based on analysts' reports and a meta-analysis by Benjamin Esty. Note that the estimates of superjumbo demand that underlie the numbers reported here fall towards the high end of analysts' forecasts.

Case a: If neither player has developed the superjumbo (case a), Airbus does not operate in the VLA segment, and Boeing continues to milk the market with its existing jumbos. Assume that Boeing sells 38 jumbos per year in each of the next 15 years (the same average number as from 1995 to 1999). At a price of $165 million per plane (rising at 2% per year for inflation), an operating margin of 20%, a tax rate of 34%, and a weighted average cost of capital of 9%, the present value of that stream of operating profits to Boeing is approximately $7.5 billion.

Case b: The second branch from the top features Airbus competing with superjumbos against Boeing with jumbos. Assume that Airbus sells about 50 superjumbos per year at a starting price of $225 million per plane and operating margins of around 15%, implying an estimated present value of operating payoffs of $6 billion. Boeing is assumed to have to drop its operating margins on the jumbo to 15%, but to continue to sell 38 planes per year, yielding it $5.6 billion from the jumbo.

Case c: The next branch from the top has Airbus staying out of the VLA segment and Boeing offering both the jumbo and a superjumbo. For simplicity (and to make a point), we assume that the operating payoffs to Boeing equal the value of a jumbo monopoly ($7.5 billion from case a) plus the operating payoffs from being the sole provider of the superjumbo, without having to worry about the cross-effects on the jumbo ($6 billion from case b). This is obviously an upper bound; the total operating payoffs (Boeing's plus Airbus's) from case b, $11.6 billion, provide a lower bound since Boeing can now coordinate pricing across the jumbo and the superjumbo, and so should be able to do at least as well as if both were set independently. Also note that innovation is "viable" in the conventional non-strategic sense for Boeing at the upper bound ($13.5b − $5.7b < $7.5b), but not at lower bound ($11.6b − $5.7b > $7.5b).

Case d: The bottom branch, unlike the others, leads to several possible product market outcomes. Three of the four possible outcomes coincide, in product market and operating payoff terms, with the cases (a-c) discussed above. The only new subcase is the one in which the two firms offer competing superjumbos. Competition is assumed to drive down the operating margins on the superjumbo from 15% to 10%, and annual sales for each player at these more competitive prices are estimated at 35 planes. These assumptions imply $2.9 billion apiece for Boeing and Airbus in terms of present values of operating payoffs from superjumbos. Boeing is estimated to make another $2 billion in operating profits from its jumbos, down sharply under the assumption that intense competition to sell superjumbos results in only 20 jumbos per year being sold at operating margins of 10% (versus 38 at 20% in case a).

(b). Given our analysis, *B* strongly prefers payoff (b) to payoff (d), although payoff (a) or (c) would be much better still.

The result that *B* should not attempt to develop a superjumbo is striking because the analysis demonstrates that it applies even if the development of the superjumbo is commercially viable for *B* (in the sense that $13,500 million − $5,700 million > $7,500 million) and *B* is far-sighted and interested in preventing *A* from entering a category that is thought to have

Exhibit 4.5   The Superjumbo Development Game: Net Present Values ($ millions)

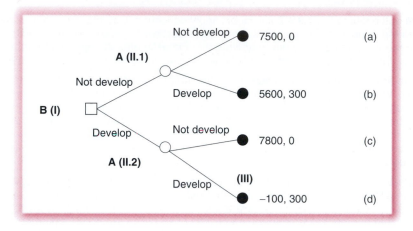

room for just one player. Boeing's existing jumbo business is the key reason *B* is interested in deterring entry into superjumbos by *A;* it is also, however, a constraint on *B*'s ability to actually deter entry. The effects of *A*'s superjumbo on *B*'s jumbo business appear bad enough by themselves (reducing its value by an estimated one-quarter). The last thing that *B* wants to do is compound competitive pressures in the VLA segment by packing in an additional product of its own because that would destroy value in terms of pure operating profits, without even accounting for the development costs that *B* would have to pay. It is therefore not credible for *B* to actually offer a new VLA as well as a jumbo to compete with the superjumbo that *A* will assuredly introduce. This would continue to be true even if *B*'s (incremental) development costs were much lower, as they were supposed to be for an intermediate-sized VLA based on stretching the jumbo's airframe, an initiative that Boeing started and stopped twice. In the model, in fact, development could cost *B* nothing at all and it still would not want to launch its own superjumbo!

Game theory clearly affords some counterintuitive insights into the case of the superjumbo. Less obviously, while there is much talk of changing the game—an important topic to which we return in the last section of the chapter—game theory is useful partly because it clarifies the constraints on the ability to shape outcomes in this sense. Specifically, while Boeing might have boosted its estimated NPV by $1,900 million (payoff a – payoff b from Exhibit 4.5) to $2,200 million (payoff c – payoff b) if Airbus did not launch a superjumbo, it is difficult to see what more it could have done to keep Airbus out. If it had gone ahead and invested in the superjumbo anyway, it might have reduced its estimated NPV by as much as $5,700 million (payoff b – payoff d). So game theory is sometimes most valuable for suggesting what is not worth attempting!

Having said as much, it is worth remembering that, even in this instance, the analysis *does* suggest some avenues for action. For example, while it might be impossible to deter Airbus from entering the VLA market, slowing it down is valuable to Boeing: based on some of the parameters in Exhibit 4.4, every year that Airbus's introduction of superjumbos is delayed increases the present value of Boeing's operating profits from the jumbo business by about $135 million. Several maneuvers that Boeing orchestrated over the years seem consistent with such an intent. For instance, in the early 1990s, Boeing secretly and separately approached two members of the Airbus consortium, Daimler Benz and British Aerospace, about the possibility of joining forces on a superjumbo. After news of these discussions leaked out, Boeing and Airbus agreed in January 1993 to collaborate on a joint feasibility study of a very large aircraft. In July 1995, however, the collaboration ended. An Airbus employee later speculated that Boeing might have participated in the joint effort only to "stall the market so that Airbus did not develop anything itself."

From a broader perspective, the Boeing-Airbus example underscores the cardinal principle of dynamic game theory: look ahead and reason back. It also illustrates the fact that applications typically involve a short sequence of stages, often two or three. Earlier stages may be thought of as literally preceding later ones. Alternatively, and this is closer to the interpretation in the Boeing-Airbus case, earlier stages of choice focus on long-term commitments, and later stages on interactions around variables that *can* be changed in the short run (most often, prices or quantities).

COMPETITOR PROFILING

So far, we have focused on interactions among players who see the business landscape in the same way and relentlessly maximize their expected net present values. While these are attractive baseline assumptions, we can obtain additional insights by relaxing them. Competitors may not be out to maximize firm value, or they may hold different beliefs about the (shifting) business landscape or may behave in ways that have a hard-wired component, reflecting **inertia** rather than purposeful choice. Attempts to predict their behavior should take such possibilities into account.

Thus, when deciding what to do in superjumbos, Boeing should have paid attention not only to value-maximizing courses of action for Airbus but also to

➤ Airbus's goal of market leadership and, perhaps, the attractions of securing a large dollop of public subsidies ("launch aid")

➤ Airbus's belief that Boeing's monopoly of very large aircraft constituted an important advantage in its competition with Airbus

➤ Airbus's history of filling out its product line plus its recent "success" in terms of market share, operating cash flow, and so on.

Because each of these considerations made it more likely that Airbus would go ahead with the superjumbo, their omission would not have misled Boeing: paying attention to them would have reinforced the prediction about Airbus's behavior derived from game-theoretic analysis. But alignment between such behavioral predispositions and the pure economic incentives that game theory focuses on cannot, in general, be assumed. Instead, behavioral predispositions and their effects must be analyzed.

Competitor profiling systematizes such analysis. It uses in-depth examination of competitors' **goals, beliefs,** and **routines** to address questions concerning

➤ What competitors really want

➤ How they might see themselves as pursuing their goals

➤ What they have tended to do historically

Exhibit 4.6 lists some of the elements of the goals-beliefs-routines framework. Compared to the formal apparatus of game theory, it clearly has a motley character. Instead of running through each of the elements of the framework, we will focus on discussing its basic logic in a way that emphasizes piercing the veil of what competitors say about themselves to uncover what really drives them, and to understand, in particular, the role of their top management.

The importance of thinking through a competitor's goals is directly related to the scope for deliberate departures from firm value maximization. Such departures may reflect an organization's charter (e.g., public enterprise, nonprofit), ownership structure (e.g., family-owned and -oriented), or **agency problems,** with managers pursuing personal goals at the expense of firm value. When there *are* agency problems, top managers tend to be the ones who matter the most in determining the direction of the departure from firm value-maximization. It is useful to recognize that their motivations are often complex: purely self-serving behavior, while perhaps more in evidence than pure saintliness, is far from universal. At an organizational level, attention may also usefully be paid to a corporation's desired portfolio of businesses/segments, to the competitive position and other operating or competitive goals it is pursuing within a business, and to its stated financial targets. (Public companies' statements about financial goals are more believable than many other promises they might make because of pressure from investors to deliver on them.)

Beliefs represent the second component of the framework for competitor profiling. The importance of thinking through a competitor's beliefs rests on room to seeing the world in different ways because of either the inherent **ambiguity** of a situation or **embedded beliefs** that are so deeply or broadly held that do not change much with new information. It is often useful to try to synthesize differences in beliefs into different **mental models:** semi-permanent, simple and often partly subliminal maps of the world that guide choices. (Of course, if beliefs are too incoherent to lend themselves to such a synthesis, that is of interest as well.) Competitors' top managers provide, once again, a very good pool in which to fish for insights into beliefs as well as to seek to pin down overall mental models.

The importance of thinking through the final component of the competitor profiling framework, a competitor's routines, is contingent on the possibility that the competitor's behavior may not be entirely purposeful even in relation to its true goals and beliefs. Philip Selznick started this line of analysis nearly fifty years ago by proposing that "Commitments to ways of acting and responding are built into the organization."[15] In other words, organizations exhibit inertial tendencies, numerous markers of the importance of which are listed in Exhibit 4.6. The precise mechanisms underlying inertia are diverse, encompassing not only the (active but "mindless") routines evoked by Selznick but also passivity/inactivity and systematic **biases**, individual and group-level, that are observed even when choices *are* made mindfully.[16] These myriad individual mechanisms make the broader point that a competitor's past routines may have considerable power to predict its future behavior.

One way to grasp the overall goals-beliefs-routines framework for competitor profiling as well as its individual elements is to apply it to an organization that you have worked for or otherwise know well. Another approach, pursued here, is to use a relatively detailed example—based on a consulting study—to illustrate the application of the framework.

Exhibit 4.6 Framework for Competitor Profiling

Questions	What do competitors really want?	How do competitors see themselves as pursuing their goals?	What have competitors actually tended to do historically?
Components	**Goals**, Stated and Latent	**Beliefs**, Explicit and Tacit	**Routines** and other Sources of Inertia
Markers of Importance	-Organizational Charter/ Ownership/Governance Structure (Scope for Deliberate Departures from Value-Maximization)	-Ambiguity/Divergence -Embeddedness (Differences in Mental Models and Their Implications)	-Size/Maturity/Complexity/ Bureaucratization/Thick Culture/ Insularity/Poor Information/ Continuity at the Top (Inertia Indicators)
Top Management (E / L)	Compensation/Incentives -Clout/Credibility/Reputation -Superordinate Goals/Intrinsic Commitment -Emotions	-Life Experiences -About Management Tools/ Practices/Principles -Consultants/Advisors -Role Models/Analogies	-Sunk Cost Fallacy -Self-Justification -Focus on Confirmatory Evidence -Advocacy instead of Inquiry
Businesses/ Segments (E / M)	-Business/Segment Mix -Status of/Linkages across Businesses/Segments	-About Profit Pools/ Industry Evolution -About Cross-Business/ Segment Scope Economies/Diseconomies	-Patterns in Choice of Scope -Endowment Effects/Organizational Attachments -Aversion/Dead Zones/ Blind Spots
(E / N)	-Type of Competitive Advantage -Share/Rank in Terms of Sales, Assets or Profits -Relative Price	-About Relative Costs/Willingness-to-Pay -About Drivers: Scale etc. -About Competitor Behavior	-Illusion of Control -Groupthink -Politics -Coalitions/Deadlocks
Strategies (T)	-Capability Development Intent	-About Key Capabilities/ Competences (Activities/ Functions/Processes) -About Improvement Possibilities	-Capability/Competency Traps
Performance (S)	-Profitability: ROS/ROA/ROE/ ROCE… -Growth: Revenue vs. Volume -Risk/Aggressiveness/Inter-temporal Tradeoffs -Social/Noneconomic Goals	-About Financial Markets and Capital Costs -About Sources and Uses of Funds -About Risk and Its Management -About Nonmarket Opportunities/ Threats	-Satisfactory/Slowly Declining Performance -Resistance to Reducing Growth Targets (Hysteresis) -Loss-Aversion: Losses that loom larger than gains -Past Social/Noneconomic Commitments

An Application: Accenture's India Strategy

The process and content of competitor profiling will be illustrated with the example of Accenture, an information technology (IT) consulting, software services, and business process outsourcing (BPO) firm.[17] The analysis was undertaken for a major Indian software services firm in 2003. It focused on reports that Accenture would begin to make large BPO-related investments in India. If Accenture was serious, it could seriously affect Indian software firms that still mostly arbitraged the cost differences between software professionals in India and in developed countries.

Too much information was available on Accenture for it all to be reviewed. So, in keeping with the principles for gathering information listed under Step 1 in Chapter 2, the analysis began with a deep-dive into the SEC filings (a common starting point) and analysts' reports. Other sources, including private ones such as customers and former employees of Accenture, industry observers, and the client, were used to fill out the picture.

Accenture's strategic intent was analyzed with a modified version of the goals-beliefs-routines framework: given the interest in figuring out whether the company was serious about a strategy shift, the analysis emphasized changes, particularly in beliefs and routines, rather than continuity. But to begin with goals, BPO had already contributed significantly to Accenture's growth after the technology bubble burst and IT consulting slumped, and management had publicly pinned hopes for satisfying future revenue growth goals on it. So the commitment to BPO itself was relatively clear.

There was, however, the question of how committed Accenture was to India as a platform for its BPO business. Accenture's announced strategy cast India as the anchor of a new offering that Accenture had traditionally turned up its nose at: a "lift & drop" offering that would relocate work without any consulting or transformation. This change could be related to Accenture's mental model of its businesses as a pecking order, with IT consulting ranking highest in terms of strategic value for clients (and margins and stickiness for Accenture), and lift & drop the lowest (see Exhibit 4.7). Accenture had managed to establish leadership in IT consulting and systems integration without getting into lift & drop. But the emphasis on BPO as the growth driver focused attention on a business much closer to lift & drop. As a senior manager pointed out, "We cannot ignore the needs of nine out of ten clients. If we don't give them a solution that meets their needs, they will go to the Indians. If they go to the Indians, we will be shut out of any higher-value work that comes along in the future." Based on such reasoning, Accenture apparently decided to offer lift & drop out of India as a loss-leader instead of simply trying to sell clients on work with more of a consulting component. It clearly held stronger *beliefs* than a few years earlier about the importance of BPO, of having an Indian component to a BPO offshoring story, and of countering the long-run threat posed by Indian software competitors.

Given what a departure the lift & drop offering was for Accenture, it also made sense to look for evidence of *changes in routines* rather than of their continuity to see whether the new offering might actually get off the ground. Commitment to the new direction seemed to have been cemented by a management shake-up in spring 2003, in which nearly one-half of Accenture's leadership team was replaced (although skeptics had not been entirely sidelined and so needed to be monitored). Since then, there had been numerous initiatives to build up the Indian operations. Thus, three of the eight BPO lines had been moved to India, with promises that more would follow, and the Fi-

Exhibit 4.7   Accenture's Business Hierarchy

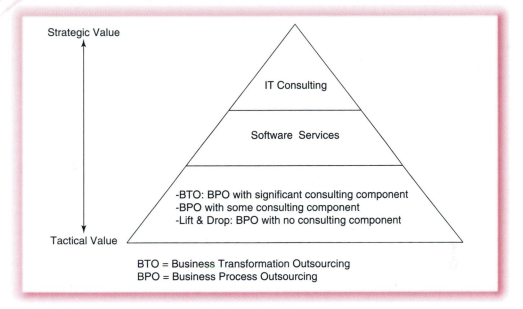

Strategic Value

IT Consulting

Software Services

-BTO: BPO with significant consulting component
-BPO with some consulting component
-Lift & Drop: BPO with no consulting component

Tactical Value

BTO = Business Transformation Outsourcing
BPO = Business Process Outsourcing

nancial Services business had agreed to spearhead the shift of work there. It was apparently also decided that all large outsourcing contracts would have an Indian component. Marketing pitches began to emphasize Accenture's Indian initiative and were supplemented with new sales and marketing training materials designed to increase internal awareness. In October 2003, management announced that 4,500 consultants and 1,700 partners had been trained with the new materials. So, while the focus on India was recent, it had considerable momentum.

The implications for the Indian software firm that was the client were crystallized by a point that Accenture executives had made to outsiders (including a client executive): by investing in India, Accenture would not only cut its costs but decrease Indian competitors' margins as well. More specifically, reports circulated that Accenture would let its Indian operations price at (operating) cost for at least their first two or three years. Such reports could not be completely verified, but they seemed worth taking seriously, because they fit with the loss-leader positioning of lift & drop within Accenture and also helped explain its extremely aggressive bidding in some recent head-to-head encounters with Indian competitors.

Assuming that Accenture would enter in a big way and would price at operating cost sounded some alarms at the client organization. Given its initial operating margins of 30 percent, head-to-head competition with Accenture pricing at cost could—even if Accenture were not differentiated—wipe out all or one-half of the initial margin, depending on whether Accenture's cost disadvantage was 0 percent or 20 percent. If Accenture enjoyed a sustainable price premium because of its differentiation as described in the preceding chapter, that made matters even worse from the client's perspective, as did the likelihood that large-scale foreign entry would push up the costs of Indian software personnel. As a result, the analysis received considerable attention—especially since Accenture has indeed built up its Indian operations, to the point where they already employ 12% of its worldwide workforce and are predicted to account for the bulk of future headcount growth.

Integration

Game theory and competitor profiling embody not only different styles of analysis but also different behavioral assumptions. Game theory, as discussed above, generally assumes symmetric value-maximization, similar beliefs, and zero inertia or routinized behavior. Competitor profiling relaxes these (reasonable) baseline assumptions by bringing in considerations related to what competitors really want, what they might—given their beliefs—see themselves doing to accomplish their goals, and what they have tended to do historically in similar situations. How should we think about the relationship between game-theoretic effects and the kinds of considerations flagged by competitor profiling?

It is useful to begin by noting that the broader assumptions about goals, beliefs, and routines brought up by competitor profiling can, in fact, be accommodated within the formal structure of game theory—so that there is no fundamental incompatibility.[18] This is clearest with regard to goals other than value-maximization. Thus, if Boeing thought Airbus was maximizing revenues rather than profits, it could replace the (present values of) profits for Airbus in Exhibits 4.3 and 4.5 with revenues and then proceed to solve the game exactly the same way as before. Differences in beliefs have been analyzed extensively by game theorists in the decade since John Harsanyi developed his theory of games of incomplete information. In particular, there is a large body of literature on information-signalling and information-jamming, as discussed briefly below. And finally, routines can also be embedded into game-theoretic models in the form of preprogrammed behavior in certain situations or by certain types of players—the focus of considerable research in evolutionary game theory, for example.[19]

We can go even further: competitor profiling is not only conceptually consistent with game-theoretic analysis but is complementary to it. As a purely statistical matter, predictive power should not go down as a result of considering both kinds of analyses rather than just one. And in fact, it will often go up rather than remain unchanged. Recognizing as much is the pragmatic way of resolving the feud about whether organizations are rational or irrational.

That is the conceptual logic for integrating insights from game theory and competitor profiling. How is integration actually to be achieved? It is sometimes possible—but not always advisable—to seek to boil considerations of both sorts down to a quantitative common denominator. Even when complete quantification is not feasible, however, things remain simple if game theory and competitor profiling point in the same broad direction. Thus, in the Airbus-Boeing example, the three aspects of Airbus highlighted by the goals-beliefs-routines framework—the goal of market-share leadership, the belief that Boeing's monopoly of very large aircraft had been very valuable to it, and a history of filling out its product line over time—actually made it more likely that Airbus would develop the superjumbo, which was also the prediction from game-theoretic analysis. There is no integration challenge here.

Cases in which the effects predicted by competitor profiling and game theory do not line up neatly with each other *and* cannot be compared quantitatively are much more difficult. One approach is to quantify what one can of the competitor's perceived value from doing one thing as opposed to another, and then implicitly weigh the results of the quantitative comparison against the qualitative differences that it might perceive between or among strategic options. The logic is that understanding the economic cost of satisfying a noneconomic predisposition is helpful in deciding whether it will be satisfied or not. A helpful practical device in this context, as Benjamin Franklin pointed out more than two hundred years ago, is to draw up a balance sheet of pros and cons:

> When these difficult Cases occur . . . [I] divide half a Sheet of Paper by a Line into two Columns, writing over the one *Pro,* and over the other *Con.* Then, during three or four Days Consideration, I put down under the different Heads short Hints of the different Motives that at different Times occur to me for or against the Measure. . . . And tho' the Weight of Reasons cannot be taken with the Precision of Algebraic Quantities, yet when each is thus considered separately and comparatively, and the whole lies before me, I think I can judge better, and am less likely to make a rash Step.[20]

Finally, the kind of integration that is probably most important is not between different types of analysis but between analysis and action. The follow-up to the competitor profile on Accenture may help make this point more vividly than an abstract discussion. The client's senior management team discussed the threat from Accenture's Indian initiative at a day-long workshop. Both adaptation by the client to large-scale entry by Accenture and how, if at all, the client might shape those entry plans were of interest. As a result, "loose bricks" in Accenture's strategy and possible disadvantages vis-à-vis the client (e.g., the liabilities of foreignness or newness, lack of focus, mixed motives, limited internal commitment, etc.) had to be examined, along with its advantages. Additionally, some weight had to be attached to preserving industry structure as well as to improving relative position, compelling consideration of cooperative as well as competitive approaches. Certain avenues of action seemed worth exploring irrespective of the approach adopted for dealing with Accenture: rethinking the supply side to keep costs under control, broadening the marketing pitch by placing more emphasis on non-price dimensions, and increasing cross-selling. The detailed analysis of Accenture was specifically helpful in this regard because it afforded insights into relationship marketing, which was an area that had proven challenging for the client. And finally, given the perceived utility of the analysis and the areas that it identified as worth monitoring, the client decided to set up a competitor intelligence system to track Accenture and other competitors continuously as opposed to sporadically.

OPENING UP THE ANALYTICAL PROCESS

The first three sections of this chapter implied a specific process for analysis:

- ➤ Start with the decision at stake and identify the players whose actions/reactions matter for the focal firm's payoffs
- ➤ Understand the other players' objectives and beliefs, and explore what they are likely to do or not do on past form
- ➤ Pick the best of one's own strategic options based on predictions about where things are likely to settle down given these assessments of competitors' actions/reactions

In addition, the preceding section broadened the bases of the analysis by looking beyond economic incentives to competitors' goals, beliefs, and routines.

A further broadening is suggested by the fact that classical game theory presupposes a "closed world" in which it is possible both to prepare a complete list of possible states, strategies, payoffs and probabilities, and to rule out unforeseen contingencies.[21] The real world, however, is "open"—and therefore too complex to consider exhaustively. Recognition of this reality suggests room for creativity in coming up with strategic options and applying a broader range of modes of analysis to them. So the first and second principles below can be seen as reformulating the first two bulletpoints from the list immediately above in ways that are more "open-minded." The third principle is meant to help keep the analysis manageable—and enhance the likelihood of useful action—in the face of all this opening up.

Principle 1. Think Broadly about the Set of Strategic Options

The first two sections of this chapter, in particular, evoked choice from a predetermined set of strategic options—that is, they assumed a closed world. But in an open world, creativity in coming up with the strategic options to be evaluated is often at a premium. Creativity can never completely be systematized, but both game-theoretic thinking and competitor profiling *can* help enrich the set of strategic options considered. Consider the two types of analysis in turn.

The large body of literature on the business applications of game theory suggests some specific dimensions of variation to consider and some of their key elements.

Variables

Game-theoretic models now span a very broad array of variables: see Exhibit 4.8 for a (partial) list of fifty. Checklists of this sort can help a company consider more of the relevant competitive variables than it otherwise might.

Asymmetries

Game theory identifies the effects of various **asymmetries**—most often leaders vs. followers, incumbents vs. entrants, or others related to size—on interactions across a broad array of strategic variables. It may thereby help surface nonobvious options for developing or unwinding such asymmetries. For example, game-theoretic models suggest that, as demand declines in capacity-driven industries, small players should at least consider hanging on and forcing larger players to shoulder most of the early capacity reductions—an outcome that, while counterintuitive, describes the Nash equilibrium.[23]

Commitment Postures

In addition to emphasizing long-run **commitments** or choices about variables that are hard to reverse and can change the terms of subsequent competitive (sub)games, game theory offers various typologies of commitment postures. For example, depending on the circumstances, it can make sense to behave like a "Top Dog" to force rivals to retreat, like a "Fat Cat" to make them less aggressive as well, or like a "Puppy Dog" to convince larger rivals not to act aggressively. These generic postures can be helpful in devising new strategic options; and so can the underlying distinction between **strategic substitutes,** for which the best response to more aggressive play by one player is less aggressive play by its rivals, and **strategic complements**, for which aggression is met with

Exhibit 4.8 Fifty Varieties of Game-Theoretic Modeling

General/Competitive Positioning

Vertical Differentiation
Market Share/Leadership
Investment/Disinvestment in Resources, Capabilities….
Raising Rivals' Costs/Reducing Rivals' Willingness-to-Pay
Signaling/Signal-Jamming

Customer/Business Scope
Customer Selection/Horizontal Differentiation
Multimarket Contact and Tacit Collusion
Strategic Substitutes versus Complements
Vertical Integration and Foreclosure

Firm Organization and Infrastructure
Organizational Structure
Centralization/Decentralization
Accounting Systems
Incentive Systems
Flow of Internal Communications
Disclosure/Public Relations
Government Lobbying

Product Positioning/Scope

Product Attributes (Quality, Durability, etc.)
Product Line
Product Variety
Product Integrality vs. Modularity
Provision of Complements

Sales and Marketing
Product Pricing
Price Discrimination/Volume Discounts
Most Favored Nation Clauses
Branding (e.g., Product vs. Umbrella)
Advertising
Couponing
Sampling
Warranties/Service Agreements
Locations
Sales Force/Service Structure
Distributor Relationships
Vertical Restraints
Slotting Allowances
Retailer Information Exchange

Procurement/Input Markets

Financial Leverage and Debt
Input Pricing/Contracting
Supplier Relationships

Operations
Quantities versus Prices
Capacity Expansion
Learning Curves
Flexibility
Inventories
Backlogs

Technology Development
Product Innovation
Process Innovation
Technology Races
Standards/Platform Competition
Innovation versus Imitation
Correlated versus Uncorrelated Strategies
Patenting
Licensing, Contracting, etc.

*This list of 50 dimensions/lines of analysis in the game-theoretic modeling of business competition is meant to be illustrative rather than exhaustive and focuses on modeling activities in industrial organization (IO) economics and in marketing. While many models along these lines are unidimensional, some do look at interactions across different dimensions, further enriching the palette. Detailed textbook treatments of many of the types of models/issues listed can be found in Tirole, Cabral and McAfee.[22] Also note that given the focus on IO, the list of internal and nonmarket issues under Firm Organization and Infrastructure is particularly abbreviated: such issues are addressed at great length by other branches of economics (which supply most of the game-theoretic treatments) as well as by other disciplines.

87

aggression.[24] Note that the specificity of competitor profiling helps pin down whether strategic substitution or strategic complementarity is likely, making up for some of the fragility of inferences based on pure economics.

Information

In addition to recognizing the possibility of asymmetric information, game theory places considerable emphasis on bluffs, feints, and more generally, strategic misrepresentation or concealment of **information.** Such initiatives often seem important to the pursuit of strategic purpose even if they are not the main course. Consider Boeing's public forecasts of demand over twenty years for large aircraft, defined as the 747 plus the stretch/superjumbo plus large cargo aircraft. Between 1990 and 1994, the forecast nearly doubled. After stagnating in 1995, however, it dropped by more than one-half in 1996 and more than two-thirds by 1999. In the words of an Airbus executive, "It's difficult not to notice the discontinuity following the termination of the collaborative [Boeing-Airbus] VLCT exercise and Airbus's announcement of the formation of a Large Aircraft Division to pursue the A3XX study." For its part, Airbus appeared not to be fooled by Boeing's apparent attempt to signal negative assessments of demand—as would be expected at the Nash equilibrium.

Competitor profiling can help generate new options and variations on existing ones in some of the same ways. An in-depth analysis of competitors may highlight additional **variables** that the competitor is leveraging that the company doing the analysis is not. It can shed more light on critical **asymmetries:** both where the competitor is vulnerable or sensitive ("loose bricks") and where it is strong ("foundations"). And as mentioned above, it helps with the articulation and evaluation of a range of *commitment postures* by helping answer the following questions:

➤ What kinds of commitments will provoke the greatest and most effective retaliation by the competitor (hot buttons)?

➤ What will evoke the most cooperative response?

➤ What commitments will the competitor have the most trouble matching (because of goals, beliefs, and routines as well as capabilities)?

➤ What future moves or strategy shifts is the competitor likely to make, and to what effect? Can they and should they be influenced?

And finally, competitor profiling can trigger new thinking by challenging the **information** or mental models of the company doing the analysis. For this and other purposes, it can even be helpful to commission a competitor profile of one's own company from the outside.

Of course, game theory and competitor profiling are not the only ways of enriching the set of options considered. Other ways of stretching strategic thinking include:

➤ *Scope changes.* Broadening and shifting the scope of the strategic scanning effort can help put one in the shoes of players other than direct competitors, direct attention to weak signals from the periphery, and foster thinking across multiple businesses or geographies through questions such as "Where else would this work?"

➤ *Shifts in perspective.* Strategic thinking can often be stretched even further through radical shifts in perspective. Ways of inducing such shifts include thinking about how one might solve a particular problem if starting afresh or, if money were no object, identifying the unwritten rules that drive the industry and competitor behavior and trying to break them, emphasizing threats (e.g., via devils' advocates or worst-case scenarios) as well as opportunities in order to increase receptivity to change, and following outside-in paths—from possible answers to the issues facing a business that they might address, as well as inside-outside paths—from issues to answers.[25] It is also helpful to bring a "can change" attitude to bear on the status quo by asking yourself "Why not?"[26]

➤ ***Organizational enablers.*** A final way to stretch thinking about strategic options involves moving beyond the "one big brain" model of strategic innovation by exploiting what we know about creativity. Recommendations include cultivating open-mindedness, risk-taking, and a commitment to learning; emphasizing rich information flows; countering known biases (e.g., the "not invented here" syndrome); and continuously revitalizing, challenging, and even unsettling the organization. Of course, organizational attributes along these dimensions affect the evaluation of new options as well as their generation.

Principle 2. Augment the Toolkit for Dynamic Analysis

The preceding sections focused on game theory and competitor profiling as ways of anticipating competitive dynamics. However, in a complex, open world, it makes sense to supplement them with insights from other tools for dynamic analysis. We shall simply mention some of these alternate possibilities and refer the interested reader to more elaborate treatments to each of them. One alternative, already discussed at some length in Chapter 2 of this book, is provided by **structural analysis,** particularly analysis of the effects of the sorts of long-run dynamics laid out in Exhibits 2.8 and 2.9. A specific elaboration that is especially worth citing in a dynamic context is **scenario analysis,** which uses structural reasoning to build distinct but internally consistent representations of the future of an industry (or company or technology).[27]

Simulation represents a tried-and-tested technique for dynamic analysis about which there seems to be some fresh excitement. For example, simulations of concentrated, capacity-driven industries facing rapid growth in demand consistently indicate a tendency toward overexpansion.[28] A bonus, proponents argue, is that building and running such simulations actually helps correct flaws in mental models (in this case, misperceptions of feedback, among others) as well as offering insight into their consequences if they go uncorrected.

Wargaming/roleplaying represents another established approach to sorting through competitive dynamics that rubs shoulder with but is less rigidly structured than simulations. This approach typically incorporates rather more of the context and richness of the real world than simulations do, to the point where unforeseen contingencies and actions represent a real possibility that may have to be dealt with by patching or fundamental redesign. Wargaming/roleplaying exercises often seem to be effective in harnessing the competitive drives of players (or teams of players) to get them to think more deeply about the competition that their company faces. The enthusiasm of Raymond Smith (former chairman and CEO of Bell Atlantic, now Verizon) for this tool is illustrative: "[In our] Red team/blue team . . . variant of the classic war game, we assign managers to teams representing major competitors and have them plan the strategies they would use to beat us. This team research increases our competitive intelligence and quickens our reflexes by building a competitive awareness into all our actions—

rather like a good chess player is always aware of what an opponent will do in response to the next move."[29]

Finally, there is the possibility of **market testing** or, more broadly, taking actions in the real world, as opposed to in some simplified representation of it, in order to generate real data. Particularly when implementation is staggered (e.g., across distinct geographic submarkets) or sequenced for other reasons, there is the possibility of learning about competitive dynamics by looking, for instance, at the pattern of actions and responses in the first few submarkets entered and making adjustments in the course of a **sequenced rollout.** On the other hand, learning by doing of this sort is costly, both in direct operating terms and, for instance, in terms of what it may disclose about one's own plans. Consider, for example, the cookie wars of the 1980s, when Nabisco's dominance was challenged by the introduction of Grandma's cookies by Frito-Lay and Duncan Hines by Procter & Gamble. Based on their results in their test markets (Kansas City in both cases), these entrants apparently caught Nabisco unprepared. However, given the constraints on their manufacturing capacities and their narrow product scope, Nabisco managed to counterattack in time by repositioning all its existing lines of cookies and launching a new one, using its superior scale and profitability to launch aggressive advertising, promotion, and trade programs, and bolstering its direct-to-store-door distribution system. In retrospect, while Frito-Lay and Procter & Gamble both learned a lot from their test marketing, Nabisco learned more—or at least enough to hang on to its dominance.

To summarize, as we move from experiments toward wargaming and testing, we move from relatively schematic modes of representing the world toward more realistic ones, and from offline/off-the-shelf modes of learning toward online/experiential learning. But the prejudice that this represents some sort of progression should be resisted: the cookie war example reminds us that taking the most "real" approach is not always a good idea. Rather, the choice of, which tools to apply will depend on the industry and company context, as discussed next.

Principle 3. Match the Analytics to the Industry and Company Context

The first two principles suggested, respectively, many sources of new ideas and additional tools for dynamic analysis. But given the risk of analysis-paralysis, it is also important to be able to narrow down this many possibilities. The third principle emphasizes an obvious way of doing so: by matching the analytics to the industry and company context. An emphasis on matching meshes well with the conclusions from more than two decades of game-theoretic modeling: that precise conclusions from models of interactions depend on, and are often very sensitive to, the details of the context. Matching also helps build a bridge between analysis and action.

Consider first how the industry context helps guide choices from the menus of possibilities provided by Principles 1 and 2. In regard to Principle 1, industry attributes, such as whether an industry is intensive in labor, physical capital, marketing, or R&D, help delimit the variables, asymmetries, commitments, and even communication strategies that are likely to be of most interest in a particular case. And as far as Principle 2 is concerned, the most important effect of industry context operates through the number (and size distribution) of competitors in an industry. Game theory and competitor profiling, in particular, tend to have a comparative advantage under conditions of industry concentration.

Turn next to the company context. This obviously conditions where a company falls along some of the dimensions discussed under Principle 1, as well as the directions that it might (realistically) pursue. Less obviously, it also affects the usefulness of the various tools for dynamic analysis discussed under Principle 2 and in the preceding sections. Very large efficiency gaps among competitors sometimes limit the value of thinking through their interactions strategically, as opposed to purely on the basis of relative efficiency. More broadly, companies are not always as receptive to offline learning from relatively abstract representations of the world (e.g., classical game theory or simulations) as they are to more textured representations or online/experiential learning (e.g., competitor profiling or wargaming). It is usually better to acknowledge and, if possible, take advantage of variations in a company's cultural receptivity to different analytical tools than to ignore them.

Because game theory has accounted for the largest part of this chapter, its status deserves special comment. The number of companies that make any use of game theory is still very small. The few that do seem to be large firms that also use other sophisticated analytical techniques and tend to cluster in particular industries (e.g., pharmaceuticals, telecom services, consulting, investment banking). Such sophisticates offer the most immediate prospects for incorporating game-theoretic modeling into strategic decisionmaking. Without such sophistication, it generally makes more sense to treat game theory as a source of insights and analogies than as a basis for serious modeling.

How long is this state of affairs likely to persist? There is often a pointed subtext to this question: if game theory is potentially valuable, why hasn't it caught on more quickly? There are at least three possible types of responses.

First, the S-shaped curves, described in the context of product substitution in Chapter 2 and also used to study the diffusion of ideas, are known to be prone to long, slow take-offs. Thus, even simpler tools that have diffused widely (e.g., discounted cash flow analysis) took decades to move from the classroom to the executive suite.

Second, several dynamics seem to favor the diffusion of game theory, even though they do not guarantee take-off by a particular date: developments in computer technology and pedagogy as well as in the theory itself, the cumulation of examples and expertise in academia and consulting, and even greater general visibility (e.g., the 1994 Nobel Prize and the book and film about John Nash, *A Beautiful Mind*).

Third, a more fundamental force for the diffusion of game theory and allied tools is related to the observation that *thinking through your best responses to other players' actions or reactions is a dominant strategy*. While the nature of your best response is likely to change as game theory diffuses, the incentives to use the theory do *not* depend on its remaining obscure. In fact, strategic complementarities seem more likely than substitution: as more competitors apply game theory to strategy, not doing so may become more costly. This is potentially very powerful.

SUMMARY

The analysis in this chapter has added a dynamic dimension to the discussion of competitive advantage and added value in Chapter 3 by examining ways of anticipating how interactions among small numbers of players will unfold. Its range of coverage can be summarized in terms of a few recommendations. Always start with a sense of relative competitive position, the general attractiveness of the industry environment, and the trends to which it is subject. Based on this understanding, try to anticipate the moves that competitors might initiate as well as how they might react to moves that you make. Anticipation typically requires integrated analysis of competitors' economic incentives and noneconomic predispositions, with game theory shedding light on the benchmark case of firms as symmetric economic maximizers, and competitor profiling adding texture in terms of their noneconomic predispositions—and both helping overcome egocentric biases. Finally, because analysis without action is not very valuable, explicitly think through bridges to action by reflecting on the industry and company context *before* making basic choices about which analytical tools to employ and how to apply them.

In terms of domain of coverage, this chapter focused on the dynamics of situations in which there are a small number of identifiable players. The next chapter takes a rather different approach to dynamics: it focuses, in a complementary way, on generic threats to the sustainability of superior performance and strategic responses to them.

GLOSSARY

- agency problems
- ambiguity
- asymmetries
- beliefs
- best response
- biases
- coalitional game theory
- commitments
- competitor profiling
- cooperative game theory
- credible precommitment
- dominant strategy
- dominated strategies
- dynamic games
- embedded beliefs
- first mover

- game theory
- game tree
- goals
- inertia
- information
- iterated elimination
- look ahead and reason back
- market testing
- mental model
- Nash equilibrium
- nonconstant-sum games
- non-cooperative game theory
- payoff matrix
- payoffs
- players

- reaction function
- routines
- rules
- scenario analysis
- sequenced rollout
- simulation
- simultaneous moves
- strategic complements
- strategic substitutes
- strategies
- structural analysis
- subgames
- variables
- wargaming and roleplaying
- zero-sum games

NOTES

1. Joel E. Urbany, David B. Montgomery, and Marian Moore, "Competitive Reactions and Modes of Competitive Reasoning: Downplaying the Unpredictable?" (Marketing Science Institute Report No. 01-121, 2001).

2. In *Co-opetition* (New York: Doubleday, 1996) Adam Brandenburger and Barry Nalebuff generate insights from both *co-operative* and *non-cooperative* game theory for business strategy, but with a focus on the former. Avinash Dixit and Barry Nale-

buff provide interesting and more general applications of game theory in *Thinking Strategically: The Competitive Edge in Business, Politics and Everyday Life* (New York: W.W. Norton, 1992).

3. Robert J. Aumann and Michael Maschler, "Game Theoretic Analysis of a Bankruptcy Problem from the Talmud," *Journal of Economic Theory* 36, no. 2 (1985): 195–213.

4. John Von Neumann and Oskar Morgenstern, *Theory of Games and Economic Behav-*

ior (Princeton: Princeton University Press, 1944).

5. John F. Nash, Jr., "Equilibrium Points in N-Person Games," *Proceedings of the National Academy of Sciences of the United States of America* 36 (1950): 48–49, John F. Nash, Jr., "Non-Cooperative Games," *Annals of Mathematics* 54 (1951): 286–95. These ideas were actually first applied more than a hundred years earlier by Augustin A. Cournot, who focused on duopoly and used a restricted version of Nash equilibrium as his solution concept. See his *Recherches Sur Les Principes Mathématiques De La Théorie Des Richesses* (Paris: L. Hachette, 1838). English translation: *Researches into the Mathematical Principles of the Theory of Wealth.* (New York: Macmillan, 1897. Reprinted New York: Augustus M. Kelley, 1971).

6. R. Selten, "Spieltheoretische Behandlung Eines Oligopolmodells Mit Nachfragetragheit," *Zeitschrift fur die gesamte Staatswissenschaft* 121 (1965): 301–24 and 667–68.; John C. Harsanyi, "Games with Incomplete Information Played by 'Bayesian' Players, I–III. Part I. The Basic Model," *Management Science* 14, no. 3 (Nov. 1967): 159–82, "Games with Incomplete Information Played by 'Bayesian' Players, I–III. Part II. Bayesian Equilibrium Points," Management Science 14, no. 5, (Jan. 1968): 320–34, "Games with Incomplete Information Played by 'Bayesian' Players, I–III. Part III. The Basic Probability Distribution of the Game," *Management Science* 14, no. 7 (Mar. 1968): 486–502.

7. John C. Harsanyi and Reinhard Selten, *A General Theory of Equilibrium Selection in Games* (Cambridge, MA: MIT Press, 1988).

8. In keeping with game-theoretic usage, strategies are defined in this section and the next as complete specifications of what players will do in all contingencies, whether those contingencies actually arise or not. This is somewhat different from the way they are defined elsewhere in the book.

9. Note that these strategies imply a sustainable level of product differentiation. Technically speaking, firm I is choosing its capacity level of production ("Cournot" game) where the optimal level of capacity depends on the perceived level of product differentiation due to marketing and sales effort by firm I.

10. Note that in the last column, payoffs are higher in the bottom cell because it assumes price increases in the excess of inflation, unlike the top cell.

11. See Benjamin C. Esty and Michael Kane, "Airbus A3xx: Developing the World's Largest Commercial Jet (A)," (Harvard Business School Case No. 201028) and Benjamin C. Esty and Pankaj Ghemawat, "Airbus vs. Boeing in Superjumbos: A Case of Failed Preemption" (Working Paper No. 02-061, Harvard Business School, 2002).

12. Contrary to the matrix representation, the game tree representation is not limited to two players.

13. This ordering of moves may be questioned. We take the pragmatic stance that because no commitments to the development of the superjumbo had been made before December 2000, either player could consider itself the first mover back then. Deciding not to develop the superjumbo yet would be equivalent to ceding the (next) opportunity to move first to the other player.

14. See Avinash Dixit and Susan Skeath, Games of Strategy (New York: W.W. Norton and Company, Inc., 1999), chapter 6, for a more elaborate treatment of combining simultaneous and sequential moves in the same game.

15. Philip Selznick, *Leadership in Administration: A Sociological Interpretation* (New York: Harper & Row, 1957).

16. Pankaj Ghemawat, *Commitment: The Dynamic of Strategy* (New York: Free Press, 1991), pp. 23–25.

17. The discussion in this section is a highly abridged and somewhat disguised version of a competitor analysis prepared for a client's private use by Ken A. Mark under the supervision of Pankaj Ghemawat.

18. Goals refer to what your competitor maximizes (i.e., its objective function); beliefs are related to the weights your competitor puts on various possible actions or outcomes; routines imply constraints on or opportunities for your competitor's opti-

mization problem that make certain choices infeasible or more likely.

19. Richard Nelson and Sidney Winter's *An Evolutionary Theory of Economic Change* (Cambridge, Mass.: Belknap Press, 1982) is a seminal book on routines and business behavior.

20. Benjamin Franklin, letter to Joseph Priestley, September 19, 1772. Available at The History Carper: *www.historycarper.com/ resources/twobf3/letter11.htm* (accessed September 30, 2004).

21. See Leonard J. Savage, *The Foundations of Statistics,* 2d rev. ed. (1954; New York: Dover Publications, 1972) and Ken Binmore and Adam Brandenburger, "Common Knowledge and Game Theory," in *Essays on the Foundations of Game Theory,* ed. Ken Binmore (Oxford: Basil Blackwell, 1990). In this context, it is interesting to read Savage's original discussion of "small worlds" versus "grand worlds" and Binmore and Brandenburger's critique of Savage's subjective expected utility theory for assuming a "closed universe."

22. Jean Tirole, *The Theory of Industrial Organization* (Cambridge, Mass.: MIT Press, 1988); Luis M. B. Cabral, *Introduction to Industrial Organization* (Cambridge, Mass.: MIT Press, 2000); R. Preston McAfee, *Competitive Solutions: The Strategist's Toolkit* (Princeton: Princeton University Press, 2002).

23. Pankaj Ghemawat and Barry Nalebuff, "Exit," *RAND Journal of Economics* 16 (1985): 84–94 and Pankaj Ghemawat and Barry Nalebuff, "The Devolution of Declining Industries," *Quarterly Journal of Economics* 105 (1990): 165–186.

24. See Jean Tirole, *The Theory of Industrial Organization* (Cambridge, Mass.: MIT Press, 1988), pp. 323–328, for a formal treatment of these effects.

25. See, for example, Edward De Bono, *Lateral Thinking for Management: A Handbook of Creativity* (New York: American Management Association, 1971).

26. Barry Nalebuff and Ian Ayres, *Why Not? How to Use Everyday Ingenuity to Solve Problems Big and Small* (Boston: Harvard Business School Press, 2003).

27. On industry scenarios, see Michael E. Porter, "Industry Scenarios and Competitive Strategy under Uncertainty," Chapter 13 in *Competitive Advantage* (New York: Free Press, 1985). See Peter Schwartz, *The Art of the Long View* (New York: Currency Doubleday, 1991), for a broader discussion of scenario thinking and Hugh Courtney, *20/20 Foresight: Crafting Strategy in an Uncertain World* (Boston: Harvard Business School Press, 2001), for an even broader discussion of McKinsey & Company's work on strategy and uncertainty. This is also the most apposite place to mention the literature on real options and strategy (e.g., Timothy A. Luehrman, "Strategy as a Portfolio of Real Options," *Harvard Business Review* 76 (5): 89–99) although it is sometimes too prone to perceive anything and everything as a real option. Real option analysis can actually be seen as a baseline for the kind of overlay discussed in this chapter because, while dynamic, it generally has trouble handling competitor interactions in nonmechanical ways.

28. See Paul A. Langley, Mark Paich, and John D. Sterman, "Explaining Capacity Overshoot and Price War: Misperceptions of Feedback in Competitive Growth Markets," unpublished working paper, Sloan School of Management, MIT (1998), on this specific point. For broader discussions of simulation and business dynamics, see John D. Sterman's textbook, *Business Dynamics: Systems Thinking and Modeling for a Complex World* (New York: Irwin/McGraw-Hill, 2000) and Michael Schrage's *Serious Play: How the World's Best Companies Simulate to Innovate* (Boston: Harvard Business School Press, 2000).

29. Raymond W. Smith, "Business as War Game: A Report from the Battlefront," *Fortune,* September 30, 1996. For a book-length reference that covers simulations and roleplays, see Clark Aldrich, *Learning by Doing: A Comprehensive Guide to Simulations, Computer Games, and Pedagogy in e-Learning and Other Educational Experiences* (New York: John Wiley, 2005).

Sustaining Superior Performance

But many that are first shall be last; and the last first.

— *MARK 10:31*

This chapter, like the preceding one, focuses on dynamics. It takes a different tack, however, which can best be illustrated by expanding upon the advice offered at the beginning of Chapter 3, to build the better mousetrap. We need to take that advice a step further and look at **sustainability** in the face of **imitation**. Because garages seem to feature many small mousetrap manufacturers as well as mice, an innovator will gain little from anticipating its interactions with any one rival in the kind of dynamic detail discussed in Chapter 4. But it *can* add a useful dynamic dimension to the analysis by recognizing that better mousetraps that have succeeded in the marketplace in the past (e.g., repeating traps and glueboards) haven't greatly enriched their respective innovators, partly because better mousetraps attract imitators as well as mice.

Recognizing the threat of imitation is the first step in thinking through whether barriers to imitation exist or can be erected around the innovation. And even if imitation cannot be blocked, its likely scope and speed should be accounted for in deciding whether to develop the better mousetrap in the first place. This chapter discusses imitation and other generic threats to the sustainability of superior performance as well as strategic responses to those threats.

Data on performance dynamics help illustrate the importance of thinking through issues of sustainability. Historically, such dynamics were understudied because they did not form part of the traditional strategy agenda laid out in the profitability grid in Exhibit 1.7. But in the last 15 years, evidence has accumulated that points to the folly of focusing on achieving superior performance while forgetting about its sustainability. This evidence suggests that above-average performance tends to subside toward the average *much more rapidly* than many managers assume.

Consider, for example, an analysis of the return on investment (ROI) reported over a ten-year period by a sample of nearly 700 business units.[1] When this sample was divided into two equally sized groups based on initial ROI, the top group's ROI in year 1 was 39 percent and the bottom group's was 3 percent. If businesses were kept in the groups in which they started out and tracked over a decade, what changes would you predict to the 36-point ROI spread between the group averages by year 10?

When managers are confronted with this question, they often guess that the initial ROI spread between the two groups shrank by between one-third and two-thirds by year 10. In fact, as shown in Exhibit 5.1, the shrinkage was actually greater than 90 percent! In another recent study, only 2 percent of the firms in a large sample managed to sustain superior performance over at least a ten-year period.[2] Such data clearly imply that in most cases, the sustainability of superior performance cannot be taken for granted.

But one should not conclude that just because sustainability is elusive, it is not worth examining. There are at least four reasons why. First, even if initially superior returns can be expected to subside to the average level by year 10, the degree to which they can be sustained in the interim—the shaded area in Exhibit 5.1—is surely of interest. Second, convergence actually *was not* complete by the tenth year for the sample: the initially top group still had an ROI advantage of 3.5 percent. This is a significant difference in long-run spreads that can, in many situations, spell the difference between significant value creation and value destruction. Third, the convergence of returns over-

Exhibit 5.1 The Limits to Sustainability
Source: Pankaj Ghemawat, *Commitment* (New York: Free Press, 1991).

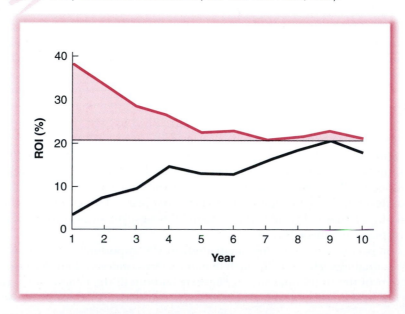

states the convergence of what is actually of interest: (economic) returns times volume. A business posting an ROI of 39 percent—again, the initial average for the top group—probably should not insist that all new investments deliver returns that high. And finally, if you are still taken aback by the extent to which the group averages in Exhibit 5.1 converged, remember that they mask tremendous amounts of variation. It is easy to cite companies that have beaten the averages by large margins over much longer periods (e.g., Wal-Mart). Understanding how they have done so will help illustrate the range of possible strategic responses to threats to sustainability.

To that end, the next section classifies threats to the sustainability of superior performance and relates them to the analytical frameworks and perspectives developed in earlier chapters. Each of the four sections that follow focuses on (1) a threatening evolutionary dynamic, and (2) possible strategic responses to it. The final section uses the example of Wal-Mart to review the discussion.

SUSTAINABILITY AND RESOURCES

In classifying threats to sustainability, it is useful to split observed performance into the two components suggested by Chapters 2 and 3, industry-level performance effects and within-industry performance differentials. Recent research suggests that superior performance that *is* sustained over the long haul is due, in large part, to stable industry-level effects, and that performance advantages over the competition tend to be less sustainable.[3] Industry-level effects were discussed in some detail—from a dynamic as well as a static perspective—in Chapter 2 and therefore will not be taken up here, beyond the reminder that dynamics such as demand saturation, technological maturation, and resource depletion do need to be taken into account. The discussion in this chapter will focus, instead, on threats to the sustainability of superior within-industry performance and ways of dealing with them.

Research in industrial organization (IO) economics is helpful in this regard: it suggests that commitments to durable, specific resources—what might be called **sticky resources**—are generally needed to sustain within-industry profit differences.[4] The deregulation of the U.S. airline industry and its subsequent experiences illustrate this link. The U.S. airline industry was deregulated in 1978 in the belief that the threat of "hit-and-run" entry would keep prices and profitability in check even in city-pairs that ended up being monopolized. Individual city-pairs were supposed to be **contestable**, that is, easy to enter and exit, on the grounds that if prices exceeded relevant costs, an entrant could fly its capital into a market and, if threatened with retaliatory price cuts, could fly it out again. (As Alfred Kahn, who headed the Civil Aeronautics Board at the time of deregulation, put it, airplanes were "marginal costs with wings.") But more than twenty-five years later, the U.S. airline industry still continues to exhibit significant, sustained within-industry differences in profitability. So the logic of contestability is revealed to be wrongheaded in the industry that was once supposed to be its leading exemplar. But the airline industry is worth examining, nonetheless, to see why differences in profitability haven't disappeared.

The summary answer is that contestability theory overlooked a range of sticky resources that have turned out to be important in the deregulated airline industry. Actually, two distinct phases can be discerned in the industry's evolution since deregulation. Through the 1980s and part of the 1990s, the established airlines fended off entrants much more effectively than the deregulators had anticipated, largely by building and leveraging such resources as hub fortresses, computerized reservations systems, and customer stickiness based on frequent flyer programs. But as prices have continued to fall—to less than half the real levels of the mid-1970s—the not-so-efficient resources that the incumbents continue to be stuck with, particularly expensive unionized work-forces, have loomed ever larger and are, in several cases, the focus of their current struggles to survive. The discount carriers that have challenged the traditional incumbents can also be looked at through the resource lens. Southwest, by far the largest creator of economic value in the airline industry after deregulation, has a uniquely standardized and fuel-efficient fleet of planes and has historically managed to keep them flying one-third longer each day than its competitors. And even the pressures that it has recently experienced related to *its* employee costs draw attention, once again, to sticky resources.

This emphasis on resources has a long tradition in the field of strategy as well as in IO economics.[5] A resource-based perspective does, however, depart from the emphasis in the previous chapters, particularly Chapter 3, on the activities that a business performs. To clarify, the present chapter shares with the others in this book an underlying stocks-and-flows conception of resources and activities. Specifically, resource stocks that can be varied only in the long run—in keeping with the traditional economic conception of resources as fixed inputs—determine the flows of activities that a business can undertake in the short run and these activities, in turn, help shape the evolution of resource stocks over time. Reinterpreted in these terms, Chapter 3 exploited the idea that even when the underlying resources are key, an activity lens may still be useful because it is hard to value fixed inputs except in terms of the flows of services they generate. In other words, activities are easier to measure and, therefore, often a better basis for analysis. But for explicitly dynamic purposes, such as understanding the determinants of sustainability, it is important to look directly at long-run factors. This involves shifting the focus from activities that can be varied in the short run to the underlying resource stocks that are fixed in the short run.

Resource-based research in strategy was slow to capitalize on these insights, partly because of an early tendency to define virtually anything as a resource.[6] As a result, traditional resource-based frameworks for thinking about sustainability often lack a clear conceptual basis.[7] Contemporary resource-based research advances matters by confirming the intuition that in thinking about the conditions under which resources will or will not continue to sustain superior performance, it is useful to distinguish between their added or **scarcity value** and their **appropriability,** or capture, of (some of) that value by the focal firm.[8] Note that these two kinds of conditions—one related to competition and the other to bargaining—are meant to be overlaid: the sticky resources that underpin superior performance at a point in time must continue to be scarce to sustain superior performance, *and* the owners of the firm must be able to appropriate some of that sustainable scarcity or added value.

The discussion in the rest of this chapter will be organized in terms of two threats to scarcity or added value and two threats to appropriability. Specifically, it will work through the **tetra-threat framework** for diagnosing the sustainability of superior within-industry performance that is laid out in Exhibit 5.2:

➤   *Imitation* of the resources underpinning superior performance to the point where they are no longer scarce is a direct threat to the sustainability of added value. Imita-

Exhibit 5.2   The Tetra-Threat Framework for Sustainability Analysis

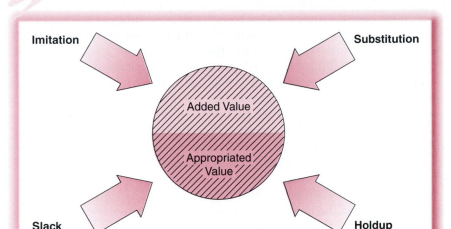

tion can be thought of as diminishing the extent to which the player being imitated would be missed if it simply disappeared—a rough measure of added value, as noted in Chapter 3.

➤ *Substitution* of the resources underpinning superior performance is an indirect threat to the sustainability of added value, driven by displacement rather than duplication. That said, substitution-related threats to scarcity are often even harder to address than threats of imitation.

➤ *Holdup* is a threat to the appropriation, or capture, of sustainable added value that is often rooted in resource **cospecialization**. Cospecialization can be essential to value creation, but it does create a problem: as a firm and its complementor (for instance) cospecialize, their added values overlap, making it impossible for both of them to appropriate the full amount. Each then faces the threat of being held up by the other.

➤ *Slack* is the internal threat to the appropriation, or value capture, that reflects a persistent tendency to dissipate potential economic surplus. The scope for slack depends on past success or current added value: firms without much of either have a hard time surviving while persistently suboptimizing.

Since the tetra-threat framework is superficially similar to the five-forces framework (imitation↔rivalry, substitution, holdup↔supplier/buyer power), the differences are worth illustrating. Compare the application of the two frameworks to the pharmaceutical industry, which was analyzed with the help of the five-forces framework in Chapter 2. A list of rivalry determinants would flag high levels of concentration, particularly within therapeutic categories, significant product differentiation, rapid growth, and so on, as contributing to the pharmaceutical industry's high average profitability. But looking at where the big money is made *within* the industry focuses attention on the blockbuster drugs that have increasingly come to dominate big pharmaceutical companies' sales and profits. Why aren't these imitated more effectively than they seem to be? Addressing this question requires attention to patents and other barriers to imitation, also rooted in underlying resources, that actually limit the number of sellers of such drugs.

Similarly, there is a big difference between the product-substitution threats which the five-forces framework emphasizes and the broader resource substitution threats—ranging from entrants using new drug-discovery technologies to the open science movement—that are one of the components of the tetra-threat framework. Considerations of cospecialization and holdup cast into sharp relief reliance on a range of suppliers of key resources: biotech and other focused firms, individual inventors, academia, and the National Institutes of Health, among others. Absent a focus on resources, five-forces analyses of supplier power in pharmaceuticals tend to split attention across suppliers of variable as well as fixed inputs—or sometimes even ignore the latter entirely. And finally, slack has no counterpart in the five-forces framework.

In addition to these differences in focus, the two frameworks also differ in terms of concreteness about the behavioral processes that threaten sustained superior performance. The five-forces framework leans heavily on statistical tendencies and regularities (e.g., the concentration of competitors as a key determinant of profitability), whereas the behavioral foundations of the tetra-threat framework are clearer (e.g., the usual assumption that imitation of a scarce resource will occur if the effort can pay for itself).[9] In other words, tetra-threat analysis operates at a level in between the macro/statistical perspective of the five-forces framework and the micro perspective, involving detailed, grounded analyses of individual players in specific situations, that was presented in Chapter 4. Given differences in the issues flagged, analysis at multiple levels is warranted, and hence this chapter supplements the preceding ones instead of superseding them.

THE THREAT OF IMITATION

Imitation is not always bad for an innovator. It can sometimes lend credibility to a new product (e.g., when network externalities or second-sourcing is an issue). In addition, the imitation of certain types of marketing moves, such as loyalty schemes and meet-the-competition clauses, does not necessarily undermine their effectiveness.[10]

Still, imitative development of scarce resources is usually bad news in added-value terms. And it seems to be endemic. Attempts by one player to increase its capacity, for example, often trigger additions by competitors intent on preserving their capacity shares. Attempts to build one's customer base tend to prompt competitors to defend or develop their own. Furthermore, attempts at product differentiation based on R&D as opposed to marketing are vulnerable on several counts; studies indicate that competitors secure detailed information on most new products within one year of their development, patent-based strategies usually fail to deter imitation, and imitation tends, on average, to cost one-third less than innovation and to get to market one-third faster. And process innovations seem, if anything, to be even more imitable than product innovations.[11]

The upshot is that the threat of imitation has to be taken seriously, even in contexts where the barriers to imitation might seem to be high. The pharmaceutical industry, for example, is characterized by product patents that are unusually effective at choking off imitation for periods exceeding a decade. But the big pharmaceutical firms still have to worry about imitation of the limited number of blockbuster drugs—typically less than five—on which their fortunes depend. (This dependence was dramatized by Merck's 2004 recall of Vioxx, its fourth-best-seller in 2003 with $2.5 billion in revenues, triggering a $27 billion, or 27 percent, drop in Merck's market value the day the recall was announced.)

Some imitative pressures reflect the big pharmaceutical companies' practice of tweaking each other's innovative blockbusters to come up with slightly different molecules that are not protected by the original patents, which they then patent and sell under their own brands. But the effects of such copy-cat molecules are moderated by the branded manufacturers' ability to contain price competition among themselves, perhaps because they recognize their mutual dependence, as in the pharmaceutical pricing game described at the beginning of Chapter 4. What are much more threatening to high prices are the generic manufacturers who enter with 30–90 percent discounts after patents expire, and typically manage to wrest the bulk of category volume away from the original patent-holder in a matter of months.[12] Concerns about generic competition loom particularly large among branded manufacturers as of this writing due to impending patent expirations and an anticipated dearth of new blockbusters over the next few years.

The diverse ways in which branded pharmaceutical companies have tried to mitigate the threat of imitation illustrate a variety of barriers to imitation, often involving early-mover advantages, that extend well beyond an prespecified period of patent protection and are at least partly endogenous, meaning that they can be influenced. The barriers listed below should not be seen as mutually exclusive: strong defenses against imitation typically rely on more than one of them.

Private Information

To the extent that superior information or knowledge can be kept private—to the extent that it is costly for would-be imitators to tap into it—imitation will be inhibited. Although being tight-lipped can sometimes ensure privacy, many other channels of potential informational leakage exist, including customers, employees, and other suppliers, spinoffs, reverse-engineering, and even patent documents. As a result, privacy is most likely to be sustainable when information is tacit rather than specifiable (i.e., doesn't lend itself to blueprinting), and when no one party can carry it out of the organization. Thus, Wyeth has managed to monopolize a lucrative hormone-replacement submarket with its Premarin drug, made from the urine of pregnant mares, for more than sixty years now even though its patent expired decades ago. A two-decade-long attempt to develop a synthetic generic version of the drug has been thwarted by the fact that nobody knows exactly what is *in* Premarin.[13]

Switching Costs/Relationships

The severity of imitation threats may be blunted by signing enforceable contracts or, more commonly, creating switching costs or cultivating relationships that secure superior access to customers, suppliers, or other important types of players. The branded pharmaceutical companies have been particularly imaginative in engaging doctors, for example.[14] They induce trials by doctors (and hospitals) of their newest and most expensive products by distributing billions of dollars of free samples. In addition, they give doctors personal gifts, provide them with generous "research" grants, and offer them consulting, speaking, and even publishing opportunities. This largesse can be thought of as leaving a residue of goodwill with doctors, with effects that linger on in their prescription decisions even after generics become available.

Size Economies

Size economies refer to the (possible) advantages of being large. They come in at least three different varieties: scale economies, which are the advantages of being large in a particular business at a particular point in time; economies associated with **learning** by doing, which imply advantages to being large in a particular business over time; and scope economies, which are the advantages of being large across interrelated businesses and which are discussed in more detail in Chapter 6.[15] If there *are* size economies, a firm may be able to deter imitation by precommitting itself to exploiting them. Deterrence depends on the possibility that if the would-be imitator tried to match the incumbent's size or resource mass, enough excess capacity might result to make it rue the effort. The pharmaceutical majors' sales forces stand out in this context: there are indications that would-be entrants shy away from categories in which they would have to achieve similarly broad reach (typically ones in which drugs have to be promoted to legions of primary-care physicians). Scale economies are also evident in the shift from print to TV advertising of prescription drugs after the rules on direct-to-consumer TV ads were relaxed in 1997.

Threats of Retaliation

Incumbents may also be able to deter imitation by threatening massive **retaliation**. But talk of retaliation is cheap. To be credible, it must be backed up by both the ability and the willingness to retaliate. The ability to retaliate is facilitated by the creation of a competitive advantage and by the maintenance of resource reserves, such as liquidity, excess capacity, "warehoused" product upgrades, and positions in competitors' other businesses, that can be used to put pressure on them. The credibility of retaliation is greatest when it is payoff-maximizing for the retaliator, but it *can* be boosted in several ways: by writing contracts that make retaliation more attractive than accommodation, otherwise binding oneself (e.g., "burning one's bridges"), cultivating a reputation for retaliating in spite of immediate losses to oneself, and so on. Thus, branded pharmaceutical companies threatened with patent expiry now often license their drugs to makers of "authorized generics" or sell their own generics through subsidiaries so as to disrupt the six months of exclusivity that are granted to the first generic manufacturer under U.S. law and are often critical to its recouping its pioneering investments.[16]

Imitation Lags

Even if the barriers to imitation discussed above do not apply, imitation typically takes time. Guesstimates of the average lead times in taking various types of actions will help underscore the importance of such lags.[17] As a rule of thumb, prices and marketing communications are among the few variables that can be changed significantly in less than one year. Changes to resource stocks tend to take longer. It takes two years or more to build and start up the typical manufacturing plant. Building a new distribution system or altering an existing one seems at least as time-consuming. Studies indicate that the mean lag in returns from R&D tends to be on the order of four to six years. And the lags in implementing major changes in human resource practices and restructuring corporate portfolios may stretch out over the better part of a decade—or longer! Changes along multiple dimensions are likely to take longer (and have a higher probability of failure), especially if they have to be executed in sequence.

In pharmaceuticals, the key lags concern generic entry, with each day of delay potentially being worth millions of dollars to the owner of a blockbuster. Instead of treating their time-in-market before generics enter as given, the pharmaceutical majors have taken a range of actions to lengthen it: "evergreening" their patents by tweaking molecules, uses, or formulations, suing generic manufacturers for patent infringement (which automatically delays approvals of generic drugs in the United States by thirty months), exploiting other loopholes that extend patent protection, such as testing drugs on children, which is worth six months, lobbying for the general lengthening of pharmaceutical patents, pressing the Food and Drug Administration to speed up the drug-approval process, and so on. The results? It has been estimated that the effective time-in-market for brand-name drugs before generic entry increased from about eight years in 1980 to fourteen years in 2000.[18]

Upgrading

Another significant barrier to imitation is based on continuous upgrading of the organization's own added value. Operationally, this involves driving a wider wedge between customers' willingness to pay and suppliers' opportunity costs over time, and often requires significant resource investments. Thus, the pharmaceutical majors continue to make major commitments to developing and introducing new blockbusters at costs that are now said to approach $1 billion per successful drug and have also been paying more attention in recent years to upgrading their product and process development capabilities (see Exhibit 5.3 for some additional discussion of commitments and capabilities). Note that upgrading makes a business a moving target in a way that compounds the difficulties or delays for potential imitators and may even permit the upgrader to break away from the pack. One way to calibrate the need to upgrade is to track the rate at which an industry's real prices, adjusted for quality, change over time. If an industry's average prices decrease by more than a threshold rate (3 percent per year, according to Jeffrey Williams), it is a "fast-cycle" environment in which advantages tend to be short-lived rather than sustainable, and more or less continuous upgrading is required.[19] The bias toward action built into upgrading also reminds us that barriers to imitation are not just forms of protection that lucky firms are blessed with; they *can* be built.

Numerous other types of barriers to imitation have also been proposed. Several are rooted in considerations of **complexity**, including **causal ambiguity**,[20] as evoked by Wyeth's Premarin, **social complexity**[21] that is supposed to put certain resources—corporate culture is the favorite example—beyond the reach of systematic management, and the challenges of achieving **cross-sectional fit,** or coherence, across many different types of choices.[22] But while insurmountable complexities can help explain barriers to imitation *ex post*, their implications for action *ex ante* are often unclear. For instance, even if it is more difficult for an imitator to copy a whole set of coherent choices instead of

Exhibit 5.3   Making Commitments and Building Capabilities

The resource-based view of strategy takes a historical perspective by stressing that the resources a business has assembled determine its menu of opportunities at any point in time. In this sense, it links what the business did in the past to what it can do well today. But to stop there would be to confine attention to the exploitation of "legacy" resources—which would be seriously incomplete, since the value of the resources that firms already have in place is often estimated to account for less than one-half or even one-quarter of their market value.[23] Thus, in pharmaceuticals, while it is extremely important for firms to exploit their legacies—blockbusters still under patent—for all they are worth, it is also essential to invest for the future by making large, relatively discrete **commitments** of resources to developing, testing, and marketing new drugs as well as more diffuse commitments to improving their R&D and manufacturing capabilities, among others.

By implication, a fully dynamic approach to strategy must not only link what a business did in the past to what it can do well today but also what it does today to what it can do well in the future. This involves explicitly considering both lumpy commitments and **capabilities** as ways for it to upgrade or shift its opportunity set. Lumpy commitments are a good way of thinking about not only market entry (and exit), major new-product introductions, significant capacity expansion/modernization, and so on, but also some less obvious categories of change, such as cultural transformation and even shifts in strategy. Thus, when Coors switched from a regional to a national strategy in the U.S. beer market in the 1970s, it had to open its first new manufacturing facility in a century, establish relationships with distributors in thirty-nine new states, improve acrimonious relationships with unions and minorities that were stronger in the new states, build a national clientele by spending more per barrel on advertising than entrenched competitors (two of which, Anheuser-Busch and Miller, also benefited from greater national scale), upgrade its marketing capabilities, and change a production-focused culture. The Coors case also illustrates the four markers of irreversibility, the true measure of significance of lumpy commitments:

➤ sunk costs that would be unrecoverable if going national did not work out
➤ opportunity costs that induce lock-out instead of lock-in, as illustrated by Coors locking itself out of certain opportunities by moving very late to go national
➤ time lags of longer than a decade in completing the switch to a national position
➤ organizational commitment to or momentum behind the new course of action that would make it hard to reverse even if reversal turned out to make economic sense

Lumpy commitments are individually important enough to warrant the full power of the analytical techniques discussed in this book—assessing fit with or influence on industry structure, and implications for competitive position, interactions, and sustainability.[24]

The development of capabilities, in contrast, involves choices that are individually small and frequent rather than individually important and infrequent. The idea is that firm-specific opportunities to perform activities more effectively than competitors or to make commitments on better terms than them can be built gradually and reinforced over long periods of time.[25]

For a vivid example, consider the success of Japanese automakers in the U.S. market. It is hard to explain this success in terms of superior product market positioning: sedans like the Honda Accord and the Toyota Camry were priced and targeted similarly to the domestic automakers' core offerings. More explanatory power is provided by the estimate that by the 1980s, Japanese automakers had upgraded their product-development capabilities to the point where they could design and introduce a new model in about *half the time* and with *half the engineering resources* required by their U.S. counterparts. This allowed them to update their products more frequently. They, especially Toyota, also managed to produce their products more cheaply and with better quality because of differences in manufacturing facilities and processes. The still unmatched Toyota Production System is protected by knowledge that is tacit and rooted in complex organizational processes,

(continued)

Exhibit 5.3   *Continued*

economies of plant scale (particularly in Japan), relationships with suppliers that are elaborated on in the section on holdup, time lags for imitators to build up comparable resources, and a deep commitment to continuous improvement.

Many different kinds of capabilities can be identified, associated with differences in product and process development efficiency, learning, speed, flexibility, mobility (across lines of business), and so forth.[26] "Metacapabilities" associated with integration, reconfiguration, and transformation have also attracted some interest but are quite hard to measure. But measurement and comparisons with competitors are important because in their absence, hubris and politics are likely to lead to excessively high self-ratings and a tendency to designate anything one cares about as a key organizational capability.[27]

Another challenge relates to the incremental nature of capability development: firms must prevent the overall coherence of such efforts from being nibbled away, choice by choice, by drop-in-the-bucket biases and the like. Somewhat paradoxically, this makes the choice of which capabilities to develop, and how, a relatively lumpy choice, just like conventional resource commitments, since commitment to a major capability-development thrust also exhibits lock-in, lock-out, lags, and organizational commitment. As a result, just like specific commitments, specific capabilities also imply specific rigidities that can, in an uncertain world, result in inferior rather than superior performance.[28] In other words, capability development and commitment may be necessary for sustained success, but are certainly not sufficient. Which is why they must be analyzed.

just one or two, is it obvious that the innovator had an easier time coming up with the coherent set in the first place? If not, there is no point to pursuing sustainability (as opposed to advantage) through intricate alignment of choices because there are no early-mover advantages to be gained thereby.

In summary, imitation is a direct threat to the sustainability of added value whose severity is inversely related to the height of barriers to imitation. Such barriers often revolve around early-mover advantages. But while moving early may reduce the threat of imitation, it can also raise costs and risks. As a result, the only sensible conclusion about early versus late timing is the one drawn long ago by Alfred P. Sloan: If you are late, you have to be better.

THE THREAT OF SUBSTITUTION

Added value may be threatened by substitution as well as by imitation. Substitution should be thought of here in terms of resource substitution, rather than the product substitution highlighted in Chapter 2. Resource substitution tends to reduce added value by displacing scarce resources instead of duplicating them, i.e., by reducing the demand for their services instead of expanding their supply. And while substitution can sometimes blur into imitation at the margin, it can also have rather more drastic effects, as emphasized more than half a century ago by the economist Joseph Schumpeter, who compared the threats of substitution and imitation "as a bombardment is in comparison with forcing a door."[29]

Substitution seems to command much more attention among business strategists today than it did in Schumpeter's era. Particularly popular are discussions of **disruptive technologies.**[30] Substitution is a related but broader idea. Thus, technological substitution encompasses not only disruptive technologies that, while suboptimal for the requirements of existing customers, are improving more rapidly, but also technological threats from above (as opposed to below). Thus, in the first twenty years of the videogame market, each new generation of consoles led to a new competitor becoming the market leader. Furthermore, as a threat to added value, substitution encompasses much more than just technological change. Other "supply-side" triggers of substitution include changes in input prices or availability and deregulation (as in the airline industry). On the "demand side," shifts in customer preferences, previously unmet needs, and changes in the customer mix can shake up things.

For a vivid example of a threat of substitution and responses to it, consider the growth of online book retailing in general and Amazon in particular from the perspective of the leader in traditional (bricks-and-mortar) book retailing, Barnes & Noble. Amazon's online store threatened to largely dispense with and displace two of the key resources that Barnes & Noble was stuck with: approximately 10 million square feet of physical selling space in stores whose value, properly capitalized, exceeded the company's annual revenues, and 15,000 in-store employees. What Barnes & Noble did and did not do illustrates the broad array of possible responses to substitution threats: acquiesce, defend, straddle, switch, and innovate.

Not Responding

One way of dealing with substitution dynamics is by not responding at all. This is *not* what Barnes & Noble did: within a year of Amazon's founding, it decided to launch its own online operation. Still, one can imagine some plausible arguments in favor of inaction:

➤ Online book retailing may prove to be just a flash in the pan

➤ Even otherwise, online will amount to only a small niche

➤ The online model underserves purchasers because it does not let them handle books or provide the physical ambiance emphasized by Barnes & Noble's Superstores

➤ Online will cannibalize the physical stores, which are already under pressure

➤ Barnes & Noble does not have the skills and expertise to make an online initiative work

These objections typify the arguments that are used more broadly to squelch consideration of substitution threats.[31] Some such squelching is in order. But the general sense—bolstered by sensitivity to such corporate sins as arrogance, myopia, bureaucracy, and sloth—is that paying too little attention to substitution threats is often more hazardous to a company's health than paying too much.

Migrating/Harvesting

Migrating and harvesting, often employed in tandem, are less passive forms of acquiescence. Migration involves redeploying resources to uses that are less vulnerable to substitution threats or more attractive overall in light of them. Harvesting requires a shift toward milking existing resources instead of building or even maintaining them. Research into disruptive technologies suggests that while harvesting is the most common response of incumbent firms, it is often accidental, at least in the early stages of the process.[32] On the other hand, it is also easy to imagine cases in which harvesting would have made sense but was not attempted. For example, questions can be raised about whether Barnes & Noble should be continuing to invest in expanding its network of physical stores despite persistently poor returns.

Defending

Defending against substitution threats means that the threatened business must either increase its willingness to pay or decrease its costs. The obvious danger with this approach, especially in the context of technological threats, is that the threats may have fundamentally faster improvement dynamics.[33] An implication from Chapter 3 that may be less obvious is also worth emphasizing: defense can be achieved not only by improving one's own economic fundamentals but also by impairing the fundamentals of competitors. Thus, Barnes & Noble attempted to squeeze competitors, particularly Amazon, in a number of ways, most notably by announcing, in November 1998, that it would acquire Ingram, which accounted for more than half of book wholesalers' sales in the United States and was also a major supplier to Amazon and others. This deal had to be called off, however, after complaints from publishers and book retailers prompted the U.S. Federal Trade Commission to launch an investigation.

Straddling

Straddling involves responding to a substitution threat by establishing a foothold in both camps. Straddling may be either a transitional hedge or a long-term strategy. Straddles can also be distinguished in terms of whether they are relatively balanced between the old and the new or are imbalanced between the two (e.g., offer only a toehold in the substitute form of competition). Perhaps the biggest risks inherent in straddling are excessive commitment to an old form of competition that may no longer be viable and an unwillingness to make tough choices. Straddling seemed to be Barnes & Noble's principal strategy between 1996 and 2000: it moved to set up BandN.com as a leading online retailer (rather than a toehold) by drawing on talent and content resources from outside the company, but kept the online venture separate, organizationally and operationally, from its traditional operations.

Switching

Switching is a more radical response to substitution threats than straddling because it involves a wholesale shift to the substitute. Despite its obvious attraction in terms of speed—and the enthusiasm for it in the disruptive-technology literature—switching is, especially in fast-moving environments, like changing horses in mid-stream: there is sometimes no alternative, but the maneuver *is* often subject to spills. Switches also raise questions that should be asked and answered *before* the fact about how the business that is switching will add value in the substitute form of competition. Given its sense that online retailing would continue to be a niche within the broader book market, it is not surprising that Barnes & Noble chose not to switch.

Recombining

Switching involves adoption of a model of how to compete that is already "out there." In many cases, however, recombining elements of existing ways of competing with some of the new possibilities implicit in substitution threats seems to work better than wholesale switching. Recombination or hybridization possibilities tremendously expand the range of possible responses to substitution threats. Barnes & Noble should probably have paid more attention earlier on to such possibilities, particularly to the obvious ones of combining its unmatched store network with elements of online book retailing by, for example, using the stores to facilitate orders, delivery, and returns for the online business. The company finally began to move in this direction in late 2000 by introducing Internet Service Counters in the stores and allowing BandN.com products to be returned there—but this move came too late to allow it to challenge Amazon for leadership online.

Leapfrogging

Leapfrogging is the most radically innovative response to a threat of substitution: it involves trying to outsubstitute the substitution threat by looking for a performance improvement or value innovation that promises even better performance.[34] Thus in 1999/2000, as it became clear that BandN.com's Amazon-like approach was not gaining ground on Amazon, Barnes & Noble invested more than half a billion dollars in two attempts at leapfrogging: an ebook initiative that required expensive software but could potentially displace physical distribution and a print-on-demand initiative that required expensive printing machinery but could potentially displace some of publishers' traditional roles. Given their desperate character, it is not very surprising that neither initiative panned out.

In summary, there are no foolproof responses to substitution threats. Nevertheless, recognition of the variety and seriousness of such threats and the array of possible responses to them should help companies go beyond the fight-or-switch dichotomy.

THE THREAT OF HOLDUP

Even if an organization can protect its added value from the threats of imitation and substitution, the ability of its owners to appropriate that added value cannot be taken for granted. There are two systematic threats to value appropriation over time: holdup and slack. Holdup, discussed in this section, threatens to divert sustained added value to buyers, suppliers, complementors, and the like, whereas slack—discussed in the next section—threatens to dissipate it.

For a simple example of holdup, consider the privately owned Ambassador Bridge, which links Detroit in the United States and Windsor in Canada and handles about one quarter of the $400 billion in annual trade between the two countries, which are the world's largest trading partners. Since the nearest competing bridge is 80 miles away, and farther from the region's economic center, the Ambassador can charge a significant premium: $34 for a gas tanker versus $18, according to one comparison.[35] Given variable trucking costs on the order of 50¢ per mile, the Ambassador does not have to be much closer to the origin or destination of a shipment to represent the better alternative.[36]

The Ambassador Bridge's ability to hold up and appropriate some of the value created through cross-border trade is easy to analyze because the size of the pie is relatively fixed and the balance of power in determining how it is sliced is very one-sided. Holdup assumes more complex forms when players' actions affect the size of the pie as well as the way in which it is sliced up and when they exhibit interdependence, often reflecting underlying resource cospecialization.[37] Bilateral monopoly represents the extreme case in which the added value of each player is equal to the total value that the two create by transacting with one another.

To reflect on these complexities, consider the relationships between automakers and their parts suppliers. Currently, efficiency requires substantial tangible and intangible investments by both automakers and their suppliers, with underinvestment potentially raising costs and reducing differentiation by limiting quality and innovation, lengthening development cycles, and even raising recall risks. The required investments are often relationship-specific and hard to reverse or recoup. But a supplier that modifies its designs, machinery, or processes to cater to a specific automaker's requirements runs some risk of being held up by it. Conversely, an automaker can leave itself vulnerable to holdup by its suppliers. Fears of holdup can, as a result, shrink the total size of the pie by reducing the amount of investment or by distorting it (by, for example, forcing inefficient reductions in investment specificity).

The evolution of automaker-supplier relationships over the last 100 years also illustrates a range of approaches for dealing with complex holdup threats.

Contracting

At the beginning of the twentieth century, U.S. automakers relied on older, more established suppliers to the bicycle and carriage industries.[38] As parts suppliers became more committed to the automobile industry and automakers undertook more coordination, the two sides shifted from transaction-by-transaction interactions toward longer-term relationships governed by contracts. Specialization subjected market-based, arm's-length transactions to market failures of the sort discussed in Chapter 6 and mandated alternative governance mechanisms. Contracting was one solution, but only a partial one, since completely comprehensive contracts enforceable at zero cost—contracts of the sort that could entirely eliminate fears of holdup—are typically impractical.[39]

Integrating

A second response to holdup threats, integration, came to the fore with the rapid expansion and consolidation of the U.S. automobile industry. Total production more than quadrupled between 1909 and 1914, and Ford achieved market dominance by increasing its volume more than twenty-five-fold with its inexpensive Model T. Ford also rethought its supplier relationships over this period. In 1909, its operations involved mounting a body, wheels, and tires (sourced from others) on a complete chassis supplied by the Dodge brothers. But by 1914, the Dodges were using their profits from the Model T to enter auto assembly, while Ford was vertically integrating backwards into parts and inputs, partly to reduce dependence on a few suppliers but also as part of a broader cost-leadership strategy. Vertical integration was meant to help efficiency by ensuring large-scale investments that suppliers were reluctant to make, easing coordination, exploiting the potential for speed unlocked by Ford's assembly line innovation, and reducing the risk of disruption (no small concern, since Ford's operations were often within a half-hour of suspension because of tardy deliveries). By the mid-1920s, Ford's vertical scope extended all the way back into mines, plantations, forests, and even sheep farms.

Vertical integration combined with specialization, scale, and process innovation to help reduce the real costs of the Model T by three-quarters between 1909 and 1924, as illustrated in Exhibit 1.3. But it also helped triple asset-intensity, increased operating leverage, and—once heavier closed bodies began to replace the Model T's open-car design in the 1920s—proved very inflexible: Ford lost long-term leadership to General Motors (GM) as it changed over from the Model T to the Model A in 1927–28.[40] Other vertically integrated auto operations also experienced pressure from independent suppliers' excess capacity and product innovation capabilities in the 1920s and 1930s. Furthermore, vertical integration did not so much solve coordination or incentive problems as transfer them from outside to inside the firm (e.g., the thorny issue of transfer pricing). In addition, vertical integration to avoid holdup by parts suppliers increased exposure to holdup by the industry's formidable labor union, the United Automobile Workers (UAW).

Increasing (and Using) Bargaining Power

After World War II, despite some deintegration at Ford, overall levels of integration remained high. GM, Ford, and, to a lesser extent, Chrysler manufactured at least some of their requirements of every basic component (and up to 100 percent in the case of such critical items as engines, transmissions, and axles), while outsourcing the rest to a number of suppliers with whom they played hardball.[41] The automakers fragmented their supplier base and further reduced suppliers' added values by maintaining large in-house R&D staffs, forcing innovators to part with their technologies, breaking down systems into parts, and making every part into a commodity through comprehensive specifications. Contracts focused on prices, rarely ran for more than one year, and often were not renewed. Other ways in which the domestic Big Three put pressure on prices included using inspection teams to estimate suppliers' costs, letting small, low-overhead suppliers make low bids that could be used in negotiations with other suppliers, linking price concessions on a particular part sourced from a large supplier to continued purchases of other parts, and even starting rumors about potential competition.

Most of these practices represented attempts to counter supplier power, as discussed in the context of the five-forces framework, so that framework does have something useful to say about the threat of holdup. Note, however, that taking just this bargaining/hardball perspective raises the risk of going too far in marginalizing suppliers, to a point where the shrinkage in the size of the pie outweighs the increased share of the pie that such efforts might secure. The other approaches discussed in this section remind us that maximizing relative bargaining power is not the only way to address the holdup problem.

Building Mutual Dependence

Large-scale entry by Japanese automakers into the U.S. market in the 1970s and 1980s forced the domestic Big Three to rethink their hardball approach, especially as the role of supplier relationships in the success of the Japanese became clearer.[42] Despite less vertical integration than their U.S. counterparts, Japanese automakers worked with far fewer suppliers with whom they maintained long-term relationships, exchanged employees and information, and partnered in innovation as well as production. Specifically, most parts supplied were "black boxes," with the automaker providing only general specifications and the supplier preparing all of the detailed specifications and blueprints, which made it difficult to switch suppliers. The suppliers, in turn, invested in assets specific to individual automakers: the typical Japanese supplier-partner relied on a single automaker for 60 percent of its sales, versus a figure of 34 percent in the United States.[43] In other words, both sides built up their confidence in each other to the level where they were both willing to invest in a profit stream that would materialize only *if* they continued to work together. Such **interorganizational relationships** can be self-sustaining only if each player is allotted a sufficiently large share of the gains from cooperation. Opportunism may then be limited by the threat of disappearance of the large profit stream available from cooperation.[44] This is very different from the approaches discussed so far in this section, all of which emphasize the minimization of dependence on others.

During the 1990s, the domestic Big Three moved to cooperate more with their suppliers. GM and Ford spun off their large internal parts operations, Delphi and Visteon, helping address independent suppliers' fears that any improvements they proposed would be passed on to the internal parts operations and their value thereby held up. But Chrysler, the least integrated to begin with, moved farthest in reshaping its supplier relationships by investing in coordination, recognizing suppliers' needs to make a fair profit, soliciting feedback and sharing the savings, shifting toward longer-term contracts, and creating the expectation of business beyond the life of the contract if suppliers performed. GM and Ford never got as far and, in the grip of the industry downturn of the early 2000s, began to revert to focusing mainly on prices.[45]

Developing Trust

The stability of cooperative relationships can also be enhanced by trust. The Japanese business environment, for example, seems to deal with opportunism by placing more emphasis on social institutions (norms, etc.) and less on legal institutions than in the United States. It is possible that Japanese automakers have benefited from this general social context in establishing cooperative relationships with their suppliers. However, researchers continue to disagree about whether the Japanese auto industry *really* exhibits trust in a sense that goes beyond self-interested calculations that recognize mutual dependence—especially given recent moves at Nissan and even Toyota toward "less Japanese" supplier relationships.

It is also worth noting that the broader context in which a business operates can create a different type of holdup threat: one reflecting unilateral **expropriation** rather than bargaining based on resource dependence or cospecialization. Social norms about acceptable levels of profit and market power, in particular, can generate legal and other nonmarket challenges that threaten the appropriation of added value. Legal restrictions are worth understanding in some detail here and in the context of some of the discussions in the preceding chapters, because along a number of dimensions, the law can be more constricting than personal conceptions of what is fair or ethical. And governmental intervention is especially worth watching out for in certain types of industries. These include industries that already feature a high level of governmental involvement (through procurement, funding, regulation, public ownership, etc.), loom large in terms of size, investments, employment, votes, or general political salience (e.g., media ownership), are considered part of the national patrimony (e.g., natural resources), or supply mass consumption staples or "entitlement" goods (e.g., food or even pharmaceuticals). Of course, in such environments, companies often strive to be involved in rule-making. At a broader level, while the origins of nonmarket threats of holdup differ from those of the market-based threats on which this section focuses, some of the same remedies (with the obvious exception of vertical integration) can be employed to mitigate them.

To summarize, holdup is a systematic threat to the appropriability of added value that tends to be based on resource dependence or cospecialization. Strategic responses to holdup vary in the extent to which they emphasize competition versus cooperation. Given the traditional strategic bias toward taking the competitive approach and increasing one's slice of the pie, explicit attention should also be paid to the possibility of growing the pie. Or to repeat one of the dicta from Chapter 2 , strategists must think about relationships both cooperatively and competitively.

THE THREAT OF SLACK

Slack is an internal threat to the appropriation of added value that can be defined as the gap between the value actually appropriated over time and the amount potentially available given the other threats to sustainability discussed above (and the strategic responses to them). In dynamic terms, slack reflects persistent suboptimization by a business that dissipates appropriable added value or even reduces added value over time. In some contexts, it is more natural to discuss the inverse of slack, what might be referred to as **organizational effectiveness.**

Although slack is relatively easy to define, it can be hard to measure. Distinguishing between slack and poor choices about how to deal with other threats to sustainability, while desirable, is often difficult. There are, in addition, a host of other complications. Some "slack" may be needed to attract customers (e.g., law offices). Some may be essential for experimentation with new strategies and innovative projects, which might not be possible in a more resource-constrained environment. Some may reflect nonmonetary compensation to employees. And so on. The broader point is that some apparent slack may be of considerable value.

These complications notwithstanding, researchers have tried to measure slack anyway. Statistical estimates, while not very precise, suggest that various inefficiencies dissipate between 10 percent and 40 percent of revenues in U.S. manufacturing.[46] Large amounts of slack are also suggested by the capability differences among direct competitors that were cited in Exhibit 5.3. But while slack is of general significance, it is of particular interest here because of its relationship to sustained success. Without current or past success, a business is unlikely to have much room to suboptimize (although well-funded startups may be exceptions to this rule). Success in the form of appropriable added value expands the scope for suboptimization and can also—as a result of arrogance or other corporate sins—compromise the quality of choice. In plainer language, rich diets are relatively likely to lead to a hardening of corporate arteries. So it is unsurprising that the most stupendous contemporary case of slack involves a company that is still, in terms of revenues, the world's largest industrial enterprise, General Motors.

General Motors' financial performance has been abysmal for some time now. Its manufacturing operation generated zero operating profits over 2001–2003, and at the

Exhibit 5.4   Market Value vs. Cumulated Strategic Investments at General Motors

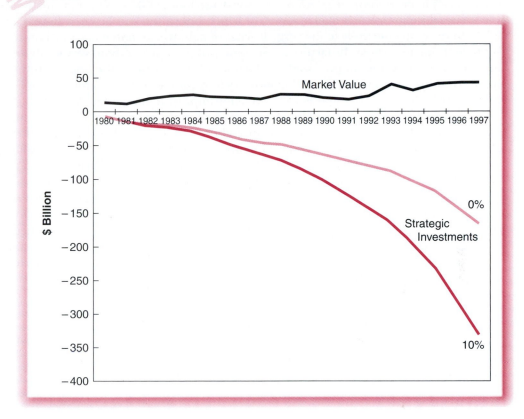

end of 2003, its equity market value was $30 billion, up only marginally from $23 billion at the end of 1983 (see Exhibit 5.4). Over the same timeframe, though, GM's strategic investments—net capital expenditures plus R&D—amounted to $277 billion if added up and $609 billion in terms of their present value in 2003 if carried forward at a 10 percent annual rate. Even if one assumes that the company's market value would have collapsed to zero in the absence of these strategic expenditures, and that it would have been unable to pay stockholders the $29 billion in dividends that it did, the amount of value destroyed at GM over this period ran into hundreds of billions of dollars![47] In other words the benefit-to-cost ratio of GM's strategic investments between 1983 and 2003 was *much* lower than 1. As H. Ross Perot, briefly a GM director, pointed out, the company could have bought Toyota and Honda in the mid-1980s for *half* of the $80 billion it spent on a program to automate its factories.

GM's poor performance partly reflects industry effects: average profit margins in the auto assembly industry have declined from 20 percent in the 1930s to around 10 percent in the 1960s and less than 5 percent in the 2000s. But that is not the whole story: the Japanese Big Three, particularly Toyota, have performed well financially over the last two decades, and even the smaller of the U.S. Big Three did not destroy as much value as GM in proportionate terms. So one must also look at GM-specific explanations.

There are many such explanations, of which only a few can be cited here. GM failed to respond effectively to the surge in sales of light trucks, and many of its car designs continue to be boxy. Its factory automation program proved both very costly and ineffective. It maintains an oversized production infrastructure in the hope of reversing the erosion of its market share. It continues to receive worse marks for its supplier relationships than Chrysler and Ford. Its relationships with the United Auto Workers have arguably been worse as well and have involved greater direct exposure, given a history of more backward integration—although the decline of labor and related expenses, from one-third of revenues in the mid-1980s to one-ninth by 2003, cast some doubt on the company's tendency to emphasize labor holdup as *the* problem.

Whatever the "real" explanation for GM's poor performance, it seems clear that value destruction on this scale would have been impossible if GM had not previously accumulated a pool of resources that afforded it large **free cash flows.** Its ability to destroy several times its assessed market value at the beginning of the 1980s presumably reflects the fact that expectations of high, ongoing levels of slack were also built into the valuation of these cash flows. And GM's ongoing struggles with slack more than a quarter-century after Japanese competition shook up the U.S. auto industry suggest that slack is often sustained by powerful inertial forces. As one might expect, GM scores high on most of the indicators of inertia flagged on the basis of organization theory in Exhibit 4.6—size, maturity, complexity, bureaucratization, thick culture, insularity, poor information, and continuity at the top—as well as on governance-related indicators of the scope to pursue goals other than value-maximization. Organization theory also suggests some remedies for sustained slack that will briefly be mentioned here.[48]

Generating Information

The difficulty of measuring slack increases, rather than decreases, the importance of generating information about it. **Benchmarking** against direct competitors or against companies that are best-in-class in certain activities is obviously useful. Simulation, experimentation, and direct investigation of the effects of changes are other ways of learning about opportunities for improvement. But an added emphasis on information gathering is unlikely to be an adequate basis for identifying all such opportunities because of what Oliver Williamson has referred to as **impacted information:** a condition in which one party to a transaction or relationship is much better informed than the other(s).[49]

Monitoring Behavior

A second response to slack, often complementary to the information-gathering option, is to increase the amount of resources devoted to monitoring behavior. Here the goal is to catch inappropriate behavior before it occurs or to decrease its attractiveness by increasing the probability of detection, backstopped by penalties (or by rewards for good behavior). One standard example is making workers punch time clocks and docking their pay if they arrive late or quit early. Note, however, that monitoring provides only limited benefits when a wide range of discretionary legitimate choices exist or when resources are what are referred to as plastic. Is a software developer sitting beside a brook with her eyes closed slacking off or having a commercially valuable vision?

Offering Performance Incentives

Even when monitoring behavior is impractical or uneconomical, it may be possible to reward good behavior indirectly by rewarding good performance. Such an approach works best when an individual's (or group's) behavior is tightly connected to the performance outcomes that are actually observed. This condition is often violated, though, when there are significant coordination requirements or other reasons why performance can be measured only in highly aggregated terms. In addition, a high degree of emphasis on financial incentives can upset norms (especially about equity), exacerbate attempts to game the system, and divert creativity from real to paper entrepreneurialism.

Shaping Norms

A fourth approach to dealing with slack involves supplementing economic rewards or punishments with appeals to norms, values, a sense of mission, and so forth. Underlying this approach is the idea that people in organizations are motivated by more than just sticks or carrots. Of course, **moral suasion** alone is unlikely to be totally effective. Given the heated debate between economists and other social scientists about the relative efficacy of economic versus "intrinsic" motivation, the safest conclusion is that a manager intent on reducing slack should consider both types of levers as opposed to fixating on only one of them.

Bonding Resources

Bonding resources is a top-down approach to containing slack. It is derived from Michael Jensen's theory of the agency costs of free cash flow.[50] According to Jensen, managers are imperfectly policed by shareholders, have incentives to grow the resources under their control, and are most able to take such steps when free cash flow is large—leading to investments that destroy shareholder value. One obvious remedy is to pile up debt so as to reduce free cash flow (by creating contractual obligations to pay fixed interest expenses). The risk is that the company may become overloaded with debt (i.e., end up with negative free cash flow).

Changing Governance

Bonding resources is just one of several top-down ways of dealing with slack. Others include creating small but well-informed and powerful boards of directors, restricting the ability of CEOs and other insiders to dominate those boards, requiring board members and top managers to own substantial amounts of a firm's equity (in relation to their personal wealth), encouraging (other) large, active investors, and unwinding cross-subsidies.[51]

Mobilizing for Change

Forcing change at the top may often be necessary to reverse slack-related problems, but it is rarely sufficient by itself. Research on change management suggests a number of complementary tactics that address inertial barriers: creating dissatisfaction with the status quo, communicating a powerful vision of what can be accomplished with change, and changing people and processes as well as organizational structure.[52]

In summary, slack is an internal rather than external threat to the appropriation of added value. This does not imply, however, that slack is easier to control than the other threats to sustainability discussed in this chapter. The scope for slack is highest in companies that have enjoyed, or are enjoying, considerable economic success. It is amplified by the difficulties of gathering information, offering high-powered incentives, or otherwise directing the organization toward value creation and capture instead of value dissipation.

AN INTEGRATIVE EXAMPLE: WAL-MART

Exhibit 5.5 summarizes the four threats to sustainability as well as responses to them. Note, however, that these threats have so far been discussed in isolation. An integrated perspective on them is of interest, since companies typically face more than one threat at a time. For an integrative example that also illustrates the value of systematically thinking through threats to sustainability even in a situation where the scope for sustainability might seem relatively limited, consider the case of Wal-Mart, which posted net income of $9 billion on sales of $257 billion in 2003, and had a market value $233 billion. These numbers made Wal-Mart the world's largest company and, with 1.5 million employees, the world's largest private employer as well.

Exhibit 5.5   Responding to Threats to Sustainability

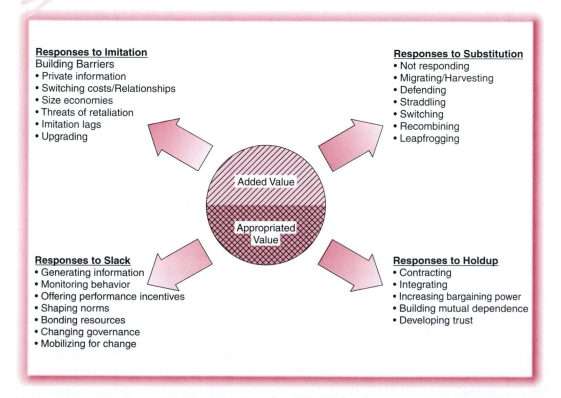

Responses to Imitation
Building Barriers
• Private information
• Switching costs/Relationships
• Size economies
• Threats of retaliation
• Imitation lags
• Upgrading

Responses to Substitution
• Not responding
• Migrating/Harvesting
• Defending
• Straddling
• Switching
• Recombining
• Leapfrogging

Added Value

Appropriated Value

Responses to Slack
• Generating information
• Monitoring behavior
• Offering performance incentives
• Shaping norms
• Bonding resources
• Changing governance
• Mobilizing for change

Responses to Holdup
• Contracting
• Integrating
• Increasing bargaining power
• Building mutual dependence
• Developing trust

To begin by linking back to Chapter 3, Wal-Mart's competitive strategy has been to outperform its competitors by achieving lower operating costs and higher asset turns/efficiency (i.e., lower fixed costs per unit). The emphasis on low costs—and the associated themes of buying in bulk, pricing low, focusing on metrics such as sales per square foot, and operating frugally, among others—have been in place at Wal-Mart for a long time now. In fact, these themes predate the startup of the first Wal-Mart store in 1962; they also characterized the Ben Franklin stores that Wal-Mart's founder, Sam Walton, operated as a franchisee in the 1940s and 1950s. So it seems to make sense to think of Wal-Mart as having been designed around a broad strategic target, low cost, with some continuity in terms of its definition and pursuit, but also some evolution in the context of an adaptive, analytical culture that searches out and spreads improvements across many physical locations.

Given Wal-Mart's focus on *discount* retailing, it is not very surprising that a low-cost/low-price position has proven to be the biggest engine of economic value creation within that industry. What *is* more surprising is Wal-Mart's ability to sustain superior performance with this apparently obvious strategy: it has posted a return on equity in excess of 20 percent in all but four years over the last three decades while growing revenues a thousand-fold. Why *hasn't* this successful strategy fallen prey to the four threats to sustainability: imitation, substitution, holdup, and slack?

To begin with imitation, Wal-Mart is protected by an array of barriers, some of which it has deliberately erected:

➤ *Scale Economies:* Wal-Mart initially tapped local scale economies by locating in towns large enough to accommodate one discounter but not two. It moved on to exploit regional scale economies by building up its hub-and-spoke distribution system, followed by the pursuit of national scale economies in dealing with suppliers and intermediaries.

➤ *Learning/Private Information:* Wal-Mart has gone to great lengths to analyze the myriad details of retailing: how to load trucks to minimize storage space, unpack boxes, schedule part-time labor, juggle fixture heights for maximum impact, etc. In addition, it aggressively "borrows" ideas from all over and maintains the second-largest customer database in the world.

➤ *Switching Costs/Relationships:* Wal-Mart is often perceived as having the lowest prices even in markets where it doesn't. Lock-in is also increased by its ability to persuade suppliers to make major Wal-Mart-specific investments in systems such as Retail Link, which furnishes them with computerized access to real-time data on the sales and inventories of their products at the store level.

➤ *Threats of Retaliation:* Wal-Mart's policy of allowing store managers to match or beat the lowest competing price on an item in their trading area by as much as 5 percent has presumably had a chilling effect on competitors/potential entrants in its local markets, as has its general reputation for fierceness.

➤ *Lags/Upgrading/Complexity:* Wal-Mart has kept competitors off balance by continuously upgrading its capabilities, particularly in information technology and logistics, and making discrete resource commitments to initiatives such as Retail Link. Imitating Wal-Mart's culture or its entire complex activity system would probably take a very long time even if it *were* feasible.

The principal substitution threats that Wal-Mart has faced have been related to the risk that its discount retailing operations might be replaced by a new format. This kind of format risk is highlighted by the theory of the "wheel of retailing," which predicts that operators of old formats will have trouble adjusting to the new ones. But Wal-Mart has actually been quite active in exploring potential substitutes for its traditional discount stores: it entered warehouse clubs in a big way, enjoyed enormous success with the hybrid food-nonfood format of Supercenters, and is exploring a smaller format with Neighborhood Markets. This kind of mobility across formats should not be too surprising, because Sam Walton started up Wal-Mart as a way of switching from one retailing format to another. Wal-Mart also tries to be a leader in figuring out how to deploy new technologies with transformational potential—such as RFID or wireless tags that can be used to track goods passively as they pass from suppliers to warehouses to stores.

As for holdup, it is useful to distinguish between suppliers of merchandise and employees. In regard to the former, Wal-Mart's extraordinary growth has allowed it to build up an unusual amount of bargaining power, even vis-à-vis very large suppliers. Thus, in 2004, Procter & Gamble derived 17 percent of its total revenues from sales to Wal-Mart, while the same dollar revenues represented 3 percent of Wal-Mart's revenues.[53] Wal-Mart does bargain hard with its suppliers by, for example, focusing on a single pricing number; getting suppliers to pay for modular displays, promotions, and the like, on top of that; and developing private labels after learning the business from them. But it also seems to afford suppliers enough surplus—in terms of real-time information and shared expertise as well as volume and terms—to induce them, for example, to invest much more in the aggregate in its Retail Link platform than the $4 billion that Wal-Mart itself reportedly spent. And companies that supply Wal-Mart seem to perform better than those that focus on other retailers.[54]

Labor holdup is more of an issue. Wal-Mart has fiercely and so far successfully resisted unionization efforts. Holding the line on wages is critically important, since a $1 per hour across-the-board increase might reduce Wal-Mart's income by one-quarter. But there has been enormous negative fallout, ranging from employee demotivation and very high turnover rates to unflattering public portrayals—for example, of Wal-Mart employees living below the poverty line. Behind the public portrayals is heightened public scrutiny of Wal-Mart now that it has become the largest company in the world and a related shift in public perceptions of the company—in former CEO David Glass's words—from endearing underdog to overbearing top dog. Wal-Mart has moved recently to address some labor-related issues by, among other things, significantly reducing turnover rates. But public perceptions of Wal-Mart's penny-pinching and power are likely to continue to be concerns—and possible catalysts of nonmarket holdup—for the foreseeable future.

Finally, Wal-Mart seems to have experienced limited slack so far, for a number of reasons. The scope for deliberate departures from value maximization is limited by the Walton family, which owns 39 percent of the company's stock (valued at $90 billion, or virtually all of the family's net worth) and whose interests are represented by Sam Walton's eldest son, Rob Walton, who serves as chairman of Wal-Mart's board of directors. Employees are motivated through incentives, particularly at the store-manager level and above, tight performance monitoring that is facilitated by the pursuit of a cost-based strategy, and social control through deeply embedded norms about frugality, performance improvement, and so on. Nonetheless, slack may become a significant issue in the future: because of the challenges of communicating with what may soon be two million employees well enough to preserve at least elements of Wal-Mart's traditional culture, doing so despite weakening bonds between store managers and employees because of larger stores and 24-hour operation, dealing with widening horizontal spans of control and increasing bureaucratic complexity (especially given the centralization of decision making at corporate headquarters), and similar factors.

In addition to creating organizational challenges for Wal-Mart, growth has become a challenge in its own right (see Exhibit 5.6). Wal-Mart's declining growth rate reflects its increasingly large share of a retailing category, discounting, that has grown at only 2–3 percent per year recently. The reason Wal-Mart has done as well as it has in the last decade is because it has built up a major growth engine outside its traditional core with its Supercenter format. It now faces the challenge of developing another new growth engine or two. Such decisions about business scope and the management of corporate portfolios of businesses are the topic of Chapter 6.

SUMMARY

Like Chapter 4, this chapter concentrated on dynamics. Unlike Chapter 4, it focused on situations in which players are more numerous or faceless and identified four evolutionary dynamics that threaten sustainability in such contexts. Two dynamics—imitation and substitution—threaten businesses' added value, and two others—holdup and slack—threaten their owners' ability to appropriate that added value for themselves.

Exhibit 5.6   Wal-Mart Revenue Growth, 1971–2002

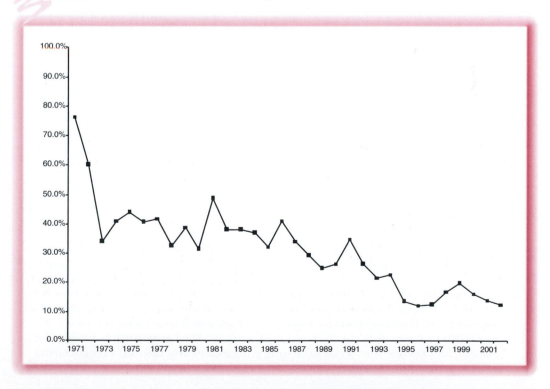

Understanding these dynamics, and looking across all of them should afford managers extra insight into the evolution of the business landscapes on which they operate and the issue of how to counter threats—or even turn them into opportunities.

GLOSSARY

- appropriability
- benchmarking
- capability
- causal ambiguity
- complexity
- commitment
- contestable
- cospecialization
- cross-sectional fit
- disruptive technologies

- expropriation
- free cash flow
- holdup
- imitation
- impacted information
- interorganizational relationships
- learning
- moral suasion
- organizational effectiveness

- retaliation
- scarcity value
- slack
- social complexity
- sticky resources
- substitution
- sustainability
- tetra-threat framework

NOTES

1. These data were originally reported in Pankaj Ghemawat, *Commitment: The Dynamic of Strategy* (New York: Free Press, 1991).
2. Robert R. Wiggins and Timothy W. Ruefli, "Sustained Competitive Advantage: Temporal Dynamics and the Incidence and Persistence of Superior Economic Performance," *Organization Science* 13, no. 1 (January–February 2002): 82–105.
3. Anita M. McGahan and Michael E Porter, "The Emergence and Sustainability of Abnormal Profits," *Strategic Organization* 1, no. 1 (February 2003): 79–108.
4. See, Ghemawat, *Commitment,* chap. 2.
5. The basic idea can be found in Kenneth Richmond Andrews, *The Concept of Corporate Strategy* (Homewood, Ill.: Richard D. Irwin, 1971), but was revived in 1984 in an article by Birger Wernerfelt, "A Resource-Based View of the Firm," *Strategic Management Journal* 5, no. 2 (April–June 1984): 171–180.
6. For example, Wernerfelt, "Resource-Based View," defined resources very broadly as "anything which could be thought of as a strength or weakness of a given firm" (p. 172).
7. Consider, for example, what seems to be the most popular resource-based frame-

work for assessing sustained strengths and weaknesses, the VRIO framework proposed by Jay Barney, where V denotes value, R rarity, I inimitability, and O organizational effectiveness. V, R, and I seem to have a high degree of overlap, especially in a dynamic context, although this framework *does* provide some interesting ways of thinking about I and about complexity that are briefly discussed later in this chapter, in the section on the threat of imitation. See Jay B. Barney, *Gaining and Sustaining Competitive Advantage,* 2nd ed. (Upper Saddle River, N.J.: Prentice Hall, 2002), chap. 5, pp. 149–192.
8. Steven A. Lippman and Richard P. Rumelt, "A Bargaining Perspective on Resource Advantage," *Strategic Management Journal* 24, no. 11 (November 2003): 1069–1086.
9. To make the connections with Chapter 4 precise, this is equivalent to replacing game-theoretic equilibrium in strategies with equilibrium defined in terms of observed outcomes and underpinned by the behavioral assumption of "one smart rival." The latter assumption embodies much weaker rationality requirements than Nash equilibrium, as explained in

John Sutton, "One Smart Agent," *Rand Journal of Economics* 28, no. 4 (Winter 1997): 605–628.

10. Adam Brandenburger and Barry Nalebuff, *Co-Opetition* (New York: Doubleday, 1996), chaps. 5 and 6.

11. The evidence on imitation is discussed in more detail in Pankaj Ghemawat, "Sustainable Advantage," *Harvard Business Review* 64, no. 5 (September–October 1986): 53–58. The article provides specific citations.

12. Stephen P. Bradley, John R. Wells, and James Weber, "The Pharmaceutical Industry in 2003," (Harvard Business School Publishing Case no. 704-470, Boston, 2004).

13. Leila Abboud, "Raging Hormones: How Drug Giant Keeps a Monopoly on 60-Year-Old Pill," *Wall Street Journal,* September 9, 2004, p. A1.

14. The details in this paragraph are based on Marcia Angell, *The Truth About the Drug Companies: How They Deceive Us and What to Do About It* (New York: Random House, 2004).

15. It is also worth noting the related category of *network externalities,* which exist when the attractions to buyers, suppliers, or complementors of joining a network increase with its size.

16. For an example of the pressure that this has put on large generic manufacturers, see the discussion of Teva of Israel in Leila Abboud, "Clone Wars: An Israeli Giant in Generic Drugs Faces New Rivals," *Wall Street Journal,* October 28, 2004, p. A1.

17. Citations for most of these sources can be found in Ghemawat, *Commitment,* chap. 5. See also Richard Hall, "The Strategic Analysis of Intangible Resources," *Strategic Management Journal* 13, no. 2 (February 1992): 135–144.

18. *Public Citizen,* "Rx R&D Myths: The Case against The Drug Industry's R&D 'Scare Card' " (2001 [accessed November 2, 2004]); available from *www.citizen.org/documents/ACFDC.PDF,* cited in Angell, *Truth About the Drug Companies,* p. 269, fn. 7.

19. Jeffrey R. Williams, "How Sustainable Is Your Competitive Advantage?" *California Management Review* 34, no. 3 (Spring 1992): 29–51.

20. Steven A. Lippman and Richard P. Rumelt, "Uncertain Imitability: An Analysis of Interfirm Differences in Efficiency under Competition," *Bell Journal of Economics* 13, no. 2 (Autumn 1982): 418–438.

21. Jay Barney, "Firm Resources and Sustained Competitive Advantage," *Journal of Management* 17, no. 1 (March 1991): 99–120.

22. Michael E. Porter, "What Is Strategy?" *Harvard Business Review* 74, no. 6 (November–December 1996): 61–78.

23. W. Carl Kester, "Today's Options for Tomorrow's Growth," *Harvard Business Review* (March–April 1984): 153–160.

24. For a book-length treatment of commitment decisions that also discusses how uncertainty can be folded into the analysis—basically, through the concept of flexibility value—see Ghemawat, *Commitment,* esp. chap. 6.

25. For the original discussion that frames these and other issues concerning capabilities, see David J. Teece and Gary P. Pisano, "The Dynamic Capabilities of Firms: An Introduction," *Industrial and Corporate Change* (1994 No. 3), pp. 537–556.

26. See, for example David M. Upton, "Flexibility as Process Mobility: The Management of Plant Capabilities for Quick Response Manufacturing," *Journal of Operations Management* 12, nos. 3–4 (June 1995): 205–224; Rebecca Henderson and Iain Cockburn, "Scale, Scope, and Spillovers: The Determinants of Research Productivity in Drug Discovery," *Rand Journal of Economics* 27, no. 1 (Spring 1996): 32–59, Kim B. Clark and Takahiro Fujimoto, *Product Development Performance: Strategy, Organization, and Management in the World Auto Industry* (Boston: Harvard Business School Press, 1991), and Gary P. Pisano, *The Development Factory: Unlocking the Potential of Process Innovation* (Boston: Harvard Business School Press, 1997).

27. For some tips on how to conduct a capability audit, see Dave Ulrich and Norm Smallwood, "Capitalizing on Capabilities," *Harvard Business Review* 82, no. 6 (June 2004): 119–126.

28. See Dorothy Leonard-Barton, "Core Capabilities and Core Rigidities: A Paradox in Managing New Product Development," *Strategic Management Journal* (1992): 111–125.

29. Joseph A. Schumpeter, *Capitalism, Socialism, and Democracy* (New York: Harper, 1942), p. 84. See also Ingemar Dierickx and Karel Cool, "Asset Stock Accumulation and Sustainability of Competitive Advantage," *Management Science* 35, no. 12 (December 1989): 1504–1511.

30. Clayton M. Christensen, *Innovation and the General Manager* (Boston: Irwin/McGraw-Hill, 1999), idem, *The Innovator's Dilemma: When New Technologies Cause Great Firms to Fail, The Management of Innovation and Change Series* (Boston: Harvard Business School Press, 1997).

31. Christensen, *Innovator's Dilemma.*

32. Ibid.

33. Richard N. Foster, *Innovation: The Attacker's Advantage* (New York: Summit Books, 1986).

34. W. Chan Kim and Renee Mauborgne, "Value Innovation: The Strategic Logic of High Growth," *Harvard Business Review* 75, no. 1 (January–February 1997): 102, reprinted in June 2004 issue.

35. This comparison and the preceding information on the Ambassador Bridge are based on John Lippert and Erik Schatzker's "Matty's Bridge," Bloomberg, March 2003.

36. The scarcity value of the Ambassador Bridge is threatened by plans to build a second bridge close by to relieve congestion caused by the tightening of borders after September 11, 2001. As of the fall of 2004, however, a consortium put together by the Ambassador's owner, Manuel Moroun, appeared to be a leading contender to build and operate the second bridge, although negotiations continued.

37. For the pioneering discussion of holdup, see Oliver E. Williamson, *Markets and Hierarchies, Analysis and Antitrust Implications: A Study in the Economics of Internal Organization* (New York: Free Press, 1975).

38. For a historical overview on which some of this discussion is based, see Susan Helper, "Strategy and Irreversibility in Supplier Relations: The Case of the U.S. Automobile Industry," *Business History Review* 65, no. 4 (1991): 781–824.

39. Reasons include bounded rationality, uncertainty about the future, and asymmetric information. See Williamson, *Markets and Hierarchies,* and the discussion in Chapter 6.

40. William J. Abernathy and Kenneth Wayne, "Limits of the Learning Curve," *Harvard Business Review* 52, no. 5 (September–October 1974): 109–119.

41. Michael E. Porter, "Note on Supplying the Automobile Industry (Condensed)" (Harvard Business School Publishing Case no. 386-176, Boston, 1986).

42. Jeffrey H. Dyer, "Does Governance Matter? Keiretsu Alliances and Asset Specificity as Sources of Japanese Competitive Advantage," *Organization Science* 7, no. 6 (November–December 1996): 649–666.

43. Ibid.

44. For a general discussion of how interorganizational relationships can lead in this fashion to sustained competitive advantage, see Jeffrey H. Dyer and Harbir Singh, "The Relational View: Cooperative Strategy and Sources of Interorganizational Competitive Advantage," *Academy of Management Review* 23, no. 4 (October 1998): 660–679.

45. Andreas Maurer, Frank Dietz, and Nikolaus S. Lang, "Beyond Cost Reduction: Reinventing the Automotive OEM-Supplier Interface" (Boston Consulting Group, 2004): 18.

46. Consult, for example, Richard E. Caves and David R. Barton, *Efficiency in U.S. Manufacturing Industries* (Cambridge, Mass.: MIT Press, 1990).

47. For more details on this methodology and an application to General Motors between 1980 and 1990, see Michael C. Jensen, "The Modern Industrial Revolution, Exit, and the Failure of Internal Control Systems," *Journal of Finance* 48, no. 3 (1993): 831–880.

48. For a more extended discussion of some of the ideas touched on here, see Paul R. Milgrom and John Roberts, *Economics, Organization and Management* (Englewood Cliffs, N.J.: Prentice-Hall, 1992), chap. 6.

49. Williamson, *Markets and Hierarchies,* 14.

50. Michael C. Jensen, "Agency Costs of Free Cash Flow, Corporate Finance, and Takeovers," *American Economic Review* 76, no. 2 (1986): 323–329.

51. Jensen, "Modern Industrial Revolution, Exit, and the Failure of Internal Control Systems."

52. For a managerial discussion, see John P. Kotter, "Leading Change: Why Transformation Efforts Fail," *Harvard Business Review* 73, no. 2 (March–April 1995): 59–67.

53. Proctor & Gamble's subsequent acquisition of Gillette did not change their situation much: Wal-Mart accounted for 16-1 of P&G and Gillette's combined revenues in 2004, and their sales to it represented 14-1 of Wal-Mart's revenues.

54. Marco Iansiti and Roy Levien, *The Keystone Advantage: Wal-Mart accounted for 16% of P&G and Gillette's combined revenues in 2004, and their sales to it represented 14% of Wal-Mart's revenues.* (Boston: Harvard Business School Press, 2004).

Choosing Corporate Scope

Pankaj Ghemawat and Jan W. Rivkin

But we must now refer to one question about systems in general, and about organization systems in particular, the answer to which is of fundamental importance. I refer to the question as to whether the whole is more than the sum of the parts ... whether there emerge from the system properties which are not inherent in the parts.
—CHESTER BARNARD, *THE FUNCTIONS OF THE EXECUTIVE* (1938), P. 79

This book has focused, for the most part, on strategy for a free-standing business in one industry. Yet large companies tend to operate in multiple industries. Procter & Gamble, for instance, expanded from its 1837 roots in the soap and candle industries to enter the markets for vegetable shortening (1911), laundry detergent (1933), hair care (1934), toothpaste (1955), toilet paper and paper towels (1957), diapers (1961), coffee (1963), pharmaceuticals (1978), and cosmetics (1989) among others. Though founded in 1892 on the basis of a handful of electrical inventions, especially electric lighting, General Electric now operates in industries as diverse as media and entertainment, healthcare, aircraft engines, energy infrastructure, household appliances, commercial and consumer finance, and insurance. This chapter examines the logic that underlies such choices of corporate scope.

Scope itself has several dimensions: horizontal scope (in what industries should a company compete?), vertical scope (should a company make its own inputs?), and geographic scope (where should a company compete?). To keep the scope of this chapter manageable, we focus on horizontal scope. (For a brief discussion of vertical scope, see the section on holdup in Chapter 5.)[1]

Systematic research suggests that the effects of common corporate ownership on the operating performance of businesses, while statistically significant, tend to be smaller than within-industry differences in performance that operate at the business level (the topic of Chapter 3) and differences in average performance at the industry level (the topic of Chapter 2). That said, **corporate strategy** cannot be ignored, for several reasons. First, the estimated corporate-level effects on performance, while smaller than direct business-level effects, are far from negligible. Second, inferences to be drawn from such estimates remain somewhat controversial. Third, the focus on ongoing operating performance used to isolate corporate effects in such studies misses out on at least some potential mechanisms for corporate value addition; for example, through one-time moves into or out of an industry, as appropriate. Finally, current corporate effects on performance seem to represent lower bounds on the strategic headroom afforded by corporate strategy, given our sense that there is a wide gap between best practice and average practice in this area. It is hard to deny that the best practitioners of corporate strategy—companies like General Electric, Danaher, and Berkshire Hathaway today, and Disney, Cooper Industries, Banc One, and Newell in the past—have boosted the performance of their business units enormously.

The next section of this chapter reviews the evolution of the practice of corporate strategy. The rest of the chapter focuses on two tests to be applied to (horizontal) corporate strategy: the **better-off test** and the **best-alternative test.** Note the parallels to the discussion, in a single-business context in Chapters 3 and 5, of the challenges of adding value and appropriating value.

THE PRACTICE OF CORPORATE STRATEGY OVER TIME

Chapter 1 described the diffusion of portfolio plannings for charting corporate strategy among large U.S. corporations during the 1970s. It also discussed some of the doubts that quickly set in about, among other things, the mechanical determination of resource-allocation patterns on the basis of historical performance data and, in many cases, an arbitrary assumption of self-financing that effectively ignored the existence of capital markets. The 1970s also saw the first systematic empirical analyses of the performance implications of different types of diversification strategies, which began to suggest that, in the United States at least, related diversifiers outperformed unrelated diversifiers.[2]

Despite these developments, portfolio planning techniques continued to hold sway through the 1980s: the decade's most celebrated corporate strategy was Jack Welch's insistence on "#1, #2 or out" at General Electric, which focused attention on the market-share axis of the growth-share matrix. Further development of corporate strategy as strategy for a portfolio of strategic business units (SBUs) was heavily influenced, however, by the revolution in U.S. financial markets in the 1980s. A rising stock market and financing innovations such as junk bonds, abetted in a number of sectors by domestic deregulation and intensified foreign competition, fueled a wave of hostile takeovers and company restructurings that forced many firms to reevaluate their strategic thinking. Specialist consulting firms began to promote "value-based management" that made heavy use of financial measures of performance. According to one such firm, Marakon,

> At least one-third, and probably more, of all units generate rates of return on equity capital each non-recession year that are significantly less than the respective costs of equity capital. Further, most of these units . . . also consistently invest equity capital at these unprofitable rates!!! Thus, they impose capital confiscation—capital losses—on their owners, not once or twice, but over and over again.[3]

By the end of the 1990s, value-based management techniques had been refined to proprietary levels (e.g., EVA, a trademarked acronym for economic value added), and 43 percent of large-company survey respondents reported that they had implemented formal value-based management systems.[4] This number was comparable to the 45 percent that had reported using portfolio planning techniques in a survey (by one of the same authors) two decades earlier.[5] The stated reasons for implementing value-based management paralleled the ones identified in the 1980s by Marakon, and were headed by "We could not clearly determine where value is created or destroyed in our company" and "Our employees did not appreciate that capital has a cost."

But the biggest change in the practice of corporate strategy in the 1990s was associated with the popularization of the concept of core competence by C. K. Prahalad and Gary Hamel.[6] In an article that went on to become the best-selling reprint in the history of the *Harvard Business Review,* Prahalad and Hamel launched a full-fledged attack on the SBU-level foundations of portfolio planning. They argued that in an SBU-based architecture, no single SBU feels responsible for maintaining a viable position in core products or competencies that cross business boundaries, competencies developed within an SBU are not shared across SBUs, and opportunities for growth are missed. As an alternative, they recommended a corporate-wide strategic architecture for competence building and asserted that the successful organizations of the future would be the ones that shifted their focus from SBUs to core competencies, because these formed the foundations of future growth.

While the model of related diversification implicit in writings on core competence was not entirely new, the suggestion that organizations reorganize around "relatedness threads" sparked considerable strategic activity at the corporate level. As of 2002, core competences ranked eleventh among twenty-five popular management tools in terms of usage in a global survey by Bain and Company; for comparative purposes, note that strategic planning was ranked first, and economic value-added analysis twenty-first.[7]

As in the case of portfolio planning, however, doubts about the doctrine of core competence began to emerge within a few years of large-scale diffusion. Two academic strategists dismissed it as "a 'feel good' exercise that no one fails." After all, "every company can identify one activity that it does relatively better than other activities and claim that as its core competence." For this reason, the definition of a firm's core competence should not be based on an "internal assessment of which activity, of all its activities, the company performs best. It should be a harsh external assessment of what it does better than competitors, for which the term distinctive competence is more appropriate."[8]

The empirical case for focusing on core competences also remains in doubt. The core competence argument implies that diversifying in related businesses will yield higher returns than unrelated diversification. Yet extensive unrelated diversification remains common, and apparently profitable, in many countries outside the United States. Even in the United States, one can find very successful companies such as General Electric that have ignored the stricture to focus on their core competences. One can also find companies that have expanded in directions suggested by alleged core competencies yet stumbled badly. Consider, for instance, the "socks and stocks" corporate strategy of Sears, Roebuck.[9] In 1981, Sears acquired Coldwell, Banker, the largest real estate brokerage firm in the United States, and Dean Witter, Reynolds, a major securities broker. The acquisitions, added to Sears's long-held insurance and consumer credit card businesses, marked the company's full-scale diversification from general-merchandise retailing into financial services. Explaining the move in the mid-1980s, Sears's CFO explained how the acquisitions would leverage Sears's expertise in data processing, its credit-card relationships with tens of millions of consumers, and the trust it enjoyed in the eyes of many customers.[10] Cross-selling efforts stalled, however, hampered by such factors as the reluctance of business-unit executives to share customer lists. Apparently distracted by the company's foray into financial services, Sears executives failed to address the company's weakening position in the retail business—a fiercely competitive industry made more challenging by the rise of Wal-Mart. By 1988, Sears was struggling to hold off hostile bidders, and in 1992, the company announced that it would exit financial services and narrow its scope to retailing. Sears shareholders paid dearly for the scope maneuvers. A $100 investment in Sears stock on January 1, 1980, turned into $746 by the end of 1994, while the same investment over the same period in a set of narrow-scope companies that mimicked Sears's industry portfolio would have produced $1,256. As one set of researchers put it, "homemade diversification outperformed Sears' diversification strategy."[11]

Sears's troubles exemplify the concerns of consultants whom we contacted to size up the state of current practice related to scope choices. As one put it:

> In our experience, most firms have stopped even thinking through all the benefits, costs and risks [of scope choices], never mind actually trying to calculate them. Instead, they've adopted "relatedness religion" in which they believe that being able to name the ways in which their business units are related means they must, by definition, be achieving synergies.

TWO TESTS

Consideration of inadequate corporate strategies, such as the one at Sears, should, of course, be balanced with recognition that cross-business strategies can also create enormous economic value. One of the most successful scope expansions of the 1990s was Wal-Mart's diversification from discounting general, nonfood merchandise—its original line of business—into discounting food as well. Wal-Mart's "Supercenter" format offers food and general merchandise under one roof. Substituting Supercenters for nonfood discount stores was not obviously a winning idea: the razor-thin margins on food would cause the new format to have lower average operating margins than the old format. Wal-Mart realized, however, that supermarkets were saddled with expensive unionized workforces and had failed to invest enough in information technology, logistics, and the like. That stirred Wal-Mart's interest in offering lower food prices as a way of growing volumes, including those for nonfood items under the same roof, to an extent that might outweigh the decrease in operating margins. Specifically, if one assumes that a mature Supercenter would have nearly double the sales of a discount store and would, because of shared infrastructure, experience lower average capital costs, then the net present value (NPV) to Wal-Mart of a new Supercenter might be 15–20 percent higher than the NPV of a new discount store. But a much bigger payoff from building traffic stems from the fact that Wal-Mart needs a population of just 75,000 people to support one of its Supercenters in the United States, versus 150,000 people to support a (smaller) discount store. Opening two Supercenters rather than one discount store in a region with 150,000 people allows Wal-Mart to quadruple its revenue in the region and raise its NPV by 130–140 percent! Operating in two industries rather than one has proven to be extremely lucrative: Supercenters are estimated to account for the bulk of Wal-Mart's market value—over $100 billion—and to have a higher return on assets than traditional discount stores do.

How can managers distinguish good opportunities to expand and exploit horizontal scope, such as Wal-Mart's move from general-merchandise retailing into groceries, from poor opportunities such as Sears's move from the same base into financial services? The two examples seem to suggest that, in any discussion of corporate strategy, managers should focus intently on the corporate strategy's impact on *individual business units*. Competition occurs at the level of the individual business unit in a particular industry. Therefore, corporate strategy succeeds or fails to the extent that it aids or undermines business units as they strive to win in their specific markets. But how can we know whether membership in a particular corporate family is likely to help or hamper a specific business unit? We find two tests to be especially telling.[12]

1. *The "Better-Off" Test:*   Do combining and coordinating the activities of multiple business units, as one can do in a corporation with broad scope, enable the units to create and capture more value than they could as independent, unassociated units? In other words, what is the corporate added value?
2. *The "Best-Alternative" Test:*   Suppose the units pass the better-off test and coordinated action is valuable. Is common ownership by a single corporation the best way to reap the benefits of coordinated action—better than alternatives like joint ventures, strategic alliances, licensing deals, and arm's-length transactions? Conceptually, this test focuses on value appropriation instead of value addition.

The better-off test asks whether a particular set of business units should be working together. The best-alternative test asks whether the set must be jointly owned in order to maximize the amount of value created and captured.

We find these tests to be useful whether one is considering the addition of a business unit to broaden horizontal scope, thinking about divesting a unit to narrow scope, or deciding how to manage an existing portfolio of businesses. In the context of adding a business unit, managers will also want to analyze the financial implications, asking whether the benefits of the addition outweigh the cost—in terms of their consequences for total profits (not just profitability, which went down in the case of Wal-Mart's Supercenters). In an efficient market for corporate assets, the answer is likely to be yes only if the two tests are passed. Similarly, when considering divestiture, managers will want to examine financials. A divestiture is likely to unlock value by freeing business units of one another only if the corporation fails at least one of the tests.

Some observers of corporate strategy suggest a third test, even tougher than the better-off and best-alternative tests: the "best-parent" test: "The appropriate benchmark for value creation is not what would happen without a [corporate] parent, but what the best available parent would achieve."[13] Taken literally, this seems too stringent. It probably does not make sense for every company to dispose of all businesses that it cannot run as efficiently as, say, General Electric could (unless GE is willing to make a high bid for the business). Having said that, we are sympathetic to a milder formulation of the third test, the "Good Parent" test, in which, even if a proposed opportunity to expand scope apparently satisfies the first two tests, it is worth asking yourself whether your company is particularly well-placed to observe or act upon the opportunity identified before you actually move to capitalize on it. In an ambiguous world marked by the possibility of the winner's curse, to do less would be deficient on diligence. Such caution also recognizes strong forces that tend to push managers toward overexpansion. These forces include the following:[14]

➤ Human beings tend to be overly confident about their abilities. In surveys, for instance, 93 percent of Americans rate themselves as above-average drivers.[15] The bias toward overconfidence may be especially prominent among successful executives, and there is evidence that this is reflected in their investment choices. A recent study shows that companies whose CEOs display overconfidence in their personal financial portfolios are particularly likely to spend free cash flow on fresh investments instead of paying out dividends or reducing debt.[16]

➤ An unexamined belief that bigger is better, a focus on "stretch goals," a failure to recognize the reality that growth rates tend to drop as organizations age, an urge to mimic the expansion of competitors and, frankly, confusion as to whether market share is a symptom of success or a valid strategic goal in and of itself—all of these may encourage corporate managers to overexpand.

➤ Even without such encouragement, poorly governed top managers may act on a personal desire to build an "empire" and to increase the resources under their control. Moreover, managers may diversify in order to reduce the unsystematic risk that they face personally—even though shareholders may not value such reductions.

➤ Managers often get advice about mergers and acquisitions from investment bankers and other parties whose fees depend on deal-making.

Building on the rest of this book, especially the discussions in Chapters 3 and 5, we examine the two tests by looking at the activities of business units across their value chains. Others have approached corporate strategy very productively by focusing not on the activities of business units but on the resources that span business units.[17] Indeed, we touch on the nature of such resources when we discuss the best-alternative test below. But, consistent with the treatment in the other chapters, we emphasize analysis of costs and benefits in terms of activity flows even when we are ultimately interested in evaluating different resource stocks that underlie them.

Our hope is that hard-nosed examination of the costs and benefits of broad scope (the better-off test) and an objective look at alternatives to expansion (the best-alternative test) can help bring the discipline of business-level strategy to bear on issues of corporate strategy. Note that the aim is not to propose a radically new point of view on corporate strategy but to use conventional theory to improve practice—an area that seems to offer large opportunities.

THE BETTER-OFF TEST

To pass the better-off test, an expansion in horizontal scope must enable a corporation's business units to create and capture more value together than they could as separate, single-business entities unrelated to one another. Indeed, the incremental value must more than offset the costs of the corporate center. Where can such incremental value come from? Obviously, a scope expansion can increase the aggregate volume of business on which it is possible to earn positive (or negative) economic margins. In view of the pro-growth biases discussed above, however, as well as the frequent business-specificity of many key resources, we remain cautious about thinking of scope expansions in purely scalar terms.[18] The better-off test forces us to look, in addition, for other possible gains related to the concepts that have been discussed in earlier chapters. Sometimes, a scope expansion can improve the structure of the industries in which a company competes. More often, an expansion can increase the added value of business units within their industries—that is, widen the wedge between the willingness to pay they generate and the costs they incur. Finally, an expansion can sometimes create value for a business by reducing the risk it bears.

Industry Attractiveness

There are two senses in which a scope expansion can improve the structure of the industries in which a company competes. First and simply, broad horizontal scope can improve structure directly by mitigating the five forces discussed in Chapter 2. Rivalry, for instance, may be muted among broad-scope firms that meet one another in multiple markets. Fearing that aggressive behavior in any one market will provoke fierce competition everywhere, they may refrain from aggression anywhere. The resulting "mutual forbearance" may lead to higher prices and profits in all of the markets.[19] In line with this argument, pairs of U.S. airlines that meet on numerous routes have been found to compete less fiercely with one another on overlapping routes than do pairs that rarely meet.[20] A similar pattern has been observed in the commercial banking industry.[21] Broad scope may also reduce another of the five forces, the threat of new entry, by denying new firms access to complementary inputs. The U.S. Department of Justice's case against Microsoft, for instance, centered on the claim that Microsoft's dominance in multiple lines of businesses (operating systems, word processing, spreadsheets, presentation software) made it difficult for new firms such as Netscape to establish themselves. A proposed remedy was to narrow Microsoft's scope, separating the company's operating-system business from its application-software operations.[22]

Second and more subtly, broad scope may give a firm an opportunity to migrate out of a structurally poor industry into a more attractive setting. Gradual experimentation over decades, accelerating in the 1990s, allowed Nokia to move from its traditional base in forest products, rubber, cables, and electricity generation to become a leading player in the fast-growing mobile handset industry. Through its diversifying merger with Time Warner, America Online (AOL) managed to take its shareholders' stake in the fast-deteriorating market for online services and trade it for assets in more stable industries like cable television, magazines, and film. Horizontal diversification can also bring efficient or creative new players into sleepy industries, sharpening skills and boosting industry performance. Cooper Industries, for example, earned high returns for decades by bringing world-class manufacturing skills and professional management to mature, low-tech manufacturing industries such as the market for hand tools.

One should be cautious, however, about industry-attractiveness rationales for broad scope. It is difficult for one company alone to change the structure of its entire industry by means of its scope choices (unless, perhaps, like Microsoft it dominates its industry). Broad scope may open up an opportunity to migrate to a more attractive setting, but decision-makers can use this as a management tool only if they have better foresight than other potential entrants about what industries will be attractive in the future. Maneuvers like AOL's presumably depend on the existence of counterparts with inferior insights into the future or internal constraints on acting on their insights.

Competitive Advantage

More common and often more compelling are efforts to use scope to improve a company's position *within* its industry. As discussed in Chapter 3, a firm's ability to create value within an industry depends crucially on its driving a wedge between the costs it incurs and the willingness to pay it generates among buyers. Competitive advantage requires that this wedge be wider than competitors'. Corporate-level scope choices often have the greatest impact by influencing the wedges that business units can attain within their individual industries. There are many ways that scope choices can widen the wedges. Some operate clearly on the cost side of the equation—reducing costs without sacrificing willingness to pay. Others almost always affect the willingness to pay side—raising willingness to pay without incurring extra costs. Yet others can widen the wedge by influencing either costs or willingness to pay. We will examine these three categories—and the various limitations and drawbacks to which they are subject—in turn (see Exhibit 6.1).

Cost Effects

Shared cost economies, the first row of entries in the exhibit, feature prominently in most horizontal diversification and can be thought of as the multibusiness version of economies of scale within a single business. Simply noting the existence of such economies is not enough, however: their significance must be assessed. This often involves analyzing the cost structures of individual businesses activity by activity, sizing up the fraction of total costs that can be shared across the businesses, and estimating how sensitive those shared cost elements are to total size. An example illustrates how one can make such estimates.

➤ The Scotts Company makes and markets a wide array of lawn and garden care products.[23] Specifically, its four business units sell grass seed and fertilizers, plant food for gardens, soil, and pesticides. In 1999, the units handled most of their procurement separately. The grass seed and fertilizer business unit purchased $30 million of pesticide inputs while the pesticide business unit bought $32 million of raw material. By combining their purchases, the unit managers felt that they could drive a harder bargain with raw material suppliers. Industry experts estimated that a doubling of purchase volume could reduce per-unit raw material costs by 5 percent. This would amount to annual savings of 5 percent x ($30 million + $32 million) =

Exhibit 6.1 Effects of Horizontal Diversification on Competitive Advantage

Component	Levers for Value Creation	Limits

Cost Effects	- Shared cost economies across businesses
	  • Shared activities
	  • Shared resources
		- Diseconomies of scale or scope
		- Costs of
		  • Conflict/politicking
		  • Compromise
		  • Coordination
		- Mixed motives
		- Cognitive conflicts
		- Reputational risk

Willingness-to-Pay/Price Effects	- One-stop shop/one-vendor sales and support - Cross-promotion/cross-selling - Umbrella branding - Bundling, particularly of complements	
Dual Effects	- Superior internal resource markets/transfer mechanisms - Other superior skills and capabilities - Cross-business learning/innovation - Size-based political influence	- Availability of market/interfirm alternatives - Typical breadth versus depth trade-off - Internal/inside-the-box biases - Antitrust laws/political backlash

$3.1 million. Moreover, the four units paid unit-level procurement personnel a total of $2.9 million in annual salaries and benefits. Centralization of purchasing, it was estimated, might permit a headcount reduction that would reduce those salaries and benefits by $0.7 million per year.

➤ Scotts also spent $16 million per year on less-than-truckload transportation to get its products from factories to retail sites. These outbound logistics costs were spread across its four business units. By consolidating the shipments, managers felt that they could shift half the volume to full-truckload shipping, which they knew to be 75 percent cheaper per unit. This could lead to annual savings of $16 million × ½ × 75 percent = $6 million.

➤ Each Scotts business operated its own sales force, ranging in size from a few people for pesticides to seventy-nine salespeople for the grass seed and fertilizer business. Each sales force, it was estimated, incurred fixed costs of roughly $3 million plus salary, benefit, and bonus costs per salesperson of $54,000. Consolidation of the sales forces would not allow much reduction in headcount, simply because the sales personnel called on different buyers and were already fully employed. Consolidation would, however, reduce redundant fixed costs associated with sales offices, sales management software, and so forth. The potential savings were estimated to be 3 × $3 million = $9 million per year.

Shared cost economies, like scale economies, can arise anywhere in the value chains of the business units. They typically occur when business units can coordinate activities for efficiency or spread the cost of some lumpy, underutilized resource over the volume of multiple business units. The resource involved might be tangible, like a piece of equipment, or intangible, like a brand, a reputation, a body of knowledge, or a capability.

It is crucial to recognize, however, that the savings from shared cost economies can be offset—to an extent that must also be examined—by *diseconomies of size or scope*. To see the possibility of such diseconomies, even for an outstanding management team, we can return to Wal-Mart. Especially with its diversification into food retailing, Wal-Mart has become massive. As the world's largest company, it now faces the challenges of hiring 600,000 new employees each year just to maintain the size of its workforce at 1.4 million as well as adding 800,000 new positions over the next five years. This has heightened public scrutiny as well as increased bureaucratic complexity, as elaborated towards the end of the preceding chapter.

The savings from shared cost economies can also be offset by the extra *costs of conflict, compromise, and coordination* that reflect heterogeneity in requirements, goals, and beliefs across businesses (which is likely to be larger than within one business).[24] Often these costs are so large that managers opt not to exploit potential economies. Consider, for instance, the Royal Bank of Scotland Group, whose recent horizontal expansion efforts have given it the fifth-largest market capitalization in the world among financial service providers. An acquisition made the Royal Bank the owner of Coutts, a bank serving 70,000 individuals of very high net worth, including the Queen of England. Managers resisted virtually all opportunities to share costs with Coutts, fearing that to do so would compromise its ability to delivery a customized service to highly discerning clients.

Wal-Mart also faced costs of conflict, compromise, and coordination between its food and nonfood businesses, but managed to overcome them in a variety of ways. It designed the Supercenter to optimize the relationship between the two businesses. (Fourteen different variants were reportedly tried out.) Moreover, Wal-Mart set up the Supercenter format as a profit center and grew it organically, but grouped it with the format that it was cannibalizing into one gargantuan division—with more than $150 billion in sales in 2003. This, along with the company's tradition of top-down strategic decision-making, aided the ongoing transfer of resources and the sharing of activities, systems, and the like.

But such conflicts et cetera *do* erect significant barriers to value creation in many cases, especially when companies are trying to redeploy existing resources or coordinate across businesses with traditions of decentralized decision-making. In the wake of the AOL Time Warner merger, for instance, the famously autonomous divisions of the old Time Warner resisted the cross-business coordination that was supposed to create much of the value of the company's expanded scope. So, in deciding whether to broaden scope by adding a business, or in choosing how to integrate a business that has already been added, managers must weigh carefully the benefits and costs of tapping potential economies.

Willingness-to-Pay/Price Effects

Willingness-to-pay and price effects, the second row of entries in Exhibit 6.1, are not quite as commonly cited in horizontal diversification as cost reductions, but they can be very important. When the Royal Bank of Scotland acquired the major rival bank NatWest, for instance, its managers planned 109 initiatives to reduce costs by £1.2 billion over three years, but they also undertook forty-three initiatives to boost revenue by £390 million over the same period. Actual revenue enhancements came closer to £600 mm.[25]

The revenue benefits of broad scope typically come from two sources: (1) increases in willingness to pay for a combined offering, and (2) improvements in a company's ability to price in a way that extracts willingness to pay. We consider each in turn. Willingness-to-pay effects include the following:

➤ Customers often value the convenience of *one-stop shopping* that comes with broad scope. In a consumer context, consider the convenience of Wal-Mart's Super-centers. In a business context, having one vendor or a single point of contact for sales, service, and other support can be a significant draw—especially when systems sales are important. When appointed CEO of a beleaguered IBM in 1993, for instance, Lou Gerstner resisted a plan to break the company into a dozen "Baby Blues." Large corporate customers valued the ability to purchase entire solutions from one vendor, he argued, and IBM's uniquely extensive scope enabled it to deliver integrated packages better than the competition. Gerstner's decision to "go to market as one IBM" is often considered one of the strategic masterstrokes of the 1990s.

➤ Much of the rationale for media conglomerates seems to derive from significant and apparently cost-effective *cross-promotion* of their properties across lines of business as well as within businesses. A vivid example was provided by Rupert Murdoch's aggressive use of his British newspapers, particularly *The Sun,* to promote his British satellite TV start-up, Sky TV, against its rival, BSB. SkyTV's war of attrition with BSB culminated in a merger of their assets into BSkyB and Murdoch's effective assumption of control of what is now a fabulously valuable franchise. Similarly, Disney undertakes cross-promotion on a massive scale. When Disney releases a new animated feature film, for instance, the film's characters appear in Disney's theme parks, in its stores, in its Broadway theater, and on its ABC television network. From its film *The Lion King,* for instance, Disney took in $1 billion of revenue at the box office and $1 billion through other businesses.

➤ *Umbrella branding* enables multiple businesses to reap the willingness-to-pay benefits of a strong brand. Virgin, for instance, has used its umbrella brand to enter businesses ranging from airlines and record stores to mobile telephony and rail service and has done quite well at some of them (so far).

Broad scope can also alter the pricing approach of a company. Microsoft, for example, benefits enormously from integrating into and offering an array of complementary products (e.g., its Windows operating system, Microsoft Office application software, Internet Explorer browser, etc.). The company's broad scope not only raises barriers to entry, as mentioned above, but it also affects pricing in two ways. As an integrated player, Microsoft can set prices in complementary markets in a coordinated manner, extracting more profits than could unintegrated players with similar market power in separate markets.

Once again, however, there are a number of limits to these levers for value creation.

➤ The issues of *conflict, compromise, and coordination* that were discussed above often also show up in the context of willingness to pay, although in the form of price penalties rather than extra costs. For example, attempts to bundle complements often lead to compromised offerings instead of ones as compelling as the Super-center, or they founder because of more fundamental coordination problems. Bundling efforts can also open opportunities for narrow-scope competitors. In the wake of the AOL Time Warner merger, for instance, rivals such as Yahoo! made considerable progress in forming alliances with competing cable providers. After PepsiCo purchased fast-food restaurants Pizza Hut, Taco Bell, and Kentucky Fried Chicken, Coca-Cola persuaded Wendy's and Burger King to switch their soft-drink offerings from Pepsi to Coke.

➤ If the offerings of different businesses are substitutes instead of complements, it is even trickier to manage across them because of *mixed motives* due to fears of self-cannibalization and similar concerns. For example, Clay Christensen's emphasis on disruptive technologies keys off the mixed motives that an incumbent using one technology faces in dealing with a new technology that underserves the needs of most of its current customers but is on a more rapid performance-improvement trajectory.[26] Or to take a somewhat different type of example, full-service airlines have failed to create a compelling "product" for the low-fare segment of the marketplace in part because they know that such an offering will draw traffic away from their existing higher-fare service.

➤ *Cognitive conflicts* in the minds of customers (or even employees) can also constrain horizontal scope if scope expansion threatens to blur a company's external (or internal) message. Thus, Disney has always been very careful about the products for which it licenses images of Mickey Mouse and the rest of its wholesome menagerie. This caution has proven to be well-placed. The 1994 release of the controversial film *Priest* by Disney's Miramax subsidiary, distant from Mickey, led the Catholic League to call for a boycott of the entire Disney corporation, not just the film. More broadly, Disney has found that actions in one domain can endanger prospects elsewhere. Disney's production of *Kundun,* a movie about the Dalai Lama, allegedly led Chinese officials to threaten in 1996 to reevaluate the full range of Disney's plans in China. And when Disney barred Miramax from distributing the controversial *Fahrenheit 9/11* in 2004, some analysts speculated that Disney feared a conservative backlash in other parts of its business. (Ironically, the action itself led to a backlash, causing some liberal groups to call for a boycott of all Disney products.)

➤ Finally, umbrella-branding efforts carry significant *reputational risk.* Think of what might have happened to Accenture if it had remained tightly coupled to Andersen Accounting, including continuing to call itself Andersen Consulting, when Andersen Accounting's dealings with Enron began to come to light.

In our experience, thoughtful managers who are considering an expansion of horizontal scope are relatively skeptical of willingness-to-pay/price effects and tend to rely more heavily on "hard" arguments about cost economies. As one management consultant told us, "If the move can't be justified on the basis of cost savings, that's a bright red flag." We are somewhat sympathetic to this point of view, given how much easier it is to dream up revenue "synergies" than to realize them. Cost synergies are subject to at least some of the same problems, however. This suggests a careful, critical analysis of both willingness to pay and costs rather than an approach that always emphasizes one over the other.

Dual Effects

Sometimes it is hard to separate opportunities to create competitive advantage cleanly into cost effects and willingness-to-pay effects. Consider, for instance, an example from the Scotts Company, the lawn and garden care manufacturer mentioned above.[27] In 1999, Scotts experimented with deploying in-store counselors at major home-improvement retailers like Home Depot. These counselors helped customers select the Scotts product that matched their needs. Stores with experienced counselors typically saw a 20 percent increase in sales of Scotts products—a major boost. Simple calculations of margin per product line revealed that only one of the four Scotts business units, the grass seed and fertilizer unit, could justify the expense of the counselor on a standalone basis. As independent entities, none of the other three units had enough volume per store for a 20 percent boost in sales to support a counselor's wages. Because they were members of the Scotts corporation, however, the three small units were able to enjoy an important advantage over rivals with narrower product lines. This advantage can be classified as a willingness-to-pay advantage, reflected in the 20 percent increase in volume, or as a cost advantage, reflected in the lower cost of a counselor's wages spread over more volume.

Such inseparabilities should not prevent a careful analysis of the impact of scope on competitive advantage; after all, advantage depends not on one or the other, but on the gap between the two. In this regard, it is useful to acknowledge, as in the third row in Exhibit 6.1, various levers of corporate advantage that widen the wedge between costs and willingness to pay, but, depending on the circumstances, can do so by influencing the cost side of the equation, the willingness-to-pay side, or both. *Superior internal resource markets, transfer mechanisms,* and *skills and capabilities* are directly relevant to the best-alternative test and will therefore be discussed further in the next subsection. *Cross-business learning and innovation* have the potential to improve both costs and willingness to pay over time. 3M, for instance, has created competitive advantages for decades by sharing deep knowledge of a handful of core technologies across tens of thousands of product lines. One such technology involves expertise in coating, where a set of more than forty specific techniques support thousands of products ranging from Post-It memo stickers to medical items—products that account for roughly two-thirds of corporate revenue. However, cross-business learning and innovation can also entail an *internal bias* that deemphasizes external know-how or thinking outside the box of the current business portfolio. Finally, there is the possibility of *size-based political influence:* a political version of economies of size. However, *antitrust laws* often constrain some of the horizontal moves that might prove the most profitable (e.g., the challenges to Microsoft's bundling strategy in the United States and Europe) and, as noted above in the context of Wal-Mart, size can actually lead to somewhat of a *political backlash.*

Risk Considerations

When asked to explain their scope choices, many corporate executives make a risk-related argument: diversification reduces volatility in overall corporate performance by averaging returns across businesses subject to different shocks, cycles, and trends. Managers of Cendant offered an explanation of this kind as they pieced together the corporation's collection of real estate franchises, rental-car agencies, hotels, tax services, relocation services, travel-distribution systems, and financial services operations. The plan, as one observer put it, was "to buy up businesses to create a company with enough size and diversity that no one shock could pummel it."[28] If a weak economy hurt the travel-related business units, for example, the associated low interest rates would boost the real estate units.

For publicly traded companies participating in well-oiled capital markets, modern finance theory has seriously undermined this type of argument. Investors can diversify inexpensively on their own, constructing a portfolio with the balance of risk and return they desire. There is no reason for the corporation to do so on their behalf. Moreover, a corporation that spots a great investment opportunity but is short on funds can raise capital in the public markets.

The risk-reduction argument does, however, hold more water in other contexts. Firms with limited access to efficient capital markets may legitimately create value by diversifying to smooth performance and create internal capital markets. The business groups that dominate many emerging economies have recently been viewed through this lens.[29] Similarly, individual- or family-owned corporations whose owners wish to retain control and avoid public capital markets often diversify for risk-reduction reasons. But except when access to efficient capital markets is seriously constrained, firms must justify their scope choices and pass the better-off test on the other grounds we have mentioned.

THE BEST-ALTERNATIVE TEST

The essence of the better-off test is to ask whether the business units of a corporation can create more value under common ownership than they would as isolated entities, even after netting out the direct and indirect costs of corporate membership. This test compares commonly owned business units with standalone business units; thus it focuses on what we might call **corporate added value.** The best-alternative test, in contrast, realizes that common ownership is not the only possible basis for coordinating across business units. Business units might, instead, remain independently owned but partner with one another, form strategic alliances, sign long-term contracts, and so forth. The best-alternative test asks, Can a corporation that owns its business units outright accomplish its ends better than the same business units coordinated in some other way? Note that, conceptually, this test focuses on value appropriation and not just value addition. For instance, in assessing the wisdom of a strategic partnership as an alternative to joint ownership, managers must not only compare the total value created under each arrangement, but must also consider whether the partner might hold up the firm and appropriate the value that was created.

Applied to some of the examples we developed earlier, the best-alternative test raises questions like the following: Could Wal-Mart have reaped most of the benefits of its Supercenters by partnering with and co-locating with local supermarket chains? Could a set of small lawn-care manufacturers, even if they are not jointly owned, band together to place sales counselors in retail stores? Could Disney exploit its animated characters by licensing the characters to theme parks and retail stores owned by others, or must it own its own parks and stores? The careful comparison of corporate ownership to alternate arrangements sheds light on whether a set of businesses should be jointly owned. As we will see below, it also helps us understand how the set might be managed.

Transactions Costs and Ownership

As the many examples of broad horizontal scope make clear, there are often times when managers judge ownership to be better than alternate arrangements. Yet at other times, managers prefer alternate arrangements; for example, when a company decides to contract out excess manufacturing capacity instead of using it to expand horizontal scope, enters into a cross-marketing agreement with another company, or licenses its intellectual property instead of using it internally. Disney, for instance, licenses its characters to McDonald's rather than operating its own fast-food stores. (Disney experimented with fast-food operations, Mickey's Kitchens, during the 1980s but abandoned the concept.) Yahoo!, the Internet portal, partners with companies like SBC and British Telecom to provide high-speed Internet access, and it has resisted the notion that it needs to own distribution resources (or be owned by a company with such resources). To expand its scope into the printer industry, Dell resells printers made by Lexmark, in sharp contrast to Hewlett Packard, which produces its own printers.

The concept of *transaction costs* can help us understand which transactions tend to take place within a corporation instead of across firm boundaries.[30] The relationship between two business units—whether they are sister units within a corporation or alliance partners or arm's-length traders—can be thought of as a set of transactions. Governing a transaction involves certain costs, including the costs of finding a transaction partner, negotiating the terms of an agreement, and making sure the transaction is completed to the parties' satisfaction. Different governance arrangements involve different transaction costs. Transactions are generally expected to migrate toward the form of governance that permits them to be completed effectively and at low cost.

Many types of transaction costs are straightforward, and comparing these costs across forms of governance is easy. Take, for example, the costs of finding a trading partner. Internal ownership often makes it inexpensive to find a partner. When Disney's film division develops a new animated character in a film and wants to market the character in a theme park, it incurs no costs in finding a willing theme-park partner. It simply turns to Disney's theme-park division.

Other types of transaction costs, however, are more subtle. Studies of corporate scope have identified one particular type of cost that explains many differences in governance choices: the cost of preventing *opportunistic behavior*. When parties enter into a relationship, each might legitimately worry that the other will exploit opportunities to take unfair advantage of the relationship—the threat of holdup discussed in the preceding chapter, but with a focus on vertical rather than horizontal integration. Thus, if Disney were to license its characters to the theme parks owned by Six Flags, for instance, it might worry that Six Flags would use the characters in ways not authorized by Disney.

A common way for companies to overcome concerns about opportunistic behavior is to write contracts that lay out clearly what each party can and must do under various circumstances. When contracts work relatively well, companies are more likely to find it cost-effective to complete transactions through arrangements that involve other parties: arm's-length purchases, licensing deals, alliances, joint ventures, and so forth. When they do not, companies are likely to prefer broad-scope and in-house deals. Researchers have identified several impediments to contracting efficiency.[31]

➤   *Contractual complexity and incompleteness.* It is very difficult to write contracts that comprehensively cover long-term business relationships in highly uncertain settings. Consider again the potential deal between Disney and Six Flags. The contract for such a deal has to cover a huge range of contingencies. What happens if the film and its characters are not as popular as anticipated? How will gains be divided if the film is more successful than expected? If there is an accident on the film-related park ride, who will be liable, and who will manage public relations? Will Six Flags be allowed to locate less-wholesome attractions near the Disney ride? Will Disney have recourse if the ride's staff is impolite or the lines for the ride get too long? And so forth. A contract for such a deal may run into hundreds of pages and still fail to cover many of the events that might arise. Because it is prohibitively costly to write a contract that covers every contingency, opportunities remain for Disney and Six Flags to take advantage of one another.

➤ *Unclear property rights.* One role of a contract is to specify who has rights to what property under various circumstances. This is a relatively straightforward task for tangible pieces of property—machines, vehicles, buildings, parcels of land, and so forth. For intangible resources—knowledge, ideas, skills, brands, innovations, and the like—property rights are much harder to define. As a result, contracting over intangibles is much more difficult, and markets for such resources are more prone to break down. Consequently, we often see intangible resources shared across business units within a corporation, while tangible resources are shared across corporations by means of other arrangements.

➤ *Poor enforcement of contracts and property rights.* A contract—even one that can easily and clearly be written down—will not allay parties' fears of opportunistic behavior unless they expect the contract to be enforced. In most developed economies, the baseline assumption is usually that courts and governments will enforce and uphold contracts and, more broadly, defend property rights. In many emerging economies, in contrast, contract enforcement and property rights seem more fragile. In such settings, trade across corporate borders can be risky. A buyer can realistically fear that a good it pays for will never be delivered. A seller can legitimately worry that it may never be paid after delivering a product or service. Where such concerns are prevalent, corporate scope might be especially broad. This appears to be another reason (in addition to risk-reduction)why highly diversified conglomerates dominate the private sectors of many emerging economies. Consider, for instance, the business houses of India, the *grupos* of Latin America, and the *chaebol* of South Korea.[32]

➤ *Relationship-specific or cospecialized resources.* The effects of the contracting hazards identified above are all amplified if, before transactions can take place, transactors have to make up-front investments whose value is specific to their relationship. Such relationship-specific or cospecialized resources were discussed in some detail in the preceding chapter, in the section on holdup, but can be illustrated once again with the potential deal between Disney and Six Flags. To consummate it, Six Flags would have to build rides in its theme parks, and Disney would have to create and market its films. Making such relationship-specific investments is risky. Before Six Flags built the ride, for example, Disney might promise that it would charge Six Flags a low fee to license its characters. Once a hard-to-alter ride is built, however, what would prevent Disney from reneging on its promise and charging a higher fee, especially after expiry of the initial contract? And knowing that this might happen, Six Flags might build a ride that is less expensive, less appealing, and less durable than would be optimal. Because of such dangers, investments in relationship-specific resources tend to be made within corporate boundaries rather than across them—although it is worth recalling from the discussion of holdup in Chapter 5 that integration is just one of several possible responses to such problems. As a result, when the resources shared by two business units are highly specific in this sense, it is more likely that the units will be owned by one corporation.

Conversely, relationships that do not involve as much resource-specificity can often be managed well across corporate boundaries. Take, for example, Disney's arrangement to license its characters to McDonald's. To incorporate Disney characters into its Happy Meals for kids, McDonald's undertakes some modest and short-lived specific investments: it buys some toys based on Disney characters, prints some bags with the characters on them, and does a little marketing. The scale of the investment it puts at risk is modest compared to the many millions of dollars of thoroughly sunk investment that might be required to design and build a theme park ride. (A ride recently added to Disney's California Adventure theme park, for instance, reportedly cost $75 million.)

More broadly, while all of these factors point to conditions in which the transaction costs of alternate arrangements might be especially high and common ownership might be especially attractive, it is important to remember, that "internal" transactions among jointly owned business units are costly as well. Even within a corporation, managers must find parties to transact with, negotiate internal terms such as transfer prices, and maintain coordination after a deal is struck. They must allay concerns, often intense, that one business unit will take advantage of another. Moreover, the biggest cost of an internal transaction may often be an opportunity cost: the cost of forgoing access to attractive transacts with third parties. For example, in the wake of the AOL-Time Warner merger, AOL's rival Yahoo! felt that it would have a significant advantage over AOL in finding Internet content. AOL would feel obliged to obtain content from Time Warner divisions, whereas Yahoo! could shift freely among content providers, selecting the best of them and playing providers off against one another. In addition to enhancing cost-efficiency, independence can also be directly valuable to one's customers. For years, Andersen Consulting (now Accenture) won information technology integration contracts over IBM because it was viewed as independent while IBM integrators were thought to push the hardware and software of sister businesses.

To summarize, one can apply the best-alternative test by envisioning the transactions that two business should undertake to maximize the wedge between costs and willingness to pay and by comparing the various ways these transactions can be governed—within a single corporation or across corporate boundaries. To justify broad scope, one must argue that common ownership makes more sense in governing the relevant transactions than arm's-length deals, licensing arrangements, alliances, joint ventures, or other options. Broad scope is most likely to be justified when contractual complexity and incompleteness are high, property rights are intrinsically unclear, enforcement of contracts and property rights is poor, and large investments in relationship-specific resources are involved.

Models of Corporate Management

The best-alternative test helps us understand not only what sets of business should be jointly owned, but also how such a set of businesses can be managed. While diversified corporations are managed in many different ways, this diversity can usefully be simplified into the three models of corporate management along the continuum shown in Exhibit 6.2. Each management model tries to meet the best-alternative test in a distinct manner.

➤ *Dominant-business corporations* consist of relatively few business units—often one or two core businesses surrounded by a coterie of peripheral units. Wal-Mart, discussed above, is one example. Dominant-business corporations strive to meet the best-alternative test and beat alternatives to joint ownership by investing in a set of highly specialized resources that separately owned companies cannot match and, often, by achieving more extensive cross-unit coordination. Thus, it is hard to imagine separate companies matching the co-location, shared logistics systems, and joint operational capabilities of Wal-Mart's general merchandise and food businesses. Because

Exhibit 6.2   Models of Corporate Management Increasing Horizontal Scope
Source: Based on David J. Collis and Cynthia A. Montgomery, *Corporate Strategy: Resources and the Scope of the Firm* (Chicago: Richard D. Irwin, 1997).

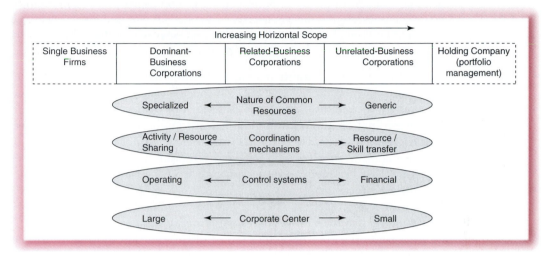

the corporate infrastructure required to develop specialized resources and to coordinate their use can be extensive, dominant-business corporations often have sizable corporate staffs.

➤ *Related-business corporations* typically have more business units than dominant-business corporations as well as a distinct bottom line for each business, but they maintain one or more common threads that link their businesses. A good example is Walt Disney, whose many businesses concentrate on entertainment and the management of creativity. Related-business corporations try to meet the best-alternative test either through one-time transfers of specialized resources or skills to new lines of business (or perhaps from them, if acquired) or, more ambitiously, through ongoing sharing of resources or activities. The collaboration across numerous units inevitably gives rise to conflicts and tradeoffs that would be difficult to govern through multilateral contracts. These, in turn, often engender a need for operating as well as financial controls, with corporate managers directly involved to achieve cross-business coordination. Consider, for instance, Walt Disney's sharing of cartoon characters, the Disney brand, and other resources across multiple businesses and its numerous mechanisms for coordination at the corporate level (e.g., a synergy committee, a corporate calendar, and so forth). If dominant-business corporations strive for deeper sharing and coordination than more loosely linked entities, related-business firms aim for broader sharing and coordination, across more businesses.

➤ *Unrelated-business corporations* often maintain sprawling business portfolios, with many units and sparse relations among them. They typically strive to satisfy the best-alternative test by building their corporate strategies around relatively unspecialized, or generic, resources. Thus, conglomerates in the United States generally emphasize tight financial controls as a way of optimizing cash management, increasing liquidity, and improving resource allocation relative to what external capital markets might be able to achieve. Given the usual limits to value creation through such approaches, they also tend to have relatively small corporate offices. A financial orientation also characterizes most other U.S. organizations involved in motley businesses, such as venture capitalists and private equity groups. As noted above, however, these conclusions seem to be very specific to country context. In emerging economies with poorly developed markets for capital and other resources and weak property rights, the best-alternative test has less bite, and highly diversified business groups can plausibly undertake a broader range of cross-business functions and sport correspondingly larger corporate offices.

Each of these models of corporate management should be thought of as a broad characterization within which there may be much specific variation. Both Disney and AOL Time Warner are related diversifiers, for example, but Disney has historically pursued far greater coordination and permitted far less autonomy across constituent businesses than AOL Time Warner. The variants within each model make the array of possibilities more a continuum than a limited set of discrete options. And companies that share the same broad model can differ not only in the variants that they implement but also in how effective they are in doing so. Among corporations with unrelated businesses, for instance, General Electric has managed its businesses much more effectively over the long run than most other conglomerates in the United States.

Despite the variation in the implementation of these broad models, there has been extensive analysis of whether any one of them consistently delivers better corporate economic performance than the others. The prevailing wisdom, based largely on research in the United States, used to be that there was a conglomerate discount (with unrelated diversifiers underperforming other firms) and, more tentatively, an overall diversification discount (with single-business firms outperforming diversified firms in general). Specifically, such studies tended to report "diversification discounts" of 10–30 percent, with larger discounts, on average, for companies that operate in less-related arrays of businesses.[33] However, much of this work does not take on board the point that profit-maximizing firms should try to maximize total economic profits (profitability times volume) rather than just profitability per se. Moreover, even if one focuses on ratios rather than measures of total value creation, recent work has raised questions about whether the U.S. data actually indicate that diversification itself causes any such discount.[34] We have also learned that the conglomerate discount may not apply universally. In a number of emerging countries, for instance, affiliates of the sorts of diversified business groups cited above can systematically outperform standalone, less-diversified local firms.[35] So instead of trying to figure out which type of horizontal diversification model is best, it seems more sensible to recognize the pros and cons of the different— and internally consistent—models for corporate management described above and to focus on the model that makes the most sense for a given portfolio of businesses in a given context.

AN APPLICATION: MERRILL LYNCH'S ANALYSIS OF THE AOL TIME WARNER MERGER

When companies announce moves that broaden horizontal scope, they inevitably publicize the "synergies" between sister units. It is important to find concrete benefits of broader scope, especially since acquisitions and mergers usually involve hefty premiums and internal expansion is often expensive. Unfortunately, many claims of synergy are logically flawed, in ways that are highlighted by the better-off test and the best-alternative test.

In order to illustrate the logic of the tests one more time, we examine one analysis of the potential gains from the 2000 merger of AOL and Time Warner. Exhibit 6.3 summarizes "You've Got Upside!" a research report published by the team of Henry Blodgett, a prominent analyst of Internet-related companies, at Merrill Lynch. (In fairness, note that the analysis was performed from the outside rather than the inside, and was completed near the height of Internet euphoria.) The Merrill Lynch report claims that, by bringing together the Internet content and access resources of AOL and the traditional media and cable properties of Time Warner, the merger could increase earnings before interest, taxes, depreciation, and amortization (EBITDA) by $1 billion. Quotations from the report, in Exhibit 6.4, explain the reasoning behind some of the items in Exhibit 6.3. The quotations illustrate several of the logical flaws we most commonly see in discussions of corporate strategy.

➤ Mutually beneficial arrangements that the companies could achieve via contracts, without common ownership, are touted as benefits of the merger. Take, for instance, the argument that AOL can cut $200 million out of its $1 billion sales and marketing budget by marketing its online services through existing Time Warner channels (item 1 in Exhibit 6.4): "AOL discs can be included in Time Warner magazines and are already displayed in Warner's Studio Stores." If this is indeed an effective or low-cost way for AOL to market itself, little prevents the two companies from completing such transactions without common ownership. The fact that AOL discs are already displayed in Warner's stores makes this especially clear. The same argument can be applied to many of the other claimed benefits, including AOL's ability to purchase content from Time Warner (item 3), the sale of Time Warner advertising through AOL sales reps (item 4), the use of cross-promotions to drive incremental subscriptions (item 5), and the use of AOL programmers to move Time Warner's magazine subscription renewals online (item 5). The best-alternative test makes clear that, in assessing broad scope, only those benefits that cannot be achieved via other arrangements should be taken as valid arguments for common ownership.

➤ *It is assumed that additional business units can tap already-heavily-utilized resources with little or no additional investment.* The shared cost economies discussed above typically depend on some multi-purpose resource that is underutilized. If the resource is too busy to be shared, however, then there is little opportunity to make two business units better off by bringing them together. Consider, for instance, the AOL customer support representatives who are underutilized early in the day (item 2). Their spare capacity seems to create an opportunity to ask the AOL reps, during their idle hours, to take on the tasks currently performed by Time Warner support reps. But what are the Time Warner support reps doing? They likely support Time Warner's cable systems, fielding telephone calls from customers whose television cables are malfunctioning. Demand for this kind of support probably peaks in the evenings . . . precisely when AOL support reps are fully utilized! (Some Time Warner support personnel visit customers' homes and repair cables, but AOL telephone support reps will surely not be able to replace those employees.)

Similarly, consider the argument that Time Warner "editorial and creative resources . . . can develop ad hoc proprietary content" for AOL (item 3). This helps the merged company pass the better-off test only if the editorial and creative resources were underutilized before the merger. Otherwise, those resources must be distracted from other tasks in order to produce content for AOL, and the resulting

Exhibit 6.3   Potential Synergies (in millions of US $) from the AOL Time Warner Merger

Revenue Enhancement	Revenues	EBITDA
Ad Sales Upside		
$200 of $600mm in estimated revenue upside at TW Online properties (CNN, CNNfn, CNNSI, Time, People, InStyle, Entertainment Weekly)	$200.0	$160.0
More deals on AOL, ICQ through TW relationships	120.0	120.0
Higher Broadband Penetration		
1mm more broadband subscriptions for TW relationships from AOL upgrades 500K average for year paying $20 more per month	120.0	72.0
Incremental Subscriptions		
New subscriptions to AOL and magazines (through cross-promotion)	25.0	12.5
New AOL Premium Services		
2mm AOL subscriptions sign up for $5 increase fee by year-end 2001 (for AOL TV, real time stock quotes, etc.)	60.0	30.0
Music		
Downloads on early generation music devices	25.0	6.3
Increased Warner Music sales using AOL platform	10.0	2.5
Total Revenue Upside	**$590.0**	**$403.3**

Cost Savings: Reduced Operating Expenses	Revenues	EBITDA
Sales & Marketing, AOL (distribution of AOL software)	$200.0	$200.0
Sales & Marketing, Time Warner (movies and music)	100.0	100.0
Reduced spending on TW online initiatives (Entertaindom)	125.0	125.0
Overhead (Finance, Legal, HR)	50.0	50.0
Reduced customer support cost (in COGS)	50.0	50.0
Reduced cost of content purchased by AOL ($600mm over 4 years)	25.0	25.0
Reduced cost of member subscription and renewal	25.0	25.0
Reduced telecom/technology costs across AOL-Time Warner	25.0	25.0
Total Cost Savings	**$600.0**	**$600.0**

Source: Stephen P. Bradley and Erin E. Sullivan, "AOL Time Warner, Inc.," (Harvard Business School Case no. 702-421, Boston, MA, 2002), p. 23.

Exhibit 6.4   Rationales for Certain AOL Time Warner Synergies

1. Sales & Marketing – AOL (distribution of AOL software)
$200 million in reduced operating expenses ($200 million EBITDA impact)
"AOL estimates that it can shave at least $200 million off of its nearly $1 billion marketing spend through a variety of cross-marketing programs and the use of remnant Time Warner advertising inventory. AOL software, for example, will likely be included on Warner Music CDs and movie DVDs. AOL discs can be included in Time Warner magazines and are already displayed in Warner's Studio Stores."

2. Reduced Customer Support Cost
$50 million reduction in operating expenses ($50 million EBITDA impact)
"We expect the combined company to achieve savings in customer support areas. AOL's 6,000 customer service representatives tend to be very busy for three to four hours late in the day, and underutilized at other times. 5% of AOL's revenues, or $400 million this calendar year, goes toward customer support.....We do not know how much Time Warner spends in support, but think the combined company can achieve at least $50 million in savings here."

3. Reduced Cost of Content Purchased by AOL
$25 million reduction in operating expenses ($25 million EBITDA impact)
"We have also assumed that AOL can save about $25 million from reduced spending on content (AOL currently expects to spend about $600 million on third-party content royalties over the next four years). Through Time Warner, AOL will have access to all varieties of content already being produced, as well as to editorial and creative resources that can develop ad hoc proprietary content."

4. Advertising Sales Upside (Time Warner)
$200 million in revenues ($160 million EBITDA impact)
"AOL management points out that Time Warner's online properties altogether generate only $100 million out of an estimated $600 million in inventory value....The Time Warner Online sites should be generating more revenue than they are....We do think some of that under-performance relates to the fact the sales efforts for those web sites come second to those of the parent business (the cable network, the magazine). Therefore, we have estimated in 2001 AOL Time Warner will capture an additional $200 million of this $500 million ad sales upside."

5. Incremental Subscriptions
$25 million in new revenues ($12.5 EBITDA impact) + $25 million in reduced operating expenses ($25 million EBITDA impact)
"The company plans to drive new subscriptions through cross-promotion of everything from AOL membership to magazine and cable subscriptions. For example, a Time Warner magazine might bundle a discounted two-year subscription with the AOL service, or AOL's sports channel might promote Sports Illustrated. Second, the company plans to move as much of the Time Warner cable and subscription renewal process online as possible, thereby reducing churn and reselling costs....Finally, the company envisions converting weekly subscribers of the Time Warner magazines to perennial subscribers—providing weekly print copies of the magazines but also providing those subscribers with magazine content online...We are estimating that AOL Time Warner can achieve $25 million in new subscription revenues....We are also estimating that the company can save $25 million from reducing the cost of subscription management and renewal."

Source: Stephen P. Bradley and Erin E. Sullivan, "AOL Time Warner, Inc.," (Harvard Business School Case no. 702-421, Boston, MA, 2002), p. 24.

content can hardly be considered "free." Likewise, the argument that AOL sales reps can sell Time Warner's left-over advertising inventory (item 4) is valid only if those sales reps are not already spending all of their time productively selling AOL ads. These objections are closely related to the next flaw.

➤ *The opportunity costs of common ownership are ignored.* For instance, when AOL promotes its new sibling *Sports Illustrated* on its sports channel (item 5), it may lose the opportunity to promote *Sports Illustrated*'s competitors. The Merrill Lynch analysis accounts for the benefit associated with the former, but it ignores the cost of the latter.

➤ *Benefits that are supposed to make the jointly owned units better off are counted twice, often once in each unit.* For example, the reduction in AOL marketing expense that comes from cross-promotion (item 1) appears to overlap with the incremental subscriptions to AOL's online services that also come from cross-promotion (item 5).

➤ *The costs and difficulty of cross-unit coordination are ignored; that is, cross-unit coordination is assumed to be free.* The Merrill Lynch analysts envision an enormous degree of cross-promotion and complex sharing of resources, which will require costly coordination efforts. Do the inevitable costs of coordination outweigh the benefits? If so, the merger fails the better-off test. And are such transactions better coordinated by contracts between independent firms than by managers within a firm? If so, the merger fails the best-alternative test.

The best antidote to logical flaws like these is a careful and dispassionate analysis of the costs as well as benefits of broad scope, weighed against a range of alternate arrangements. It seems that analysis of this sort could have identified the limited synergies from the merger of AOL and Time Warner ahead of time, and perhaps even helped predict that it would, as a result, be unstable even if it were consummated—as has turned out to be the case.

SUMMARY

Both the stakes and the level of difficulty are high when a management team chooses the range of businesses in which a corporation will compete. Perspectives on such choices have evolved over time, and we see progression towards a view in which corporate-level scope choices are best seen as an overlay on business-unit strategies: corporate choices of scope are treated as effective or ineffective to the extent that they contribute to the success or failure of individual business units in their specific industries.

Broad scope that contributes to success passes two tests. First, the breadth must bring together business units that are made better off by their union. More specifically, it must increase the ability of units to add value, net of any incremental costs. Increased added value might derive from an increase in volume, improvements in industry structure, a widened wedge between willingness to pay and costs, or—occasionally—a reduction in risk.

A choice of broad scope that passes this first test must also clear a second one. Joint ownership must capture the benefits of breadth better than alternate arrangements such as arms'-length trade, licensing, strategic alliances, and joint ventures. We discussed circumstances that are likely to favor joint ownership over the alternatives, including contractual hazards and major investments in relationship-specific resources. We also considered how various models of corporate management address this best-alternative test in distinct ways.

The examples in this chapter illustrate the enormous power of corporate strategy both to create and to destroy value. We are likely to continue to see examples of both given the complexities of scope choices. Yet managers can improve the odds of value creation and capture by rigorously asking whether, and if so, why, business units might be better off under the same corporate umbrella than they would be if separated...or coordinated by some alternative to outright ownership.

GLOSSARY

- best-alternative test
- better-off test
- corporate added value
- corporate strategy
- good-parent

NOTES

1. For a discussion of the distinctive strategy issues that arise in the context of geographic scope, see Pankaj Ghemawat, "Semiglobalization and International Business Strategy," *Journal of International Business Studies* 34, no. 2 (March 2003): 138–152

2. See, for instance, Leonard Wrigley, "Divisional Autonomy and Diversification" (D.B.A. thesis, Harvard Business School, 1970), and Richard P. Rumelt, *Strategy, Structure, and Economic Performance* (Cambridge, Mass.: Harvard University Press, 1974).

3. Marakon Associates, *Commentary* 11 (June 1983).

4. Philippe C. Haspeslagh, Tomo Noda, and Fares Boulos, "Managing for Value: It's Not Just About the Numbers," *Harvard Business Review* 79, no. 7 (July–August 2001): 64–73.

5. Philippe C. Haspeslagh, "Portfolio Planning: Uses and Limits," *Harvard Business Review* 60, no. 1 (January–February 1982): 58–73.

6. C. K. Prahalad and Gary Hamel, "The Core Competence of the Corporation," *Harvard Business Review* 68, no. 3 (May–June 1990): 79–91.

7. Darrell K. Rigby, *Management Tools 2003: An Executive's Guide* (Boston: Bain, 2003).

8. David J. Collis and Cynthia A. Montgomery, "Competing on Resources: Strategy in the 1990s," *Harvard Business Review* 73, no. 4 (July–August 1995): 118–128.

9. Pankaj Ghemawat, "Sears, Roebuck and Co.: The Merchandise Group" (Harvard Business School Case no. 794-039, 1993).

10. Videotape of Richard M. Jones, President and Chief Financial Officer of Sears, Roebuck, addressing an Advanced Management Program class at Harvard Business School, November 11, 1985.

11. Stuart L. Gillan, John W. Kensinger, and John D. Martin, "Value Creation and Corporate Diversification: The Case of Sears, Roebuck & Co.," *Journal of Financial Economics* 55, no. 1 (January 2000): 103–137.

12. For others who employ similar and related tests, see Michael E. Porter, "From Competitive Advantage to Corporate Strategy," *Harvard Business Review* 65, no. 3 (May–June 1987): 43–59; Michael Goold, Andrew Campbell, and Marcus Alexander, *Corporate-Level Strategy: Creating Value in the Multibusiness Company* (New York: John Wiley, 1994); and David J. Teece, "Economies of Scope and the Scope of the Enterprise," *Journal of Economic Behavior & Organization* 1 (1980): 223–247.

13. Goold, Campbell, and Alexander, *Corporate-Level Strategy*, p. 14.

14. For further discussion of some of these points, see Pankaj Ghemawat, "The Growth Boosters," *Harvard Business Review*, (July –August 2004): 35.

15. Ola Svenson, "Are We All Less Risky and More Skillful Than Our Fellow Drivers?" *Acta Psychologica* 47, no. 2 (February 1981): 143–148.

16. Ulrike Malmendier and Geoffrey Tate, "CEO Overconfidence and Corporate Investment," (NBER Working Paper No. w10807, 2004), available from www.nber.org/papers/w10807. For related theoretical work, see Simon Gervais, J. B. Heaton III, and Terrance Odean, "Overconfidence, Investment Policy, and Executive Stock Options" (Rodney L. White Center for Financial Research Working Paper No. 15-02, 2003), available from http://ssrn.com/abstract=361200.

17. See, for instance, David J. Collis and Cynthia A. Montgomery, *Corporate Strategy: Resources and the Scope of the Firm* (Chicago: Richard D. Irwin, 1997).

18. Having said that, we reiterate—here and elsewhere—that performance has to be looked at in terms of total economic profits rather than just profitability or margins.

19. B. Douglas Bernheim and Michael D. Whinston, "Multimarket Contact and Collusive Behavior," *Rand Journal of Economics* 21, no. 1 (Spring 1990): 1–26.

20. Joel A. C. Baum and Helaine J. Korn, "Competitive Dynamics of Interfirm Rivalry," *Academy of Management Journal* 39, no. 2 (April 1996): 255–291.

21. Arnold A. Heggestad and Stephen A. Rhoades, "Multi-Market Interdependence and Local Market Competition in Banking," *Review of Economics and Statistics* 60, no. 4 (1978): 523–532.

22. Robert M. Grant, *Contemporary Strategy Analysis: Concepts, Techniques, Applications,* 4th ed. (Malden, Mass.: Blackwell, 2002), p. 457.

23. Brian S. Silverman and Michael E. Porter, "Scotts Company: North American Corporate Strategy" (Harvard Business School Case no. 701-002, Boston, 2000).

24. This typology was first proposed by Michael E. Porter; see Porter, "From Competitive Advantage to Corporate Strategy."

25. Nitin Nohria and James Weber, "The Royal Bank of Scotland: Masters of Integration" (Harvard Business School Case no. 404-026, Boston, 2003).

26. See Clayton M. Christensen, *The Innovator's Dilemma: When New Technologies Cause Great Firms to Fail, The Management of Innovation and Change Series* (Boston: Harvard Business School Press, 1997).

27. Silverman and Porter, "Scotts Company."

28. Ryan Chittum, "Cendant Hopes Simpler Model Will Lift Stock," *Wall Street Journal,* May 20, 2004, p. C1.

29. Tarun Khanna and Krishna Palepu, "Why Focused Strategies May Be Wrong for Emerging Markets," *Harvard Business Review* 75, no. 4 (July–August 1997): 41–51.

30. Ideas concerning transaction costs were pioneered by Ronald Coase and Oliver Williamson. See especially Ronald H. Coase, "The Nature of the Firm," *Economica* 4, no. 16 (November 1937): 386–405; Oliver E. Williamson, *The Economic Institutions of Capitalism: Firms, Markets, Relational Contracting* (New York: Free Press, 1985); Oliver E. Williamson, *Markets and Hierarchies, Analysis and Antitrust Implications: A Study in the Economics of Internal Organization* (New York: Free Press, 1975).

31. The description of these circumstances draws in part from Bharat Anand, Tarun Khanna, and Jan W. Rivkin, "Market Failures" (Harvard Business School Case no. 700-127, Boston, 2000).

32. Khanna and Palepu, "Why Focused Strategies May Be Wrong . . . ," *op cit.*

33. Larry H. P. Lang and Rene M. Stulz, "Tobin's Q, Corporate Diversification, and Firm Performance," *Journal of Political Economy* 102, no. 6 (December 1994): 1248–1280; Philip G. Berger and Eli Ofek, "Diversification's Effect on Firm Value," *Journal of Financial Economics* 37, no. 1 (January 1995): 39–65.

34. See also Jose Manuel Campa and Simi Kedia, "Explaining the Diversification Discount," *Journal of Finance* 57, no. 4 (2002): 1731–1762, and Belén Villalonga, "Does Diversification Cause the 'Diversification Discount'?" *Financial Management* 33, no. 2 (Summer 2004): 5–27 (who address self-selection biases in the previous literature).

35. On India, see Tarun Khanna and Krishna Palepu, "Is Group Affiliation Profitable in Emerging Markets? An Analysis of Diversified Indian Business Groups," *Journal of Fi-*

nance 55, no. 2 (2000): 867–891, and also Pankaj Ghemawat and Tarun Khanna, "The Nature of Diversified Business Groups: A Research Design and Two Case Studies," *Journal of Industrial Economics* 46, no. 1 (1998): 35–61. Tarun Khanna and Jan W. Rivkin, "Estimating the Performance Effects of Business Groups in Emerging Markets," *Strategic Management Journal* 22, no. 1 (January 2001): 45–74, provide a much broader perspective on the performance consequences of group affiliation in a broad range of emerging markets. And on highly industrialized countries other than the United States, see Eric R. Gedajlovic and Daniel M. Shapiro, "Management and Ownership Effects: Evidence from Five Countries," *Strategic Management Journal* 19, no. 6 (1998): 533–554. and Karl Lins and Henri Servaes, "International Evidence on the Value of Corporate Diversification," *Journal of Finance* 54, no. 6 (1999): 2215–2239.

Name Index

Company Index

Subject Index